India Briefing, 1988

India Briefing, 1988

edited by
Marshall M. Bouton
and Philip Oldenburg

Published in cooperation with
The Asia Society

Westview Press / Boulder and London

Published in 1988 in the United States of America by Westview Press, Inc., 5500 Central Avenue, Boulder, Colorado 80301, and in the United Kingdom by Westview Press, Inc., 13 Brunswick Centre, London WC1N 1AF, England

Library of Congress ISSN: 0894-5136
ISBN: 0-8133-0740-6
ISBN: 0-8133-0741-4 (pbk.)

Printed and bound in the United States of America

The paper used in this publication meets the requirements of the American National Standard for Permanence of Paper for Printed Library Materials Z39.48-1984.

10 9 8 7 6 5 4 3 2 1

Contents

Preface

While India continues to play key roles on the international stage, 1987 was a year of primarily domestic preoccupations in India. Severe drought and floods, combined with a sluggish economy, complicated the task of economic reform. Separatist terrorism and sectarian violence increased at home and among Tamil militants in Sri Lanka, where India sent troops to enforce a settlement of civil strife. Charges of corruption against members of Prime Minister Rajiv Gandhi's government, defections from his ruling Congress (I) party, and regional electoral defeats threatened the government's popularity and support. At the same time, there appeared to be little prospect of serious economic setback or political breakdown.

India Briefing 1988 is the second volume in a new series of annual assessments of key events and trends in Indian affairs. Encouraged by the reception of *India Briefing 1987*, The Asia Society and Westview Press decided to continue this effort to offer the general reader an overview of Indian politics, economy, and foreign relations in 1987, as well as in-depth examination of other important topics in Indian life. The special topics covered in 1988 are national security, science and technology, and education.

This year, Philip Oldenburg joins Marshall M. Bouton in the co-editorship of the series. Marshall Bouton and The Asia Society are deeply grateful to Professor Oldenburg for agreeing at a late date to help bring the volume to press and for consenting to be part of this venture in the future. We look forward to the collaboration.

The editors wish to express great appreciation to the authors of *India Briefing 1988*. Their forebearance and cooperation under the extraordinary circumstances that surrounded the completion of the volume were exemplary. Their work is the heart of our effort. We are also grateful to Susan McEachern and her colleagues at Westview Press for their dedication to the enterprise and for their patience and understanding in completing this project.

Several individuals at The Asia Society helped make *India Briefing 1988* possible. Sarah Beckjord skillfully managed the final editorial and manuscript preparation tasks, despite being new to her job and to this project. Earlier Linda Griffin Kean provided valuable assistance. Donatella Lorch carried out important research assignments and prepared the chronology. Andrea Sokerka, Rose Wright, and Chip Gagnon were crucial to the manuscript preparation.

Marshall M. Bouton
The Asia Society

Philip Oldenburg
Columbia University

23 August 1988

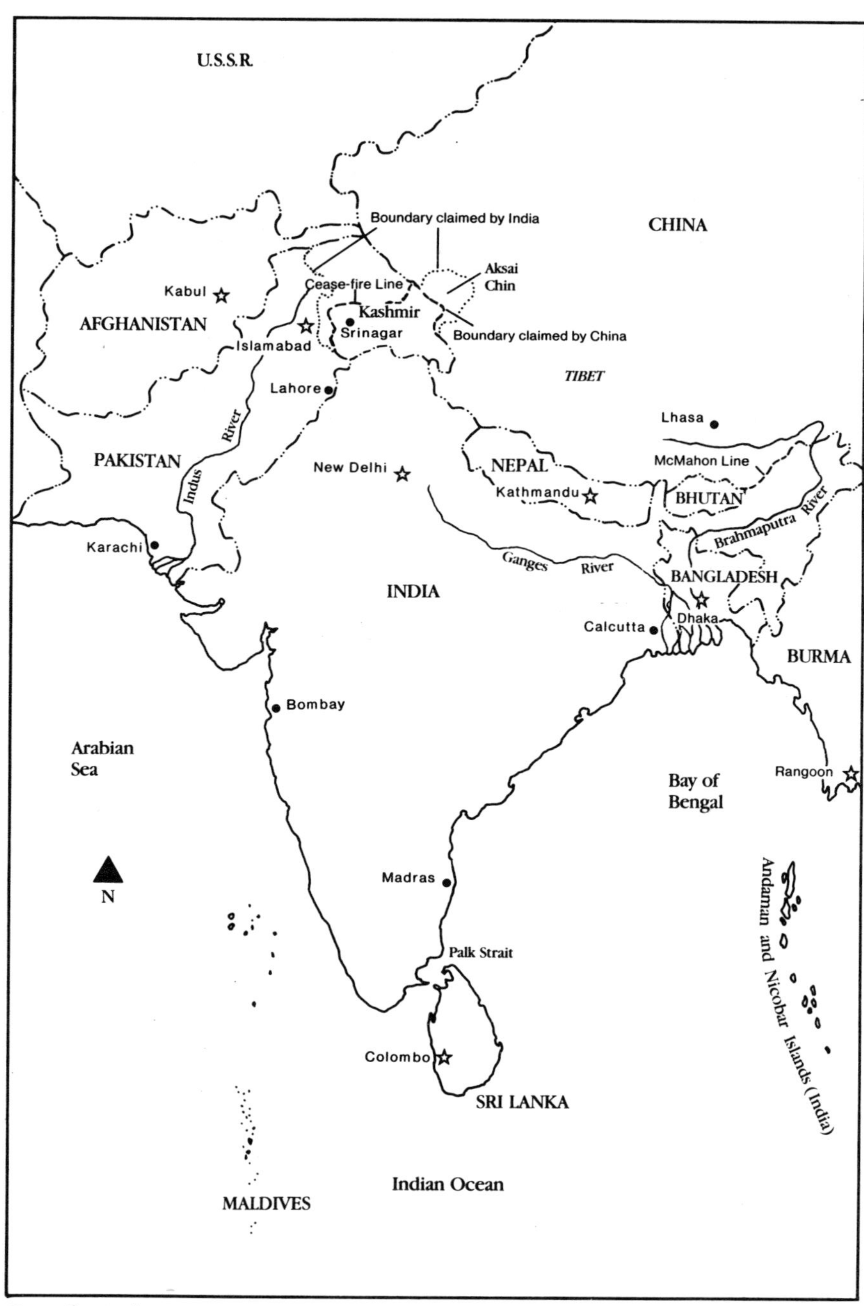
U.S.S.R.
CHINA
Boundary claimed by India
Aksai Chin
Cease-fire Line
Kashmir
Srinagar
Boundary claimed by China
Kabul
AFGHANISTAN
Islamabad
Lahore
TIBET
Lhasa
PAKISTAN
Indus River
New Delhi
NEPAL
McMahon Line
Kathmandu
BHUTAN
Brahmaputra River
Karachi
Ganges River
BANGLADESH
INDIA
Dhaka
Calcutta
BURMA
Bombay
Arabian Sea
Rangoon
Bay of Bengal
N
Madras
Andaman and Nicobar Islands (India)
Palk Strait
Colombo
SRI LANKA
Indian Ocean
MALDIVES

South Asia

U.S.S.R.
Boundary claimed by India
AFGHANISTAN
CHINA
Cease-fire Line
Aksai Chin
Kabul
Islamabad
Srinagar
JAMMU AND KASHMIR
Chinese Line of Control
Amritsar
HIMACHAL PRADESH
Lahore
PAKISTAN
PUNJAB
Chandigarh
Boundary claimed by China
TIBET
Lhasa
McMahon Line
HARYANA
ARUNACHAL PRADESH
New Delhi
NEPAL
Aligarh
Thimpu
SIKKIM
BHUTAN
Jaipur
Agra
Kathmandu
RAJASTHAN
Lucknow
ASSAM
UTTAR PRADESH
MEGHALAYA
MANIPUR
Patna
BANGLADESH
BIHAR
Ahmedabad
Bhopal
INDIA
MIZORAM
GUJARAT
WEST BENGAL
Dhaka
MADHYA PRADESH
Calcutta
BURMA
TRIPURA
ORISSA
MAHARASHTRA
Bhubaneswar
Bombay
Hyderabad
Bay of Bengal
Rangoon
ANDHRA PRADESH
GOA
N
KARNATAKA
Bangalore
Madras
ANDAMAN AND NICOBAR ISLANDS
Port Blair
TAMIL NADU
Kavaratti
KERALA
LAKSHADWEEP
Palk Strait
SRI LANKA
Trivandrum
Colombo
MALDIVES
Indian Ocean

India

1
Politics: Ambiguity, Disillusionment, and Ferment

James Manor

In 1987, India celebrated the completion of four decades of self-government. It was a year in which it was easier to see how important political leaders, forces, and initiatives had run into trouble than to discern how they and India's democracy might extricate themselves. It was, however, a year of ambiguity rather than of negativity and decline. There was plenty of political and social ferment, some of which led to destructive conflict and violence, but much of which appeared to have creative promise. It was a year of further disillusionment with Prime Minister Rajiv Gandhi, and of continuing doubts about the possibility of broad opposition unity. But India's political system ended 1987 no less open or stable than it began the year, despite the worst drought of the twentieth century, terrorist outrages, severe communal violence, statist overreactions, populist extravagance, the deaths of two major political leaders, electoral humiliation for the party in power in New Delhi, revelations of monumental corruption, and much more. That is no small achievement.

It became apparent during 1987 that Rajiv Gandhi had largely abandoned his efforts, undertaken in 1985, to rebuild formal political institutions which had suffered damage in preceding years such as the cabinet ministries, the bureaucracy, and the courts. He was more than ever at a loss as to how to rebuild his Congress party, which had once been India's most important political institution, but which has been in a wretched condition since the mid–1970s. It also became clear that his current five–year term as prime minister, which extends until the end of 1989, will be distinguished neither by a sustained liberalization of the economy nor by creative new state–led programs to promote development or social welfare. This means that he will be very short of programmatic achievements on which to base his reelection campaign in the next year. He will therefore have to depend on his own waning appeal and the possibility of opposition disarray; and—since these may not suffice, given the maturity and impatience of India's mass electorate—upon huge political gambles that rarely produce spectacular achievements.

Problems that Did Not Arise

Before plunging into a discussion of India's political dilemmas, it is worth mentioning five problems which India did *not* face in 1987 and is unlikely to encounter soon, as a way of suggesting the scale of its political achievement over the last 40 years. First, India was not threatened by the prospect of a military coup. This owed a little to logistical factors. The size of the country and the structure of the armed forces, which prevents close contact between officers from different services until they reach senior ranks, make a coup difficult to coordinate. More important, the armed forces had enough confidence in civilian elites and in open politics that they were disinclined even to contemplate such action. They had also learned, by observing Pakistan and Bangladesh, the inadequacy of armies as instruments of government in complex societies.

Nor, despite much ill–formed comment to the contrary, was India about to fall apart. In part, the coercive power of the central government is more than sufficient to prevent regions or states within India from breaking away. But the threat of secession has never seriously arisen and is unlikely to do so—except perhaps in the remote, hilly states of the far northeast which are ethnically and culturally distinct. Elsewhere, in mainstream India, secessionist movements of substance (as opposed to secessionist rhetoric) are unlikely to arise because would–be secessionists cannot generate enough solidarity at the state or regional level to sustain such movements. Perhaps *the* most distinctive feature of Indian society is its extreme heterogeneity, the ubiquity of variegated sub–groups within sub–groups. That means, at one level, that the states and regions within India differ markedly from one another, which leads some observers to prophesy balkanization. But they overlook great heterogeneity *within* each of these varied states. It is for that reason that the current crisis in the Punjab is essentially a problem not of separatism but of bitter alienation between Sikhs and Hindus, and between Sikhs and the current government in New Delhi.

India was also free of any serious threat of revolution. Groups of leftists seeking to promote insurrection could be found in a few pockets, but their strength has declined since the early 1970s. One such group made headlines in late 1987 by kidnapping a few senior officials in the southern state of Andhra Pradesh. But nowhere did they pose a significant danger to the existing political order. This was partly because of the strength of the security forces, but mainly because conditions did not exist for potent insurgencies to develop. India is still a predominantly agrarian society in which discontented urban elements—which might be mobilized by extremists of the left or right in an effort to seize power—are still a manageably small portion of the population. The continuing strength of the joint family sometimes mitigates the suffering and discontents of would-be rebels. And in an overwhelmingly rural society such as this, the regime is unlikely to be overthrown unless a revolt could mold large numbers of disadvantaged rural dwellers into a solid revolutionary force. This would be very difficult to achieve in India because the rural poor are badly fragmented by social divisions, especially the *jati*—a small caste group (of which there are many thousands in India) beyond which a person is not supposed to intermarry or share food. Remarkably resilient, this institution has not wasted away in rural areas in the manner of pre–existing social institutions in much of the rest of Asia and Africa.

This is not to say that revolution cannot happen in India. *Jati* is sustained by important material supports that could give way. If the political system were to become far less responsive than it now is, if the rural economy were to go into prolonged decline, or if the proportion of rural dwellers who are landless were to increase dramatically over wide areas, then the outlook might change. But for the present, this is not a serious issue.

Nor was India faced with major problems of social disintegration of the kind which assail many governments in sub–Saharan Africa. There is great variation in the capacities of long–standing institutions in various parts of the non–Western world to survive colonialism, the development of modern market economies, and the modern state. In much of Africa, social institutions have often grown heavily dependent on the state, so that the decay of state institutions has thrown society into severe dislocation.[1] This is far less true in India where institutions—especially *jati*—have survived and in some cases even gained vitality by adapting to new circumstances. Rural society in India is thus far less dependent upon the state than its African counterparts, so that when political institutions undergo decay in India, far less social havoc is wrought as a result.[2]

Finally, despite a drought that devastated much of Indian agriculture, the nation avoided widespread starvation. The drought, which resulted

---

[1] See for example, Nelson Kasfir (ed.) *Race and Class in Africa* (London, 1982).

[2] James Manor, "Anomie in Indian Politics," *Economic and Political Weekly* (Bombay), annual number 1983.

from a catastrophic failure of the monsoon rains on which the agricultural sector largely depends, affected nearly all of India's states and was then compounded by severe floods in four states. It is too early to make a definitive assessment of its impact, since data are still being gathered and its effects will continue to be felt beyond 1987. But despite immense suffering among vast numbers of landless and land–poor people and no small amount of bungling and corruption by state and central governments, the system worked well enough to prevent large numbers of deaths.

This is partly explained by the enormous increase in food production in India, thanks to the green revolution. Since Independence in 1947, wheat production has increased sevenfold, while rice production and food grain production generally have nearly trebled. This has been accompanied by an impressive effort to create reliable storage facilities, free of rats, damp, and other threats, and by the government's stockpiling of vast food grain reserves—more than 23 million tons—for just this sort of crisis. Linked to this is an enormous government program to procure food from farmers and a network of government–controlled outlets for food distribution which since 1980 have increased by nearly a third to about 340,000. The working of this system is often marred by corrupt practices, but in most areas this year it made a significant contribution on three fronts: (1) channelling stocks of grain to people in villages, (2) preventing acute shortages of grain which would drive prices on the open market (the primary distributor) beyond the reach of those at risk, and (3) delivering food to people who have turned to the government's food–for–work program in order to survive. The diversion by state and central governments of resources from other sectors to meet the emergency and the diversion of electricity away from industry to the rural sector were criticized by some—perhaps rightly—as inadequate, but they nonetheless made a difference.

Understanding Rajiv Gandhi

Great leaders seldom exercise decisive influence over socio–economic forces and huge, complex political institutions. But when power has been inordinately centralized in the hands of the leader of a political system, as occurred under Mrs. Gandhi for the benefit of herself and her son, then those who understand the system must assess the behavior of that leader. Rajiv Gandhi has become less important in Indian politics since he assumed office after his mother's assassination on October 31, 1984. This is partly because he has at times sought to rebuild some of the institutions which his mother systematically weakened, and because he wants to reduce the overdependence of the political system on him.

Unlike his mother, he sees such overdependence as a problem and not as an ideal mode of governance. He is also less dominant on the political scene because he has often been confused—institutions and rivals have a way of reasserting themselves when leaders are hesitant—and because people have grown somewhat disillusioned with him. Initial public expectations were so unrealistic that he was bound to disappoint, but the disillusionment has long since passed that point.

The problem is, which Rajiv do we discuss? We have seen at least three since he took office, and the only way to represent him adequately is to deal with each in turn. The first Rajiv is quiet and magnanimous. We caught occasional glimpses of him during the Emergency which his mother imposed in the mid–1970s. There was the occasion when he called aside a judge who had recently been transferred to a highly undesirable outpost because one of his rulings was not to the liking of Mrs. Gandhi and Rajiv's vindictive brother, Sanjay. Rajiv astonished the judge by apologizing for their behavior and saying that in a free country, the judiciary should not be intimidated in this way. We also saw plenty of the magnanimous Rajiv in the year following his election victory at the end of 1984. He forged accommodations with the leaders of the deeply alienated Assamese in the northeast and of the Sikhs in the Punjab by offering them generous concessions. He also departed from his mother's ways by adopting an accommodating approach to state governments that were in the hands of opposition parties.

And yet, only a few weeks earlier, during the 1984 election campaign, they had encountered a very different Rajiv, an aggressive, illiberal slasher. He had mounted slanderous attacks on the opposition parties as collaborators with Pakistan and anti–national forces. He also indulged in public gestures which many took to be anti–Sikh and chauvinistically Hindu, and he allowed anti–Sikh innuendo into his party's election advertisements.[3] No Indian prime minister had ever undertaken such a negative, confrontational election campaign. This second Rajiv was reliably reported to have taken a hard line a few months earlier when advising his mother to confront opposition–run state governments, and to send troops into the Golden Temple, an action which inflamed Sikh opinion and led ultimately to the assassination of Mrs. Gandhi.

The third Rajiv is impatient and dismissive. It was this Rajiv who, at the centennial celebrations of his party, the Indian National Congress, denounced not only the opposition parties but the Congress itself as parasitic, sanctimonious and riddled with corruption. He seemed to dismiss the possibility that *any* party might perform acceptably. It was

[3] James Manor, "Rajiv Gandhi and Post–Election Politics in India." *The World Today* (London), March 1985.

this Rajiv who has shuffled and reshuffled his Cabinet so often that the central government has known little stability, and few ministers have had time to learn their jobs. It was this Rajiv who, during a nationally broadcast press conference, insulted his senior foreign ministry official by announcing that he would soon be replaced. It was this Rajiv who began cutting back on government controls and red tape, but then gave up in exasperation after a few months when those with an interest in the old system offered resistance.

One common tendency unites these three very different faces of the prime minister: he tends to pursue them to extremes. He will move impulsively in one direction, find that he has gone too far, and then over–correct by rushing headlong in another. This often lands him in political trouble. For example, the anti–Sikh themes in his 1984 election campaign alienated Sikhs and created high expectations among chauvinistic Hindus. After the election, he made concessions to Sikhs, but then discovered that if he delivered on them he would pay too high a price among Hindus. He therefore failed to deliver, generating still greater anger among the Sikhs, but leaving Hindus dismayed that he should have made such a deal in the first place.

We have caught sight of all three Rajivs during 1987, though magnanimity was in short supply because he was often on the defensive. But the fact that all three still emerge suggests that inconsistency and impulsiveness born of inexperience—he began dabbling in politics only three years before becoming prime minister—remain severe problems. In 1987, he was still failing to give clear, sustained signals on at least three crucial fronts, and with a nationwide election due in late 1989, time is running short. First, he needed to decide how he was to make a creative impact on Indian society. Like his mother in her later years, he has lost confidence in the public sector as an agency for positive action in society. Consequently, he has done very little in the way of programs to catalyze social change or provide resources to the disadvantaged. It seemed at first as if he would place his faith in free enterprise, but his sudden disinterest in liberalizing the economy has left the private sector still swathed in red tape. Unless the prime minister moves forcefully and soon in one of these two directions, it is difficult to see what advancements for Indian society he will be able to point to when he next faces the voters.

Rajiv Gandhi must also decide whether he intends to present himself as an enlightened protector of religious minorities (mainly Sikhs and Muslims) and as an advocate of tolerance and cultural diversity, which is the traditional posture of Congress leaders, or as a Hindu chauvinist. His mother—astonishingly for a daughter of Jawaharlal Nehru—had adopted the latter approach in the last two years of her life. After she was murdered by members of the Sikh minority, Rajiv Gandhi continued to pursue the same themes and in response, an estimated 200,000 members of the R.S.S., the Hindu extremist organization, worked for the first time for Congress at the 1984 election.[4] Since then, he has at times wooed Muslims and Sikhs, but he has also returned often enough to Hindu chauvinist themes so that in 1987, the R.S.S. endorsed his party—an event that would have disgusted Nehru. Once again, the prime minister must decide which way he will turn if he wants to cultivate a reliable constituency at the next election.

Finally, he needs an instrument through which to govern this complex society, which means that he must revive his party, now in dire difficulties. Here again, inconsistency has caused him major problems. This topic is important enough to warrant a separate, detailed discussion.

The Troubled Congress Party

Rajiv Gandhi inherited a political party which had undergone severe decay since its heyday in the period up to the mid–1960s when it was one of the most formidable political machines that the world had ever seen. His mother viewed it mainly as a threat and had centralized power within it, starved it of political resources, and abandoned its long tradition of internal democracy. She tended, especially after 1975, to appoint as party officers large numbers of flatterers whose competence and probity were in doubt. Indeed, her son Sanjay—who killed himself doing aerobatics over New Delhi in 1980—actively sought out recruits with a history of violent and even criminal behavior. When Rajiv Gandhi succeeded his mother in late 1984, he knew that in many parts of India his party was afflicted by corruption, vicious factional quarrels, or both. But in the intervening years he has not succeeded in cleansing it, partly because he has been uncertain about how to tackle the problem, and mostly because he has often been irresolute.

It should be emphasized that the condition of the party varied considerably from state to state, as most things tend to do in this bafflingly complex country. For example, in Rajasthan during the 1984 election campaign, parliamentary candidates pleaded with Rajiv Gandhi to keep campaign funds out of the hands of the corrupt chief minister, lest they vanish. The prime minister complied and gave a highly effective former chief minister control of the campaign—which went

[4] The organization's full title is Rashtriya Swayamsevak Sangha. These comments are based on extensive interviews with political activists during the 1984 election campaign.

well—and later of the state government. The Congress party there has shown considerable improvement as a result.

Unfortunately it is difficult to find other such success stories. In some states—Kerala and Maharashtra are examples—Rajiv Gandhi has had good managers available to replace leaders who are unpopular, ineffective, or worse. But he has been unable to bring himself to impose on them because the undesirable incumbents have too many backers in their faction of the party. This probably cost Congress control of Kerala in the 1987 state election. In other states, the prime minister *has* appointed people he trusts but then has failed to offer them anything more than moral support when they need money and patronage to survive in the rough world of Congress politics. Several such men have been quickly eaten up by party strongmen, in episodes that have made Rajiv Gandhi appear naive and weak.

In several states, however, things are so far gone within Congress that there seems little that any leader can do. In West Bengal, violent conflict between Congress factions has long been a matter of routine. They even managed to stage a riotous melee on the other side of the country, in Bombay, at the centennial celebrations of the party, and numerous murders have occurred during their factional ructions. In Uttar Pradesh in the early 1980s, no fewer than 155 Congress members of the state legislature were convicted criminals—people convicted of actual crimes, not honorable veterans of Gandhian civil disobedience.[5] The Congress organization in neighboring Bihar is far more decayed than that of Uttar Pradesh.

One option which was long discussed by Rajiv Gandhi before he finally abandoned it in 1987 was the holding of elections for offices within the Congress party for the first time since 1972. There is disagreement among political analysts about the impact that this would have on the party.[6] Some contend that although it would entail the enrollment of bogus members and other questionable practices, they would on balance strengthen the Congress. Elections would force the party into unaccustomed actions: mobilizing members (which implies some role for them in the workings of the party), building coalitions of support, opening itself up to interaction with interest groups, and having to set priorities concerning which groups to reward and which policies to advocate. This whole process would, for a time, increase conflict within an already conflict-ridden party, but it is argued that this

[5] I am grateful to Paul Brass for revising Indian press reports on the number of convicts.

[6] I am grateful to Myron Weiner for help in clarifying this disagreement. He tends to the former view and I to the latter.

would be healthy, creative conflict rather than the destructive squabbling of recent years.

Other analysts claim that if elections were held before some of the unsavory elements in the party were expelled—and this means hundreds of people, not the mere handful that have been thrown out—intraparty elections would be won by those with the money and the muscle to secure victory by foul means. Elections in the absence of a purge would institutionalize, legitimize and strengthen the worst elements in the Congress. What these analysts do *not* disagree on is that if neither intraparty elections nor a large-scale cleansing occurs, then the Congress organization will remain riddled with corruption and destructive factionalism. And yet that is precisely the way that things have turned out.

Rajiv Gandhi's main opportunity—perhaps his only major opportunity—to take his party in hand arose immediately after his mother's murder in the run-up to the national election in December 1984. He enjoyed so much support in the party and the country at large that for a short time there were scarcely any limits on his freedom of action. He could have systematically ousted from the party, or at least from his list of parliamentary candidates, people with established records of misconduct. In one of his most serious errors of judgement, he failed to do so. Many incumbent members of Parliament from the Congress party *were* denied renomination—no less than 37 percent of them. But the criterion used was their perceived chance of winning. Some corrupt and divisive persons were ousted since they seemed likely losers, but many were kept on. The prime minister was so certain to win the election that he could have risked the loss of a few seats by ridding himself of undesirables. But he lacked the confidence to do so and, thereby, probably scuttled any hope of a significant revival of Congress.

Since then, he has handled the party so hesitantly and inconsistently that little improvement has been possible. During his first year in office, he did little to the party other than building up a computerized profile of every constituency in the land. Since the collection of data was left to often dubious Congress activists, the exercise was frequently worse than pointless. He eventually realized this, and it dented his initial belief that technology and the science of management could serve as substitutes for a necessarily untidy party organization. At the end of that first year, he put a tough and experienced organizer—Arjun Singh—in charge of the party with a mandate to whip it into shape.

Rajiv did not fully grasp, however, that in the short run this was bound to cause bitter resentment among those who lost out. By late 1986, the inevitable avalanche of complaints persuaded him that it had all been a terrible mistake. In a characteristically dismissive reaction, he removed Arjun Singh to a minor Cabinet post, sacked the team of party general secretaries who had served under him and—for several weeks as state elections in Kerala and West Bengal loomed—left the party headquarters in New Delhi virtually unattended. Later in 1987, when Gandhi found himself besieged on several fronts, he appointed a new team of general secretaries and brought men of fetid reputation back into the high command for the first time since Mrs. Gandhi's day.[7] It seems highly unlikely that the Congress party will experience an organizational revival under its present leader.

The Condition and Prospects of the Opposition

It is best to begin by identifying the opposition parties, or—since they are a legion—those parties which possessed at least modest importance during 1987. They can be roughly broken down into three categories: (1) *"hard" parties* which are well disciplined and manned by committed grass roots activists who take the parties' clear and elaborate ideologies seriously; (2) *consensual parties* which have more internal diversity of view, and pay less attention to ideological clarity and discipline; and (3) *avowedly regional parties* which operate within single states and are often dominated by a single leader. It should be clearly understood, however, that this is a very rough breakdown. Several parties do not fit neatly within a single category. For example, some of the "consensual" parties suffer frequent bouts of intolerant assertiveness from their leaders, and one of the three main "hard" parties has liberalized somewhat in recent years. Despite such ambiguities, it is still worth briefly surveying the field.

The three "hard" parties that count for something are the Bharatiya Janata Party (BJP) to the right of center, and two parties of the left: the Communist Party of India (CPI) and the Communist Party of India–Marxist (CPI–M). The BJP, which has lately liberalized, began life as the Jan Sangh with a far more aggressively Hindu chauvinist line than has been evident in recent years. Like the "hard" parties of the left, the BJP's leaders came to appreciate liberal rights and open politics when these were taken away during the Emergency in the mid–1970s. Unlike the Communists, they merged themselves into the ruling Janata Party between 1977 and 1979, and when it broke up they abandoned the centralized, disciplined, "hard" constitution of the Jan Sangh and opted for a freer, more consensual set of rules for the new BJP. They retain enough of the old, cadre–based organization to be included among the "hard" parties, but their position is now ambiguous. They also adopted

[7] See, for example, *India Today*, October 30, 1987.

more liberal policies toward religious minorities and on other fronts. When Indira and Rajiv Gandhi adopted Hindu chauvinist postures between 1982 and 1984, the BJP found itself in the curious position of being more tolerant of minorities than Congress was. The BJP has not altered its position much since then, but Congress and Rajiv Gandhi have veered back and forth between Hindu chauvinism and concessions to minorities.

The BJP suffered serious losses at the national election in 1984, as many Hindu extremists deserted it for Congress and as anger at Indira Gandhi's murder by Sikhs made many Hindu moderates into temporary extremists. Since then, however, the party has stuck assiduously to the patient organizational work at which it has always excelled, and it is quite capable of taking advantage of whatever opportunities may arise in the regions where it is strongest. These are mainly the states of Rajasthan and Himachal Pradesh, and the union territory of Delhi. Elsewhere, the BJP continues to have difficulty extending its base beyond the urban, middle class, high caste groups that have always backed it. But its success as part of the victorious coalition in the Haryana state election in June 1987 showed it to be a useful ally, even though it was clearly the junior partner there—winning 15 seats alongside its Lok Dal partner's 58. It became embroiled in the vituperative exchanges with the communist left in 1987 that probably hurt both groups, but if the BJP can find a place in the main opposition coalition at the next national election, it may once again enjoy a spell in power in New Delhi.

Today more than ever, the CPI–M predominates over the Moscow–oriented CPI, from which it split in 1964. It ended the year as the ruling party in three states: Kerala, West Bengal, and the tiny hill state of Tripura, a Bengali–dominated state east of Bangladesh which fell to Congress in questionable circumstances in early 1988. The CPI–M is far less attentive to Soviet interests and inclinations than is the CPI, and on most issues it stands to the left of the CPI. But both parties are relatively moderate as communist parties go, seeking substantial reform through electoral and parliamentary politics. The Maoists who broke away from these parties two decades ago have, through failure and repression, been reduced to a few minor pockets of influence.

Nineteen eighty–seven was a good year for the communist parties, especially for the CPI–M, which won reelection as the ruling power in West Bengal and ousted the Congress–led coalition government in Kerala where it had previously held power. The latter victory was the more surprising, since the party had taken what many regarded as a rash gamble by refusing to forge an electoral alliance with parochial parties representing Christian and Muslim minorities and certain castes, as it had done repeatedly in recent years. But its widely anticipated reelection in West Bengal was—in historical terms—the more important, since it reconfirmed that for the first time in India a communist party had built itself a solid rural base which made it virtually unassailable at election time. This produces intense anxiety among the Congress party's national leaders. The CPI–M and the CPI also managed largely to avoid the squabbles that have divided them in the past, and at year's end, they mounted the most massive leftist rally ever held in New Delhi, drawing mainly on the surrounding Hindi region where they are supposed to be weak.

It is unlikely, however, that these parties will make major advances anytime soon beyond the traditional CPI–M bastions of West Bengal and Kerala. (Indeed, they have a long way to go before establishing themselves as the predominant force in the latter.) Experience indicates that a party's ability to mobilize huge numbers at political rallies is a poor guide to electoral prospects. It is also probable that the communist parties will fight the next national election largely alone, cut off from a broad coalition of opposition forces which is likely to form—after a fashion—and which might well defeat the Congress (although they will reach informal agreements to avoid pointless contests in certain regions). These two parties may even find it impossible to stick together, given the CPI–M's view of itself as the senior partner and the CPI's tendency to strike deals with Congress.

Three "consensual" parties are important enough to discuss here: the Lok Dal, which split during 1987, and the Janata Party. They claim to have a national role, and while this is not entirely spurious, their support is heavily concentrated within specific regions. The Janata Party, a descendant of the ruling party of the late 1970s, is a heterogeneous assemblage of forces clustered around the center of the political spectrum. During 1987, it provided reasonably clean, effective government in the southern state of Karnataka and had scattered pockets of significant strength elsewhere. But it lacked any real hope of forming further state governments except as part of an anti–Congress coalition of the kind that it will probably join as the next national election approaches. The party is troubled by personal rivalry between its leader, Chandrashekhar, who aspires to high office in New Delhi, and the impressive Karnataka chief minister, Ramakrishna Hegde, whom many regard as a potential prime minister. His state government ran into heavy weather in 1987, after several successful years, but it is unlikely that these problems will do much damage to Janata's potential as a useful coalition partner.

The Lok Dal, which used to form the second "consensual" party, was the creation of Charan Singh, who for two decades had opposed

Congress on behalf of Hindi–speaking India's cultivating peasants and who served as caretaker prime minister for half a year between the Janata and Indira Gandhi governments in 1979. His death in May 1987 caused his party to split, with the "Lok Dal (A)" led by his inexperienced son Ajit and the "Lok Dal (B)" by the veteran H.N. Bahuguna. His passing and this schism heralded important changes within the opposition, some of which are still obscure. It is worth asking two questions about these developments because the answers will give the reader a taste of the complexities that lie just beneath the surface of Indian politics.

First, what are the implications of these events for opposition unity in national elections? Charan Singh's departure simplifies the task of the unifiers because he was a man whose fierce quest for national preeminence repeatedly created irritation and even crisis among the opponents of Congress. Among other things, his ambition brought down the Janata government in New Delhi in 1979. At the same time, however, the Lok Dal split has added a further division to an already fragmented opposition, and the acute antagonisms between the two successor parties will make it very difficult for them to make common cause at national elections any time soon.

Do these events mean that the two Lok Dals will perform less well than in Charan Singh's day, and that North India's cultivators and others whose interests he championed will be less effectively represented? On the one hand the votes and financial resources which used to go from his peasant constituency to his party will now be divided, which will mean a certain dilution of their effect. But this negative impact may be outweighed by a surprising gain that has already carried the Lok Dal (B) to a spectacular election victory in the state of Haryana in June 1987. While Charan Singh lived, he ruled the Lok Dal with a heavy hand. This prevented powerful state-level leaders in the party from conducting campaigns tailored to conditions in their states rather than to Charan Singh's preoccupations. His passing liberated such men, as one of them—Haryana's Devi Lal—vividly demonstrated in June when his campaign, directed at issues particular to his home state, subjected Rajiv Gandhi's Congress to one of the worst political thrashings in its history, reducing it from a majority to a rump of five seats in a 90–seat legislature. His landslide victory will enable him to attend to the interests of Charan Singh's peasant constituents better than might have been possible had the old man lived.

This brings us, finally, to the avowedly regional parties of Tamil Nadu, Kashmir, Assam, and Andhra Pradesh.[8] All of them are beset by major uncertainties, most of which pose problems for Congress. In the last week of 1987 the death of the film star and chief minister of Tamil Nadu, M.G. Ramachandran, destabilized the politics of his state and his regional party, the All India Anna Dravida Munnetra Kazhagam (AIADMK)—both of which he dominated. This might appear to give Congress an opportunity to reestablish itself in the state, but will probably hurt Congress since a fragment of MGR's party or its rival, the regional Dravida Munnetra Kazhagam (DMK), will likely take over, and neither may be as willing as he was to treat with Rajiv Gandhi.

In Kashmir, chief Minister Farooq Abdullah of the main regional party, the National Conference (F)—who was first forced out of office and then drawn into a ruling alliance by the Congress—ended the year in serious difficulty. An unwise decision in October inflamed Hindu–Muslim and sub–regional antagonisms in this communally polarized state. His Congress partners in government then sought unwisely to exploit this against him, and rioting and widespread protests occurred. The beneficiaries were more extreme parties on each side of the communal divide.

In Assam, the largest state in the far northeast, the resentments of native Assamese against immigrants threatened to convulse the state by year's end. The regional party, the Asom Gana Parishad, which had ridden the issue to an election victory over Congress after a tense and sometimes violent movement in the early 1980s, had become deeply frustrated over the inadequate implementation of their 1985 accord with Rajiv Gandhi which set out ways of dealing with the immigration issue. Most people in Assam appear to blame this on deliberate foot–dragging by the authorities in New Delhi, and Congress is unlikely to profit from whatever disruptions may arise there.

Only in Andhra Pradesh, where the other film star chief minister, N.T. Rama Rao, and his regional Telugu Desam party faced major trouble, did Congress seem likely to gain advantage over the opposition. Serious allegations of corruption and the award of ministerial offices to a second Rama Rao son–in–law and his astrologer intensified long–standing discontent over his inaccessibility, impulsive decision–making, and an expensive free lunch scheme that crippled the exchequer and weak party organization. Congress is the only serious alternative in the state.

---

[8] I exclude parties which have very little hope of gaining power at the state level, the parties in the tiny northeastern hill states, and the Akali Dal in Punjab which is dealt with later.

Efforts to promote cooperation among opposition parties during 1987 made little headway. Attempted conferences among opposition leaders were more notable for absentees than for anything else. But this should not be seen as a deeply serious matter—yet. With only one–fifth of the seats in Parliament, even a united opposition could accomplish little at present. The key question is whether they can coalesce at the next national election, due in late 1989.

There is certain to be at least one serious division within the opposition ranks at the time of the elections. The two communist parties and the BJP detest one another so thoroughly and have clashed so noisily in 1987 that they will not cooperate. Instead, one or the other of these forces is likely to join an electoral alliance with many of the centrist opposition parties—the Janata Party, one or both of the Lok Dals, the regional parties, probably V.P. Singh's group (which will be discussed later), and perhaps some Congress defectors. This could amount to a formidable force if major leaders are kept in check, if the distribution of nominations and campaign funds is seen by most or all parties to have been reasonably fair, and if political activists at the grass roots are not so embittered by past conflicts that they will not cooperate. Such a coalition would be even better placed if it decided, pragmatically, not to oppose candidates from anti–Congress parties outside the coalition, where such parties had the best chance to win the seat. But all of these are big "ifs." India's opposition parties have been more effective at uniting when they were motivated by *fear*—in 1977, after nineteen months of the Emergency—than when faced with *opportunity*. In 1989, it is likely that they will encounter only the latter.

What do the three *state* election victories of the opposition against the Congress in 1987 imply about the next *national* election? There are two main views on this question. Some analysts argue that although the opposition's chances should cause Congress leaders concern, they do not imply that the party faces defeat at the national level.[9] They base this view on the belief that state and national elections evoke markedly different responses from voters. State elections tend to be decided on issues particular to the state, and since Congress is often seen as a national party, opposition parties which concentrate on only one state or a few states often win at the state level. Those who hold this view recognize that the Congress party is overly–centralized and ineffective. But they claim that Congress nevertheless wins national elections because it is led by a person of national stature and is the only genuinely national party. In their eyes, the 1977 election—in which the Janata

[9] Again, Myron Weiner tends to the former view, and I to the latter. A reliable opinion poll in August 1987 lent credence to his view, but the next election is still far away.

Party defeated Congress after the excesses of the Emergency—was an aberration from the norm of national Congress victories.

Others disagree, arguing that recent state election defeats carry grave implications for Congress. They contend that although state and national elections differ in character, they have (with one exception) tended to follow the same logic since about 1972. Since then, both types of elections have usually been decided by voters' judgements of the concrete performance of incumbents. The awakening electorate has grown increasingly impatient with parties in power, and political decay makes ruling parties less able to respond effectively to pressure from voters. As a result, the norm at both state and national elections changed around 1972. Before that, incumbents—mostly Congress incumbents—were usually reelected. Since then, in most state elections and in two of three national elections, incumbents have been defeated. Every state in India has now experienced at least one spell of non-Congress government, and in some states, effective performance by opposition parties in power has earned them reelection. So despite the appeal of Congress as a national party, Rajiv Gandhi could face defeat at the next election if he and his party perform poorly in office, as they are doing. For this set of analysts, the 1984 election—when Rajiv Gandhi's inspiring freshness as the only leader unencumbered by an ambiguous past and the intense emotions unleashed by his mother's murder caused voters to ignore the indifferent performance of his party—was an aberration from the norm of stern judgments on incumbents.

Finally, no review of the opposition could exclude Gandhi's imaginative attempt during late 1986 and early 1987 to coopt erstwhile opposition leaders and parties. He first reached out to ex–Congressmen in an effort to reincorporate them into the ruling party, and here he scored a major success by drawing the Congress (S) back into the fold. This was the potent opposition party in the large western state of Maharashtra where its leader, the formidable ex–chief minister Sharad Pawar, had a solid base. Gandhi then made overtures to opposition leaders who were more remote from Congress, seeking not to draw them into his party but to forge alliances with them. Again he succeeded when Farooq Abdullah, whose ouster as chief minister of Kashmir Rajiv Gandhi had helped to organize in 1984, joined forces with Congress in a new ruling coalition in that state.

Compared to Mrs. Gandhi's confrontational and sometimes unconstitutional approach which often backfired by creating public sympathy for her adversaries, this was a much more subtle strategy for dealing with the opposition. Had Rajiv been able to carry it further, he would soon have removed enough parties from the opposition ranks to make Congress very difficult to defeat at future national elections. He certainly tried. There is evidence that he tempted the Janata Party's chief minister of Karnataka, Ramakrishna Hegde, with an important post in New Delhi that would have taken him out of party politics. But his efforts were in vain, mainly because opposition leaders no longer believed that Congress would remain the dominant force in national politics. In Nehru's time, Congress's dominance enabled it to incorporate many opponents, but times have changed. By the end of 1987, the prime minister's fortunes had declined sufficiently to scuttle his chances of further gains of this type. His increasing reversion to the caustic, confrontational rhetoric toward the opposition which had marked his election campaign, his willingness to tolerate the punitive transfer of judges, and increasing pro–Congress partisanship by state governors whom the Constitution requires to be neutral, suggested that he would not resume attempts to bargain with the opposition.

The Case of V.P. Singh

V.P. Singh, who began the year as Rajiv Gandhi's finance minister, ended it as his most formidable opponent. He needs to be considered as standing adjacent to but separate from the opposition parties, since he chose neither to join nor to form one. Instead, he founded the *Jan Morcha*, or People's Movement, which was a crusade open to members of various parties rather than a party in its own right. By adopting this approach he could claim that he stood above the pettiness of party conflict, seeking to cleanse politics rather than to gain power. This has genuine appeal in India where it echoes the style of Mahatma Gandhi and Jayaprakash Narayan who never held any office and who gained enormous moral authority by their detachment from such ambitions.

This stance also had more mundane advantages, however. By not joining an opposition party, he keeps open the possibility of reentering Congress should Rajiv Gandhi decide to invite him back on satisfactory terms. Alternatively, a large bloc of Congress members of Parliament and party activists might desert Gandhi out of exasperation with his leadership and despair over his election prospects. There is a very large number of disgruntled people in the party—especially in what Ramakrishna Hegde has called the "obese" Congress majority in Parliament—and if they defected, V.P. Singh would be the obvious choice as leader.[10] If the prime minister's standing does not improve significantly, such a breakaway may even become a probability as the 1989 election approaches. V.P. Singh is also well placed should the post of prime minister fall vacant. This could happen if Rajiv Gandhi decided to retire

[10] Interview with Hegde, January 7, 1985.

from politics—a possibility that should not be entirely ruled out, since he is often deeply frustrated—or if, tragically, another assassination attempt were to succeed, or in the unlikely event of his ouster by Congress members of Parliament. And by standing above party politics for a time, V.P. Singh can remain a plausible leader of an opposition coalition in the run–up to the next election or in the next Parliament should no party obtain a majority—which at this writing seems a distinct possibility.

Since leaving office, V.P. Singh has constantly stressed that he was driven out because he was too committed to combatting corruption, and the facts tend to bear him out. In January 1987, he was moved from the Finance Ministry to Defense, in part because he had organized too many tax raids on wealthy industrialists and others. A few weeks later his position as defense minister became untenable when it was revealed that he had initiated an investigation by a U.S. company of possible kickbacks to prominent Indians by the Swedish armaments firm, Bofors, at the time India made a huge purchase of howitzers from that company—kickbacks which appear to have found their way into Swiss bank accounts. His righteous campaign thereafter was anathema to the prime minister who until then had been much admired as India's "Mr. Clean," and V.P. Singh was expelled from the Congress party.

A few words of caution are in order, however, about V.P. Singh's effort to establish himself as a convincing alternative to the prime minister. First, the group of dissidents expelled from Congress around the time of his ouster—men with whom he has associated since—do not all enjoy the popular admiration which he does. Among them was a man who is reliably reported to have been the main custodian of the vast payments of ill–gotten funds which Congress state chief ministers were forced to send to Mrs. Gandhi during the last decade of her life.[11] Little of that money has ever been properly accounted for. That group also included V.C. Shukla, the most prominent muzzler of the Indian press during the Emergency, and Arun Nehru—relative of Rajiv Gandhi—who had deeply alienated many Congress members with arrogance and bullying prior to his dismissal. These people do not have well–cultivated power bases and they may turn out to be serious liabilities for V.P. Singh.

Second, it is important not to overestimate Singh's potential appeal to the great mass of voters. In most of India—that is beyond the north–central Hindi belt from which he comes—he is little known outside the small urban middle class. He has had some success at attracting crowds in western India, but on present evidence his impact in the non–Hindi

[11] This is based on extensive interviews with the late D. Devaraj Urs in the late 1970s.

states may be limited despite the sizable press coverage that he has received. It is not even clear how effective he can be in the Hindi belt where the opposition most needs help. The geographic area that might be described as his personal power base there is quite small. But the caste cluster from which he comes—the Rajputs—enjoy considerable political, economic, and numerical strength across the Hindi–speaking states. If he can forge ties between them and other key groups that have lately opposed Congress and Rajiv Gandhi—most notably the Jats (mainly peasant proprietors) and groups involved in animal husbandry—then Congress will lose many seats in the Hindi belt.[12] It could suffer an electoral catastrophe if Scheduled Caste (ex–untouchable) and Muslim voters who used to back Congress continue recent swings to narrow protest parties.

Finally, it is not clear how much damage the allegations about high level involvement in kickbacks from Bofors and other sources will do Rajiv Gandhi. At this writing, they are no longer the central issue in public debate. Despite brave investigations in the face of aggressive government harassment, the *Indian Express* newspaper group and others have not yet succeeded in convincing the public that Rajiv Gandhi was closely linked to this scandal. But a reliable opinion poll in mid–1987 suggested that he may be less able than his mother to emerge unscathed when scandals ensnare his close associates.[13]

The Sri Lanka Initiative and Domestic Politics

One of the developments which distracted public attention from the Bofors scandal was India's initiative in Sri Lanka. The decision to act and its political impact within India yield insights into domestic politics. This complex episode has been assessed in detail elsewhere (see "India's Foreign Relations: Problems along the Borders," by T.P. Thornton in this volume) and it is necessary here to simplify somewhat.[14] The Indian authorities had several reasons for deciding to intervene in Sri Lanka. They were concerned with the 130,000 or so Tamil refugees who fled across the straits to the Indian state of Tamil Nadu to escape the civil war. It was difficult to see how large numbers could return unless something was done to promote peace and reconciliation in Sri Lanka, and New Delhi rightly concluded that polarization between Sinhalese and Tamils on the island had gone so far that the resources no longer

[12] I am grateful to Paul Brass for this information.

[13] *India Today*, August 31, 1987.

[14] Nor did it later lead to extensive atrocities against civilians by Indian forces in Sri Lanka, as has been falsely alleged by both Tamil and Sinhalese extremists on the island.

existed there to achieve those goals. It was feared that the refugees' plight might excite disturbances in the South Indian state of Tamil Nadu, and armed militants among the refugees had already engaged in acts of banditry and violence within south India. With troubles in the Punjab, and the high incidence of collective violence across much of India, Rajiv Gandhi and his circle were intensely conscious of the need to act firmly to prevent outbreaks elsewhere.

By June 1987, Sri Lanka's Army stood at the gates of Jaffna, the main city in northern Sri Lanka containing nearly one million unarmed Tamil civilians. If the army moved in to try to break the power of armed Tamil militants, as seemed probable, it was likely that large numbers of noncombatants would be massacred, since the Sri Lanka security forces had engaged in such atrocities on many previous occasions. If that occurred, riotous reactions in Tamil Nadu would be almost inevitable. The widespread killing of civilians was also plainly unacceptable on humanitarian grounds, and Indian leaders were very anxious to prevent it. This was characteristic of India's long-standing concern with the welfare of people of Indian origin overseas. But thanks to proximity and military superiority, India had seldom been in a position to embody that concern in effective action.

Another element was the desire among some politicians, foreign affairs advisers and senior military figures in New Delhi that India assert itself more forcefully as the dominant power in South Asia. These sentiments were evident in their extreme sensitivity to Sri Lanka's arrangements with foreign broadcasting agencies, its failed attempt to persuade the United States to make greater use of Trincomalee harbor, its hiring of small numbers of British ex–commandos and members of the Israeli security services for training of security personnel, and its unproductive overtures to Pakistan.

Finally, it is no accident that the initiative in Sri Lanka occurred soon after the humiliations suffered by Rajiv Gandhi's Congress party in the Haryana state elections. After the V.P. Singh affair and allegations of illegalities in the arms purchase from Bofors, that election result left the prime minister badly in need of a major success. Sri Lanka was meant to provide it and in the short run at least, it yielded considerable benefits.

The accord signed by Rajiv Gandhi and President Jayewardene of Sri Lanka on 29 July was imposed upon unwilling extremists in both the majority Sinhalese and the minority Tamil communities on the island. It is to be welcomed since it probably prevented massacres in Jaffna[15] and

[15] This is based on reports from *The Hindu* (Madras) during May and June, 1987, and on numerous interviews with key Indian and Sri Lankan officials and with Tamil extremist sources.

it provided—over the medium term, after an initial backlash from both linguistic groups—the first real hope of reconciliation in Sri Lanka since 1981. Well-placed sources in both countries indicated that, contrary to claims by both governments, India compelled Jayewardene to accept the accord by issuing something close to an ultimatum. He was told that Indian forces would move into the predominantly Tamil Northern Province and Jaffna, and into the mixed Eastern Province, with or without an invitation from Sri Lanka.

There is no other way to explain Jayewardene's sudden abandonment of the acutely anti-Indian posture that he had long adopted to generate popular support among the Sinhalese, at the very moment that his army was poised—after years of inconclusive struggle—to take Jaffna. Jayewardene agreed partly because resistance was pointless and partly because he could see that the accord might possibly take hold, despite opposition from Tamil militants and most Sinhalese. The Indian Army would deal with armed Tamil separatists, and the ghastly civil war might be brought to an end. If that occurred, national unity would be preserved, he could retire as the statesman responsible, and his party might—after a period of intense unpopularity among the Sinhalese—reap some benefit. But despite these considerations, he signed the accord under duress.

In the first few weeks after the signing, Rajiv Gandhi won plaudits within India from those (especially in Tamil Nadu) who had agonized over the fate of Tamils in Jaffna, from those who enjoy seeing India assert itself in the international arena, and from many who had come to doubt that he was capable of forceful, creative action. After mid-October, when Indian forces in Sri Lanka were driven into a prolonged and bloody assault on the main Tamil extremist group, some doubts emerged. By year's end, concern had begun to mount about the long stay on the island that appears to face the Indian forces, and about antipathy toward them in both the Tamil and Sinhalese communities in Sri Lanka. But on balance the initiative in Sri Lanka was still widely appreciated as an exercise in peacemaking, and it was useful to Rajiv Gandhi as a counterweight to problems such as Bofors, V.P. Singh, and his party's electoral performances.

Riots, the Punjab Crisis, and the Statist Response

Over the last decade, India has been afflicted by serious violence which could provoke an abandonment of open politics. In part, this has taken the form of riotous clashes between caste or religious groups, or between these groups and police. The number of such incidents fluctuates from year to year, but since 1979 the level of violence has been high. Of equal concern has been the tendency of corrupt and demoralized police to compound the problem by running away, overreacting or joining in with one set of rioters. This has forced the authorities to ask the army to reimpose order on an enormous number of occasions. Official figures indicate that it was called out in aid of civil authority on 82 occasions in 1982–83, on 96 in 1983–84, and on a staggering 175 occasions in 1984–85.[16] These statistics would have been unimaginable in the Nehru years.

We have no official figures on the number or the intensity of violent clashes during 1987, but an initial rough estimate suggests that there were fewer than in recent years. India certainly experienced nothing this year to rival the disorders that gripped much of urban Gujarat in the second quarter of 1985, creating something approaching the Hobbesian state of nature—a war of all against all with clashes between a baffling array of castes, class groups, religious groups, and sects within religious groups. For the first time on that occasion, the presence of the army over a period of several weeks was insufficient to quell the disturbances.

Nonetheless, hair–raising violence still erupted in 1987, most especially in the northern city of Meerut where the acute Hindu–Muslim tensions that gripped much of the Hindi–speaking areas through the year produced grisly results. A major riot between Hindus and Muslims was rendered far worse when the predominantly Hindu state police went on a "killing spree" in the Muslim quarter. An experienced Indian journalist who had seen enough riots in his time to be hardened wrote about Meerut:

> . . . I am writing this piece in sheer anguish . . . With all that has happened in Meerut I do not think we can call ourselves civilised, let alone citizens of a great nation with a rich heritage. We are simply barbarians who take pleasure in killing each other. It is sheer sadistic pleasure. Loss of life and destruction of property has been unprecedented. I have investigated many riots but have not seen the things that I saw in Meerut. Believe me, I am not exaggerating.
>
> What is sad, Hindus told me how many Hindus were killed and Muslims how many Muslims were slaughtered. No one was genuinely concerned about human life as such . . .[17]

Such violence should not yet be seen as an example of the irreparable rending of the social fabric. It is best understood as a result of the social and political awakening that has been occurring over more than two

[16] *India Today*, 15 May 1985. See also Kuldip Nayar in *The Times* (London), May 18, 1984.

[17] Asghar Ali Engineer in the *Indian Express*, June 22, 1987.

decades at the same time as political institutions have undergone decay.[18]

There was a time when such institutions, especially the Congress party's organization before Mrs. Gandhi weakened it, were able to anticipate simmering conflicts between social groups and to act to reduce tensions before violence broke out. They would promote dialogue and bargains between leaders of social groups, and offer exasperated groups concessions and patronage to cool tempers. This is far less easy today, partly because political institutions are less able to identify and respond to mounting tensions, but also because the awakening that has occurred makes social groups more aware that they are in competition with others, and more assertive in their efforts to satisfy enlarged appetites for resources. When leaders of social groups seek help from politicians and find them short of resources, hungry for exorbitant bribes or even thuggish in their responses, they are naturally repelled—so that something of a divergence between politics and society has occurred of late. Social groups have tended to turn inward and to batten on parochial identities and resentments which can be manipulated by extremists and can easily lead to violence.

The source of the most unnerving violence in recent years has of course been the crisis in relations between the Sikh minority (2 percent of India's population) and both the Hindus and the Indian authorities. The most serious outrage in this sad business occurred in 1984—the assassination of Indira Gandhi in the eyes of many Hindus and the authorities, and for Sikhs the Indian Army's invasion of their sacred Golden Temple and the massacres of over 3,000 Sikhs after the assassination. But 1987 also witnessed its share of baleful incidents: the massacres of Hindus on bus routes in Punjab and neighboring Haryana and at garden parties in Delhi, scores of assassinations by Sikh extremists in Punjab and allegations that police there had murdered many Sikhs in faked encounters.

Several political decisions and events in 1987 deepened the alienation of Sikhs. The most serious was the June decision in New Delhi to impose President's Rule in Punjab, the one predominantly Sikh state. This is a constitutional device which allows the President of India, on the advice of the prime minister, to dissolve an elected government in an Indian state for up to one year if disturbances or irregularities arise and to rule it through civil servants answerable to the state governor, a presidential nominee. The government which was dissolved in Punjab consisted of moderates from the Sikh Akali Dal party. Rajiv Gandhi and his col-

[18] James Manor, *Collective Conflict in India*, Institute for the Study of Conflict monographs (London, 1988).

leagues had previously had the vision to see that it was better to have a Sikh administration trying to impose order on their own extremists than to have New Delhi bear that odium. But the prime minister was desperate to avoid defeat in the crucial state elections in neighboring Haryana where the huge Hindu majority harbored acute anti–Sikh sentiments, and the ouster of the Sikh government was meant to gain their support. It failed utterly when Haryana voters humiliated Congress, and left New Delhi with a fresh problem in Punjab. Thereafter, its regime in the state employed extremely harsh police tactics which have angered many once–moderate Sikhs. This approach took a heavy toll among Sikh extremists, but at year's end they were still capable of creating considerable havoc.

The New Delhi government compounded this problem further by failing to mount satisfactory investigation of the murders of more than 3,000 Sikhs in a post–assassination pogrom in 1984. Two authoritative citizens' inquiries have alleged that Congress party activists assisted the mobs that did the killing. No one has been brought to book for these atrocities, however, and two men allegedly involved hold ministerial rank in Rajiv Gandhi's government. The authorities refused for many months to launch an inquiry into the riots. When they did, its anodyne and tangential findings inspired still more cynicism among Sikhs. This does not mean that reconciliation with the Sikhs is impossible—a serious effort might well bear fruit, although that might require a change of government in New Delhi. But events such as these clearly make further violence over the medium term more likely.

The increase in various forms of violence in recent years has caused considerable anxiety in India and has, not surprisingly, evoked a hard-line statist reaction in some quarters—that is, response favoring forceful or draconian action by central authorities to maintain law and order, if necessary at the expense of traditional liberties. Indians have long demonstrated the capacity to face substantial violence without being panicked into draconian reactions which might make things worse by weakening or destroying political institutions that can eventually promote accommodation. Indians have experienced clashes between religious and caste groups for many decades, and they have tended to believe that in such a heterogeneous society, disturbances are bound to occur. They need to be firmly dealt with by security forces, but they do not prefigure the collapse of society or the political order. But given recent levels of violence, some politicians and intellectuals—including persons close to the prime minister—have concluded that the unity of India and the survival of the Indian nation–state are at serious risk. Some of them see violence by Sikh extremists and inter–caste or Hindu–Muslim riots as part of a common pattern, perhaps even of a conspiracy. Some also believe that these incidents are linked to a desire by foreign powers—usually Pakistan and the United States—to undermine or destroy India. For evidence, they point to the assistance which Pakistan has clearly and unwisely provided to Sikh terrorists,[19] Pakistan's efforts to build nuclear weapons, and American willingness to give Pakistan massive aid despite these things.

Many who hold this fearful view propose a more assertive role for the state on two fronts. They believe that the current constitutional system places too many constraints on powerholders, and those with a technocratic bent often argue that democracy is untidy, that it impedes the efficient application of management science. Their second theme is the need for the state to intervene more within society, to take command and abandon the restrained posture which prevailed during the British period and through most of the years since Independence.

Such suggestions are based on a naively over-simplified notion of Indian society, and if implemented they would produce increased violence—the opposite result to that intended. Witness the way the dispute with the Sikhs was rendered worse by Mrs. Gandhi's intervention in the Golden Temple. Nevertheless, these statist ideas have acquired a certain currency amid conditions that might incline political incumbents to seize upon them. Many members of the current regime are under explicit threat from Sikh assassins. The loss of public office would entail the loss of the heavy protection that they now enjoy. This could provide a compelling reason to follow these statist prescriptions. For this reason an attempt by civilian elites to maintain themselves in power by autocratic means must be seen as the main threat to the survival of open representative politics in India.

The Capacity for Political Regeneration

This paper has mainly addressed India's political troubles, but these must be seen in the context of the proven ability of political institutions there to recover after suffering damage. This is something at which India is noticeably more adept than most of the less developed countries. This has become especially apparent in recent years, mainly at the state level, but within the central government as well.

In the early part of his premiership, Rajiv Gandhi sought to rebuild at least three sets of formal institutions which had been seriously undermined by his mother's centralizing ways. He sought to reactivate the ministries and bureaucracy of the central administrations which had

[19] This is based on authoritative reports by journalists known to the author, confirming official Indian allegations.

tended to wait for Mrs. Gandhi to make even minor decisions. He sought to restore the autonomy of the judiciary, partly in order to attract talented lawyers to the bench. And he sought to reestablish an accommodative relationship between New Delhi and state governments controlled by opposition parties. During 1987, he reversed direction on all three fronts when he found himself beleaguered, but all these institutions retain more substance than they possessed when he took power.

Nineteen eighty–seven saw the Indian presidency—which performs a role akin to the Crown in the British parliamentary system—reinvigorated. Five years earlier, Mrs. Gandhi had filled that office with a man of unsavory reputation because his political blunders—which included a speech to Parliament in praise of Adolph Hitler—had rendered him so abject that by raising him up, she ensured fulsome gratitude and loyalty from the president. Rajiv Gandhi regarded this man with intense distaste and allowed the institutional tie between the prime minister and the president to deteriorate badly. But in 1987, as the old president's term ended, Rajiv selected a widely respected man who—since taking office—has demonstrated a sophisticated grasp of constitutional subtleties and a sure sense of the balance between restraint and independence of mind which his office requires.

It is, however, at the state level where the system's capacity for political regeneration has been most evident. Here too, when destructive leaders and regimes have given way to more creative successors, institutions have regained substance and effectiveness. Two states—Maharashtra and Karnataka—were for several years governed by Congress chief ministers who operated roughly in the manner of Ferdinand Marcos. But in each case, those who replaced them allowed institutions to recover considerably. Similar trends were apparent during 1987 in other states where former regimes were less notorious—in Rajasthan, Haryana, and Kerala for example.

The main reason that institutions revive in this way is the large number of highly skilled political operatives that can be found in most regions and political parties. Time and again, politicians have shown a remarkable ability to comprehend subtle social changes and to adapt old methods of bargaining, patronage distribution, and coalition–building to new circumstances that are products of the political awakening of recent years. These skills, and at least a partial understanding that strong institutions and checks on the arbitrary use of power serve the long–term interests of power–*holders* as well as others, have repeatedly facilitated the regeneration of institutions. It is possible that the forces unleashed in this hierarchical society by a political system based on the egalitarian notion that everyone has one vote may someday destroy that very system. But for the present, this seems way off.

2
The Economy: Stresses, Strains, and Opportunities

T. N. Srinivasan*

Introduction

This chapter is devoted to economic and political developments in India in 1987 and their implications for meeting the challenge of India's development: transforming a slow–growing and agricultural economy in which two-fifths of the world's poor live into a rapidly growing, modern one that generates productive employment opportunities outside of agriculture. Perhaps the major event of 1987 from an economic standpoint was the failure of the summer monsoon, and consequently the severe drought in most of the country. We will discuss the likely impact of the drought on agricultural output (particularly of food grains) and on agro–processing industries, the purchase of food grains for and the stocks in the public distribution system, the budgetary consequences of drought relief programs, the need for imports of grains and other agricultural commodities, and the resulting demand for foreign exchange. Given the possibility of a disappointing monsoon in 1988, precautionary action may be required. A longer–term assessment of past investment (particularly in irrigation) to insulate the agricultural sector from ravages of drought will also be attempted.

In the political arena, the major domestic developments were the festering scandals, one relating to alleged payoffs on defense contracts by the Swedish firm Bofors, and the other relating to the appointment of the private U.S. investigating agency Fairfax to inquire into suspected illegal foreign exchange transactions by Indian companies and nationals. The stalemate in the struggle against Sikh separatism in the northwestern state of Punjab and the continuing violence there, apart from threatening national integrity, also constitutes an unproductive use of

*Thanks are due to J. Bhagwati, M. Bouton, S. Guhan, L. Kean, and R. Saah for their valuable comments on an earlier draft.

resources. The ongoing upgrading of Pakistani defense forces by the United States, ostensibly to meet the threat arising from Soviet intervention in Afghanistan, has prompted a 20 percent increase in India's defense budget for 1987–88 compared to the revised figures of 1986–87. And the economic cost of the Indian Peace Keeping Force (IPKF) in Sri Lanka, in what appears to be an open–ended commitment, is likely to be substantial.

We must also consider the erosion of the political support for Rajiv Gandhi's government, and the effect this will have on economic policies. Scandals have claimed a number of victims, the most prominent being Mr. V. P. Singh, the former finance (and later defense) minister in Mr. Gandhi's government. The architect of a number of economic policy initiatives during his tenure as finance minister, Mr. Singh was dismissed, first from the government and then from the ruling party, by Mr. Gandhi. He has now started his own political party. Others, perceived as threats to Mr. Gandhi's leadership, have been expelled from the ruling party.

Most of the economic policy initiatives of the Rajiv Gandhi government relate to external trade and industrial sectors. An assessment of these is facilitated by an understanding of the basic features of the Indian economy and India's development strategy since Independence in 1947, which will be reviewed in the following sections. The prospect of these initiatives in the changed political climate will be discussed in turn.

Basic Features of the Economy in Perspective

With a population of about 795 million in mid–1987, India is the second most populous country in the world. Although eleventh largest in terms of total gross domestic product (roughly $204 billion in 1986 at official exchange rates), India is also among the poorest of nations, with an average per capita income of about $290. Real national income grew at an average annual rate of under 4 percent from 1950 to 1980. Some—the government, in particular—have claimed that India has achieved an average growth rate of 5.6 percent during 1980–85 due to changes in economic policy. However, in part because this growth rate is misleadingly high (it represents a recovery from a steep decline of over 5 percent in 1979–80), and in part because the changes in policy are less of a break with the past than the government has claimed, it is still premature to pronounce a definitive increase in growth. Fortunately, the rate of growth of India's population has averaged only about 2.2 percent per year since the 1960s, a modest rate compared to many developing countries. Moreover, there is increasing evidence that fertility rates have started to decline. But given the growth momentum in the population of reproductive age, the decline in fertility will not result in an immediate drop in the rate of growth of population, but rather a long–term decline.

This is not the occasion to discuss the possible two–way relationship between population growth and economic development. It suffices here to say that India's relatively slow growth cannot be attributed to diverting resources away from investment to sustain a rapidly growing population. Nor can one foresee a sufficiently rapid decline in the population's growth rate in the short term to affect aggregate growth. With a declining rate of population growth, even an unchanging growth rate of total national income will mean a slightly faster rate of growth of per capita income than before. (See Table 2.1 for comparative statistics on India and other developing countries.)

Table 2.1

Selected Economic Indicators: India and Some Other Countries

	India	China	Brazil	Mexico	Korea
Population (millions) (1985)	765	1040	136	79	41
Geographical Area (thousand sq. km.)	3288	9561	8512	1973	98
Gross Domestic Product (GDP) (billions of US$) (1985)	176	266	188	177	86
Gross National Product (GNP) Per Capita US$ (1985)	270	310	1640	2080	2150
Share in GDP (Percent)					
Agriculture (1985)	31	33	13	11	14
Industry (1985)	27	47	33	35	41
Services (1985)	41	20	54	54	45
Value Added in Manufacturing (billions of US$) (1984)	30	144	57	43	27
Gross Domestic Investment/GDP (percent) (1985)	25	38	16	21	36
Gross Domestic Saving/GDP (percent) (1985)	21	34	22	26	38
Life Expectancy at Birth (Years) (1985)	56	69	65	67	69
Crude Birth Rate (1985)	33	18	29	33	21
Crude Death Rate (1985)	12	7	8	7	6
Infant Mortality Rate (1985)	89	35	67	50	27
Total Fertility Rate (1985)	3.0	2.1	2.6	2.8	2.1

	India	China	Brazil	Mexico	Korea
Labor Force in Agriculture (percent) (1980)	70	74	31	37	36
Labor Force in Industry (percent) (1980)	13	14	27	29	27
Merchandise Exports (billions of US$) (1985)	10	27	26	22	30
of which Manufactured Goods (billions of US$) (1985)	6	13	9	7	28
Merchandise Imports (billions of US$) (1985)	15	43	14	13	31
External Capital Inflow (Net) (billions of US$)	2.8	—	0.2	0.3	4.0
of which Public & Publicly guaranteed (millions of US$)	2.4	—	1.0	0.9	2.7
Total Outstanding External Debt (1986) (billions of US$)	41.1	22.7	110.7	101.7	45.1
Long-term Debt	34.5	17.2	97.2	91.0	34.3
of which (Public & Publicly guaranteed)	31.9	17.2	82.5	75.0	34.3
Use of IMF Credit	4.3	0.7	4.5	4.1	1.5
Short–term Debt	2.3	4.8	9.0	6.6	9.3
Total External Debt/Exports (percent) (1986)	276	75	438	428	108
Total External Debt/GNP (percent) (1986)	19	9	41	84	47
Total Debt Service/Exports (percent) (1986)	18	8	33	37	17
Total Debt Service/GNP (percent) (1986)	1	1	3	7	7
Central Government Revenue (Percent of GDP)	14.0	—	24.7	17.6	19.0
Central Government Expenditure (Percent of GDP)	16.7	—	21.1	24.9	18.4
Overall Government Deficit (Percent of GDP)	−8.4	—	−4.4	−7.7	−1.3
GDP Per Capita Growth Rate (1965–85)	1.7	4.8	4.3	2.7	6.6
Inflation Rate (1980–85)	7.8	2.4	147.7	62.2	6.0

Source: World Bank, *World Development Report*. New York: Oxford University Press, 1987.

Agriculture continues to be the dominant sector of the economy, accounting for more than one–third of the real gross domestic product (GDP) and two–thirds of employment. The manufacturing sector, although growing more rapidly than agriculture, has experienced a decline since the mid–1960s. Growth has recovered recently, though not to the rates attained during 1950–65. The share of manufacturing in real GDP has stagnated at about 15 percent for more than a decade. Indeed, the only sectors that have grown relatively rapidly in recent years are public administration and defense. Given this trend and the lack of any significant support in the commodity–producing sectors, some caution is warranted in assessing the long–term significance of the alleged upward shift in India's growth curve.

For such a poor country, India has substantially increased the gross domestic savings rate from under 10 percent of GDP in the early 1950s to nearly 22 percent in 1985–86. Low–income countries other than India and China saved on an average only 6 percent of their GDP in 1985, a decline from a rate of 15 percent in 1965. The Indian savings rate in 1985 of 21 percent compares favorably with the rate of 19 percent in the lower middle–income and 26 percent in the upper middle–income countries. The rates of gross domestic investment in India were 10 percent in the early 1950s, and 25 percent in 1985–86. Thus external borrowing and aid financed a relatively small part—about 8 percent—of gross domestic investment. The fact that more than a doubling of the investment rate since the early 1950s has not appreciably increased the aggregate growth rate reflects the increasing capital costs of India's pattern of development. This is largely due to the adoption of a strategy that emphasized self–reliance in almost total disregard for costs. A commanding role was assigned to the public sector which turned out to consume, rather than generate, resources. The Indian development strategy will be discussed in the following section. Substitution of imports (actual or potential) by domestic production through protection meant penalizing export sectors. The penalties were somewhat offset by a variety of implicit or explicit export subsidies. Nonetheless, India's share of world exports, and manufacturing exports in particular, steadily declined from about 2.5 percent in the early 1950s to less than 0.5 percent in the late 1980s.

One distinguishing aspect of Indian strategy, in contrast to other large countries which also emphasized import substitution such as Brazil or Mexico, is its conservative macroeconomic policies. This can be seen in the relatively slow growth in monetary holdings, which grew at an average annual rate of 15.3 percent during 1965–80 and 16.7 percent during 1980–85. The corresponding figures for Brazil were 43.4 percent and 175.6 percent; for Mexico 21.7 percent and 61.4 percent; and for Korea 35.5 percent and 18.4 percent. Macro–conservatism meant that inflation (as measured by the consumer price index) was negligible until the mid–1960s, when a concatenation of circumstances (two consecutive droughts, a massive increase in defense expenditures following skirmishes with China in 1962 and with Pakistan in 1965, devaluation of the rupee in June 1966, and a subsequent reduction in external aid) activated inflationary tendencies. Nonetheless, the inflation rate averaged only about 5 percent per year during 1965–80. Although it roughly doubled in 1980–85, hyperinflation of the Latin American variety did not develop in India. Another feature of macroconservatism is a reluctance to borrow extensively from foreign commercial banks at high and variable rates of interest. It is true that, unlike Brazil or Mexico, India as a poor country had access to concessional loans from the World Bank–affiliated International Development Association (IDA). Yet in the post–oil shock era, India's share of IDA loans went down dramatically after China's entry into the World Bank. Non–concessionary World Bank loans did not rise to offset the reduction in IDA loans. Even when credit was easily available from the private capital market prior to the onset of the debt crisis, India borrowed only limited amounts from foreign commercial banks despite pressures, particularly from the United States, to do so. The net result is that debt owed to private creditors amounted to less than 20 percent of total outstanding debt as of the end of 1986. Servicing long–term debt cost roughly a quarter of India's export earnings in 1986.

From the very beginning of national development planning in 1950, India's policymakers have been concerned with alleviation of poverty. With more than two–thirds of the population living in rural areas and dependent on agriculture, poverty is a predominantly rural problem. The proportion of the rural population with consumption below a modest poverty line (about $10 per capita per month) has fluctuated at about 50 percent, on an even level with fluctuations in agricultural income per capita until the late 1970s. Government calculations suggest that this proportion fell dramatically by the mid–1980s. Nongovernmental economists dispute the extent of the fall, but concede that some progress has been made in alleviating poverty.

To sum up, Indian economic development has neither been a spectacular success like that of some of the East Asian countries (e.g., South Korea, Taiwan) nor a dismal failure like that of some of the African countries (e.g., Ghana). However, relative to India's potential, there is no doubt that achievements have fallen short. The failure to build a rapidly growing manufacturing sector that exploits India's abundant labor resources has meant that employment opportunities outside of low–productivity agricultural occupations have grown too slowly to make a serious dent in poverty. Indeed, the major challenge facing India's policymakers is to change a primarily inwardly oriented, expensive, and technologically backward industrial sector into an internationally competitive, efficient, and rapidly growing sector of the economy. Whether this challenge will be met or not depends largely on whether the recent hesitant steps towards liberalizing the economy will become part of an extensive economic reform program or will be abandoned, as in the past, at the first sign of economic or political setbacks. Of course, the external environment is pivotal: increasing protectionism in the United States and other industrial countries, their lackluster economic growth, and failure to grapple with developing countries' debt and to ensure a positive and increasing net resource transfer from developed to developing countries cannot but reinforce the already strong predilection of Indian policymakers for inward orientation.

India's Development Strategy

The Directive Principles for State Policy as stated in the Constitution of India enjoin the state to strive to secure "a social order in which justice—social, economic and political—shall inform all the institutions of national life" and "to minimize inequality in income, status, facilities and opportunities, amongst individuals and groups." The Constitution also requires the state to ensure "that the ownership and control of the material resources of the community are so distributed as best to subscribe the common good; that the operation of the economic system does not result in the concentration of wealth and means of production to the common detriment." Article 43 of the Constitution seeks to secure the right to work, to education, and to public assistance in case of unemployment, disability, or sickness.

The strong egalitarian and redistributive thrust of these principles is evident. They assign a dominant role for the state in economic activity. Although the principles are not enforceable by any court of law and their objectives are yet to be attained in full measure, they have always been invoked in political and public policy discussions. Indeed the government resolution which established the Planning Commission in 1950 to articulate a national development strategy explicitly raised them. The first Five–Year Plan for the period 1951–56 set out the task of development as to "translate . . . the goals of social and economic policy prescribed in the Directive Principles of the Constitution . . . into a national program based upon the assessment of needs and resources" (as quoted in the Draft Sixth Five–Year Plan 1979–83). So far, six Five–Year (and three Annual) Plans have been completed. The Seventh Plan covers the period 1985–90, and preliminary work on the formulation of the Eighth Five–Year Plan has already begun.

The three basic objectives of Indian development strategy are economic growth, self–reliance, and social justice. The ideals of social justice expounded in the Directive Principles were later given substance in the form of a commitment to achieving a "socialistic pattern of society." The choice of the word "socialistic" rather than "socialist" was deliberate: it implied not only a realization that the Indian economy was a mixed economy with a significant private sector, but more important, it reflected the belief of many Indian leaders, most prominently the late prime minister Jawaharlal Nehru, that India's chosen democratic political framework could not be sustained without an economic framework in which the private sector played a significant role.

In agriculture, organization of production through small peasant farms was deemed preferable to agricultural capitalism based on large private farms or Soviet–style collectivization. In industry, the spheres of activity for the private and public sectors were clearly demarcated through the government's industrial policy resolutions of 1948 and 1956. Broadly speaking, industries were divided into three groups: those to be developed exclusively by the public sector, those reserved for the private sector, and those open to development by either or both sectors. Industries allocated to the public sector included the key infrastructural industries such as railways, telecommunications, and electrical power. Industries supplying key industrial raw materials and capital goods such as steel, petroleum, electric generators, and heavy machinery were also delegated to the public sector. The basic philosophy behind this choice was that by controlling the "commanding heights" of industry, the state would be able to direct industrial development as a whole. It was also believed that by choosing a pricing policy for goods and services supplied by the public sector, surpluses would be generated for investment. This emphasis on government control, guidance, and extraction of surpluses paid little attention to the possibility that, if operated inefficiently, the public sector could end up constraining economic growth, and instead of generating surpluses, might drain resources from the rest of the economy to finance its deficits. The public sector ended up not only operating in industries assigned to it under the industrial policy resolutions but in others as well. For instance, enterprises that were about to go bankrupt in the private sector textile industry were acquired by the public sector in order to protect the workers' jobs. But the losses in these enterprises continued to mount under public sector management. The actual performance of India's public sector over the last four decades has been to drain resources from the rest of the economy.

Any attempt to reduce the size of the public sector, even marginally, generates political resistance. Part of the resistance is ideological. It arises from a refusal to recognize that increasing the public sector's share in the economy has not led to the more egalitarian distribution of income which it was in theory supposed to achieve. Resistance has also come from the vested interests that have grown around the public sector in the form of powerful labor unions, the bureaucracy, and those reaping benefits from the pricing policy of public sector enterprises.

In addition to the private–public split of industrial activities, certain products were reserved for small–scale and cottage industries. This policy, perhaps unique to India, was a legacy of Mahatma Gandhi's vision of a self–sufficient village economy in which basic commodities were to be produced using labor–intensive techniques and employing village labor. Small-scale plants were distinguished from large–scale ones in terms of the value of investment, which was revised periodically to reflect inflation, among other things. To the extent a small–scale operator suffered disadvantages regarding access to markets for inputs, outputs, credit, or capital, but possessed technology equal to that of a large–scale operator, state intervention to offset these disadvantages might be appropriate. But in practice, the technology of some, if not most, of the small–scale plants appears to be inferior in the sense of requiring more capital, labor, and material inputs per unit of output than its large–scale counterpart. This has meant that resources could have been saved by not producing these commodities in the small–scale sector. Indeed, in cases where small–scale production is grossly inefficient, paying those employed in such firms an income subsidy and shutting down their operation could be considered socially worthwhile! Those small–scale producers that succeeded in upgrading their technology could not expand beyond the line of division separating the small–scale from large–scale firms without losing their privileges. In addition to sustaining inefficient resource use, the policy has not fulfilled its other objectives, such as diffusion of ownership and regional dispersion of location, to the extent envisaged.

The pursuit of self–reliance, combined with the objective of channelling industrial growth in 'planned' directions, led to the setting–up of an elaborate bureaucracy to regulate industrial investment and foreign trade. Government–issued industrial licenses are required for establishing anything other than a small–scale operation. An import license is needed for importing equipment and raw material. These controls were also used to serve other objectives such as avoiding concentration of market power and achieving balanced regional development. Large industrial houses were precluded from certain activities or had to pass additional bureaucratic hurdles. In an effort to obtain regional balance, licensed capacity in an industry was often divided into a number of plants located in different states. Each small plant was inefficient, whereas a single large plant would have been able to serve the national market. Details of the regulations have varied over time, but their broad features have remained essentially unchanged for more than 30 years. In the past, liberalization has usually not meant that the system was radically changed, but that it was operated in a less irksome way.

It is evident that the regulation of private economic activities through administrative controls creates incentives for their evasion and for corruption. In India, incomes earned from such illegal activities are called "black" incomes. Estimates of black incomes vary, but an authoritative study prepared by the National Institute of Public Finance and Policy estimated that they accounted for 18 to 21 percent of GDP in 1980–81, representing an increase of 3 percent over the range in 1975–76. There is no doubt that there has been a further increase since 1980–81.

The Likely Impact of the 1987 Drought

There is some truth to the cliché that Indian economic policy is a gamble on the monsoons. As pointed out earlier, nearly two–thirds of India's labor force depends on agriculture for their livelihood—a proportion not much lower than that of more than a century ago! With irrigation in less than one–third of total cultivated area, agricultural output depends significantly on rainfall. Except for some parts of South India which receive the major portion of their annual precipitation during October–November, the rest of the country depends largely on the summer (July–September) monsoon, and to a considerably lesser extent on the winter (January–February) rainfall. While the *average* or *trend* of growth in output is determined by investments in the expansion of the cropped and irrigated areas, cultivation of high–yield varieties, and use of fertilizers, manures, and pesticides, *fluctuations* around the trend have been associated with the vagaries of the monsoon.

With most of the arable land already in use, expansion of cropped area has been of minor significance in recent years. However, with irrigation, the same land can be planted more than once a year. With the expansion of irrigation facilities over the last four decades, multiple cropping has led to a modest increase in total area cultivated. The introduction of high–yield dwarf varieties of wheat and rice in the mid–1960s with the assistance of the Rockefeller Foundation, and the subsequent development of other varieties by Indian scientists, ushered in the so–called "green revolution." The use of chemical fertilizers also expanded rapidly. As a result, agricultural output has continued to grow at a trend rate of 2.5 to 3 percent annually, in spite of a marked slowdown in the growth of cropped area.

In recent years, agricultural economists have debated whether this growth, which is mostly due to an increase in crop yields per unit area, has been accompanied by greater instability in year–to–year fluctuations in output. The available data do not permit a clear–cut conclusion, mostly because it is not easy to disentangle factors contributing to this instability such as the year–to–year shifts in crop area among states, and between crops within states, in response to price fluctuations. However, it appears unlikely that the technology associated with the high–yield varieties has contributed significantly to the increase, if any, in instability.

Assessing the significance of a monsoon failure for crop output is not a simple matter. For example, a significantly below–normal aggregate amount of rainfall, if well distributed throughout the season (i.e. without short bouts of heavy rainfall separated by long dry spells) and across major agricultural regions of the country, will result in a lower loss in output than a badly distributed 'normal' rainfall. Compounding this is the fact that different crops (and different varieties of the same crop) can withstand drought to different degrees. Although, as stated earlier, the summer monsoon is the primary source of rainfall for most of the country, there are two major crop seasons: the monsoon or *kharif* season (May–October), and the winter or *rabi* (November–April) season. If the monsoon failure is not too severe, a shortfall in *kharif* can be offset by a larger *rabi* output. The extent of the recovery depends on soil moisture at the end of *kharif*, whether irrigation reservoirs have sufficient water left, and whether winter rainfall is normal. Table 2.2 shows the extent of droughts since the mid–1960s and their impact on output.

Table 2.2

Rainfall and Food Grain Production

Year	Composite Rainfall Index % Departure From Normal	% Fall From Previous Year	% Falls in Output From Previous Year Kharif	Rabi	Total
1965–66	−18.6	−23.3	−18.7	−17.7	−18.4
1979–80	−20.2	−27.3	−19.0	−13.7	−17.0
1982–83	−13.2	−13.4	−12.5	+9.2	−2.9
1987–88	−27.7	−15.9	*	*	*

Source: National Council for Applied Economic Research, New Delhi.
*See postscript

It is evident from Table 2.2 that offsetting of loss in *kharif* output by an increase in *rabi* output has been achieved in the last two droughts. Also, roughly the same aggregate deficiency in the rainfall index led to a loss of total output of about 3 percent in 1982–83, but no loss at all in 1986–87. One has to keep this in mind in assessing the impact of the 1987–88 drought. By December, the *kharif* crop had already been harvested, and *rabi* crops sown. The latest available estimates suggest that the *kharif* output may reach 73 million metric tons, a fall of about 13 percent from last year's estimated harvest of 84 million tons. The shortfall is less than feared at first. On the other hand, estimates of *rabi* area are not yet available. Indications are that the soil is unusually dry, water levels in irrigation reservoirs are very low, and there may be little power available to run pumps. If so, the prospect of completely offsetting *kharif* losses in *rabi* appears unlikely. If the *rabi* harvest is no higher than last year's 66 million tons, the 1987 shortfall will be 8 million tons, compared to the revised estimate of 147 million tons for last year's harvest and a whopping 22 million tons compared to the target output for 1987–88 in the range of 160–163 million tons.

Fortunately, the current agricultural year (July 1987–June 1988) began with a stock of more than 21 million tons of food grains. According to a statement attributed to the Civil Supplies Minister, Mr. H. K. L. Bhagat, the stocks had been depleted to 14.1 million tons as of January 1, 1988, compared to 23.5 million tons a year earlier. These figures suggest that government procurement from the *kharif* harvest was below last year's level, though some earlier news reports had suggested that purchases of paddy have been considerably above expectations. The same statement reports that the offtake from the public distribution system of rice and wheat ran at about 1.75 million tons a month in 1987, compared to the 1986 average of 1.43 million tons. Assuming that procurement for the year may fall by about 5 million tons (less than half the estimated shortfall in output) to about 15 million tons, public food grain stocks by the end of the agricultural year may be around 15 million tons, if none are imported. However, if the offtake is larger and procurement lower, then stocks will have to be depleted much further.

An end–of–year stock of 15 million tons may prove a narrow margin should the monsoon fail miserably again next year. Food grains may need to be imported to bring stocks up to prudent levels. And planning such imports before stocks are actually depleted will avoid panic buying and the associated higher costs. Estimates of *kharif* output for other major crops are not yet available. It is likely that oil seed and sugarcane outputs are below normal, although if scattered news reports are to be believed, the shortfall will not be significant. Since the late 1970s, increasing quantities of edible oils have been imported. Large–scale imports of sugar were made in 1985–86. The offtake of cooking oil from ration shops is reported to have been 1.52 million tons in 1987, compared to 1.22 million tons in 1986. That of sugar was 8.7 million tons in 1987, compared to 8.29 the year before. It is reasonable to assume that, given the likely losses due to drought, substantial amounts of edible oil and possibly sugar may have to be imported in 1987–88 and 1988–89. Depending on international market prices, this will require a larger or smaller amount of foreign exchange than last year.

There is some evidence that Indian import demand is raising prices in world markets. According to *World Bank News* of February 25, 1988, world food prices climbed by over 10 percent between January 1987 and January 1988 in response to Asian drought. It reports further that the Indian State Trading Corporation's weekly purchases of vegetable oil continued to be large, with one tender in mid–January 1988 for 112,000 tons. Indian purchases of U.S. soybean oil under the U.S. import enhancement program are also reported to be growing. All this led to an across–the–board increase of more than 25 percent in prices of fats and oils between January 1987 and January 1988. Sugar prices also rose by 16.5 percent during the same period in expectation of greater sugar exports by India, China, Pakistan, Ecuador, and Venezuela. In the absence of firm data, it is impossible to hazard a guess on the impact of drought on the output of fibers (jute and cotton) and beverages such as tea and coffee. A rough estimate of the foreign exchange needed for additional agricultural commodity imports is on the order of $1 billion.

In addition to reducing crop output, the drought resulted in shortages of fodder and drinking water. There are reports of cattle dying or being slaughtered. Reduction in the water table due to drought has increased the cost of pumping water. Obviously, any shock that adversely affects agricultural production will affect income and employment of agricultural producers and workers. The fact that an overwhelming proportion of the population depends on agriculture for employment and that an even larger proportion of the poor are landless agricultural workers, small peasants, and rural artisans means that, unless relief measures are organized effectively and in time, there will be serious consequences to the income, health, and survival of large numbers of rural people.

Drought relief by providing those affected with employment in construction of public works has been an element of Indian public policy since colonial times. In post–Independence India, and particularly since the early 1970s when prime minister Indira Gandhi made the abolition of poverty a major plank in her electoral platform, several programs for chronically unemployed as well as underemployed rural laborers have been initiated and sustained on a regular basis. Two such programs are the National Rural Employment Programme and the Rural Labor Employment Guarantee Programme. In addition, the Drought Prone Areas Programme was undertaken in regions most susceptible to drought to restore ecological balance and reduce vulnerability to drought. Given the present drought, expenditure on this kind of program will have to be increased substantially. The $1.5 billion proposed in November 1987 for drought relief and related measures is likely to prove insufficient by year's end. A supplementary budget announced in September 1987 imposed additional "temporary" taxes to the tune of $420 million and proposed to cut expenditures by $500 million. The World Bank and its soft loan affiliate, the International Development Association (IDA), are loaning $150 million and $200 million respectively for drought relief–related activities, though not all of this is additional to the funds committed earlier for fiscal year 1987–88.

The impact of drought on different states in India is likely to be uneven for several reasons. First, not all of the country's 35 meteorological regions were stricken to the same degree. In 14 of the 35 regions—accounting for 37 percent of the area of the country—rainfall was not deficient or scanty. But, for many regions, this is the third or fourth successive year of poor rainfall. Second, the percentage of crop area that is irrigated, and hence relatively protected from drought, varies substantially between the states. In 1980–81, this was only 11.5 percent in Madhya Pradesh, 12.5 percent in Maharashtra and 13.4 percent in Karnataka. In contrast, 85.5 percent of the crop area in Punjab, 60.6 percent in Haryana, and 50.9 percent in Tamil Nadu was irrigated. Third, partly because of the variation in the proportion of irrigated area and partly because of differences in cropping patterns, the impact of the drought on statewide agricultural output is likely to be uneven. Finally, per capita income and the extent of poverty vary between states. For instance, in 1971–72 the percentage of rural households deemed absolutely poor varied from 22 percent in Haryana to 64 percent in Tamil Nadu. Since the poor are the first victims when a severe drought erodes employment opportunities, the variation in the extent of poverty means that some states are more affected by drought than others. Different state governments compete for drought relief funds provided by the central government and augment these funds with some of their own. The differences in the fiscal strength of states and in the efficiency of administration influence the extent and quality of relief provided. Also, since several states are governed by opposition political parties, the allocation of central drought relief funds and the performance of different state governments in implementing relief projects have a political dimension as well.

Apart from providing employment and income to those affected by drought, the government has instructed the nationalized commercial banks to provide them with consumption loans on easy terms. Essentially, the policy will enable the poor to consume even if they do not earn. But because these loans are unlikely to be repaid, they can threaten the financial viability of the banks and result in loss of income to depositors, if provided on a massive basis. Apparently prudence seems to have prevailed, and so far, consumption loans are said to be relatively insignificant.

In spite of repeated pronouncements that austerity measures will be taken and the government's noninvestment expenditure will be kept in check, this has not yet happened. Because of a drought–induced drop in the output of taxable commodities as well as in income and corporation taxes, a shortfall in revenue can be expected. The prime minister's assurance that the government deficit will not exceed the $4.37 billion allotted in the annual budget presented to Parliament in late February 1987 cannot be kept unless investment expenditures are cut, thereby jeopardizing growth. To avoid this, the government has recently decided to sell bonds (the so–called "drought relief bonds") which yield a tax–free return of 9 percent and are repayable after five years. However, borrowing from the public to finance an incipient government deficit diverts resources that would have otherwise been invested by the private sector. Thus, total investment will be reduced, unless the terms of the bonds are deemed so attractive as to increase the savings of the private sector, a very unlikely event. In any case, it is extremely improbable that the government deficit will be kept at $4.37 billion—the finance minister backed away from such a commitment in a statement in late November, promising only that he would restrict the deficit to unspecified "reasonable limits."

In a monetary framework such as India's, where budgetary deficits tend to get monetized directly or indirectly, the inflationary potential of deficits is substantial. Reinforced by anticipated shortages due to drought, inflation has been creeping up: by the third week of January 1988, the wholesale price index had risen by nearly 9.8 percent over its value at the beginning of the fiscal year on April 1, 1987. Data on cost–of–living indices for industrial workers and urban non–manual employees are available only until September. These show a rise of 8.6 percent and 7.8 percent respectively between March and September. The cost–of–living index for agricultural labor available for August shows a rate of 8.4 percent. With the emoluments of government servants and workers in the organized sector linked to these cost–of–living indices, the government's salary bill will go up, thereby further adding to the deficit.

Without up–to–date data on industrial production, it is hard to provide an estimate of a drought–induced fall in this sector. If indeed the fall in output of oil seeds, sugar, cotton, and jute is not significant, there will not be a shortage of raw material for agroprocessing industries. However, available data suggest that because of low water levels in reservoirs, electricity generation from hydroelectric plants has fallen compared to last year. But thermal power generation has increased significantly. It is not clear whether the shortage of power will reduce the growth of industrial production. According to news reports of the president's address which opened the budget session of the Indian Parliament on February 22, 1988, the government announced that industrial growth during April–November 1987 was 10.2 percent, and the expected rate for 1987–88 was 8 percent. These growth rates refer to gross industrial output. The rate of growth of real value added or real income generated by the industrial sector is likely to be lower. As such, taking agriculture, industry, and services together, it is likely that aggregate real national income will grow by no more than 2 percent during 1987–88 (compared to a target exceeding 5 percent) and may in fact not grow at all, given that agricultural income may fall by about 8 percent compared to the previous year. With the population growth rate exceeding 2 percent, per capita income in 1987–88 will at best be unchanged, or more likely, fall by 0.2 percent to 0.5 percent, compared to that of 1986–87. The income shortfall in 1986–87 due to drought is likely to affect demand for industrial products with some time lag, given that they are not competitive in world markets. If so, the effect of drought will be seen in industrial output of 1988–89.

The *Economic Times* share–price index (1984–85 = 100) reached a peak of 276.3 at the end of August 1987 after a low of 213.7 in the middle of June. Since August, prices have steadily slipped at a trend rate of about –9.1 percent per year. Yet, according to the news magazine *India Today* (January 15, 1988), the private sector is cautiously optimistic about the economy.

It is generally believed that the massive increase in irrigation from 23 million hectares in 1950–51 to 70 million hectares in 1985–86, coupled with investment in research on improving rain–fed farming through better seeds and improved methods of moisture conservation, has increased India's capacity to withstand drought. This belief, while undoubtedly valid, is perhaps optimistic. Available irrigation water can be spread thinly over a wide area to protect a number of crops against drought, or alternatively, concentrated in a smaller area to raise the yield of fewer crops. This is the age–old distinction between protective versus productive irrigation, and its implications are several.

First, the so–called green revolution technology—which involves the use of high–yield dwarf varieties that can withstand large dosages of yield–raising chemical fertilizers—was largely confined to wheat and rice, which have a relatively high value. Second, the best results are obtained under conditions of controlled irrigation. Both these factors meant that cultivated area, and particularly irrigated area, was shifted to these two crops. Third, whenever there is a shortage of irrigation water due to low rainfall or to wells drying up because of drought, the available water is likely to be channelled to these crops at the expense of other crops. Thus, greater and perhaps more stable output of rice and wheat were achieved at the expense of slower and more unstable output of other crops. Of course, the fact that the output of different crops grew at different rates need not have induced a similar pattern in the domestic use (for consumption and stock accumulation) of these commodities. International trade could have been utilized to offset domestic surpluses and deficits arising from drought or other causes, as long as these shocks were uncorrelated with global shocks. But Indian grain markets were separated from world markets, with foreign trade in food grains controlled by a public sector monopoly. This, together with government intervention in domestic grain markets (through price support and purchases for public distribution) meant that domestic wheat and rice prices bore no relation to world market prices. For this reason, and the fact that other crops (coarse cereals and pulses) were grown only in India, international trade did not play a significant role. This situation can change, now that domestic wheat and rice prices are closer to international prices than they have been in a long time. The slow growth of, and greater fluctuations in, the output of coarse cereals which are highly vulnerable to drought had a disproportionate effect on the poor since they are the major consumers of these cereals. With the public distribution system operating mostly in urban areas, the rural poor have little or no access to subsidized wheat and rice from ration shops and depend on purchases from the more costly open market. Therefore, paying part or all of the wages for those working on drought relief public works projects in rural areas in food grains makes sense.

Prospects for Economic Liberalization in the Industrial Sector

The industrial sector of the Indian economy is by far the most regulated. The more important regulations and constraints are investment licensing requirements; restrictions on foreign collaboration and investment; controls on foreign exchange transactions; licensing of imports of technology, capital goods and parts, and raw materials; restrictions on investment by the so–called monopoly or large industrial houses; and restrictions on choice of location of industrial plants. In addition there are problems associated with the quality, quantity, reliability, and prices of key inputs supplied by the public sector such as electricity, petroleum products, coal, steel, railways, air transportation, and telecommunications.

The ostensible purpose of these regulations is to ensure that investment corresponds to the "priorities" laid down in the Five–Year Plans and, given a continuing scarcity of foreign exchange, that imports conform to Plan "priorities" and above all are consistent with planned import substitution. Given the many objectives of the planners and the complexity, timeliness, and reliability of the information required to make licensing decisions and monitor their implementation, laying down priorities is an Orwellian task! In any case, the regulatory framework on the one hand has vested power in the bureaucracy, leaving producers little or no recourse against bureaucratic decisions. On the other hand, because resource allocation directed by the government (rather than by a unified market) created wedges between the prices for the same resource paid by different users, there is room for arbitrage, which by definition violates the system. Thus, the quotas on some imports, such as the plastic PVC, synthetic yarn, and some categories of steel, were so far below market demand that they (and hence, the licenses to import them) carried premiums in domestic (gray or black) markets.

In effect, these premiums constituted rents that bureaucrats or their political bosses conferred almost at their discretion. Individuals would try to influence the allocation of these monies by fair or foul means. Time and effort, as well as material resources, were diverted to rent–seeking and corruption rather than production. Apart from inducing corruption, the power to confer rents also enabled the party in power to generate electoral campaign funds. Consequently, the regulatory framework is supported by powerful interest groups consisting of politicians in power (as well as those who naively associate controls and the public sector with "socialism"), the bureaucracy, and above all, industrial entrepreneurs who fear competition and who have the connections to make the regulations work in their favor. Since none of the major opposition leaders including V.P. Singh have recognized the need for abandoning the regulatory framework in order to contain corruption and rent–seeking, the prospects for broad liberalization under a unified opposition government, in the unlikely event it comes about, are not very bright.

The two domestic scandals mentioned earlier are in many respects the results of rent–seeking. The regulations governing foreign exchange transactions by individuals and companies generated powerful incentives to avoid or evade them. Indeed, the belief that illegal foreign exchange transactions and export of capital by enterprises and individuals were substantial led to the decision to appoint Fairfax, an investigative agency located in Virginia (of which no written record seems to exist in government files), to examine the matter. Among the individuals suspected of illegally exporting capital and/or receiving funds abroad was Ajitabh Bachchan, younger brother of Amitabh Bachchan, a film actor and close friend of Mr. Gandhi. The elder Mr. Bachchan was elected to Parliament on the Congress ticket in 1984. As more and more revelations were published about his younger brother's illegal financial transactions in Switzerland, the elder Mr. Bachchan resigned from Parliament. The scandals relating to defense contracts also involved allegations of kickbacks to politicians. The accusations against Prime Minister Gandhi and his party made by the opposition and in the press since the beginning of the year have not been dispelled by the commission that investigated the Fairfax scandal. Nor has there been an end to the government's harassment of the owner and editor of *Indian Express*, the major newspaper that relentlessly investigated and publicized the scandal.

In many respects the latest scandals reflect the decline in norms of behavior in politics and administration since Independence. This decline, already evident in the final years of prime minister Nehru's administration, accelerated under Indira Gandhi. In addition to engineering a split in the ruling Congress party twice, basically for reasons of personal political power, she systematically destroyed rival sources of state power by imposing and removing at her pleasure chief ministers of states in which her party had a legislative majority. Independence of the judiciary and upper echelons of civil service were eroded through her politicization of judicial and administrative appointments. Her declaration of a state of emergency in 1975, again in response to a perceived threat to her power, is the culmination of years of assault on democratic institutions and concentration of power in the prime minister's person. The Emergency saw the unbridled and arbitrary exercise of power by Indira Gandhi and her late younger son, Sanjay. The power of the Parliament, the quality of its membership, debates, and committee reports, and even the quality of drafting of legislation have declined since the first Parliament, which earlier, as the constituent assembly, had drafted India's constitution. While the rents and interest groups created by the regulatory system are not the only causes of this decline in public standards, they contributed significantly to it. When Mr. Gandhi came to power, he was viewed as "Mr. Clean," not beholden to any faction or group. Yet in three years, he and his regime are facing serious charges of corruption.

It is not surprising that Gandhi feels politically threatened under these circumstances, and that some members of his own party opposed to his policies have been emboldened. He has been forced to mend fences with the old guard as well as the left wing of his party. He has asserted his "socialist" credentials and commitment to strengthening the public sector and denied any shift away from planning towards market–oriented policies. All this appears to be a retreat from his pronouncements after his massive victory in the 1984 elections. At that time he talked about upgrading technology, taking India into the twenty–first century, and removing the bureaucratic shackles on entrepreneurship and creativity. Some of the economic policy changes introduced then appeared to move further away from controls and regulation toward the economic liberalization that began under his mother's government. Since those opposed to such a policy have exaggerated its extent and those in favor of it have argued that it has been too limited, it is worth a brief look.

The strategy of import substitution buttressed by a regulatory framework governing investment and foreign trade has succeeded in producing a diversified industrial structure and a certain level of technological maturity. But it has been achieved at a substantial cost. Capital intensity and inefficient use of capital have risen. There is evidence that total factor productivity (i.e., productivity of labor and capital combined) has been growing very slowly, if not actually declining. The regulatory system has considerably blunted the incentive to produce at the lowest cost and highest quality by restricting competition from imports and confining it to a few domestic producers in many products. Plants use outmoded technology, often domestically designed, and capacity is fragmented into plants of uneconomic scale in the interests of balanced regional development. The structure of indirect taxes, which are the major source of government revenue, did not leave inputs free of taxes so that it had a cascading effect on the cost of final output. The net result of all these policies is a relatively slow–growing, high–cost manufacturing sector, the size of which is pitifully small by international standards and decreasing all the time. Measured by value added, it is about equal to that of Korea and Argentina and only 20 to 30 percent larger than that of Sweden and Belgium.

As was pointed out earlier, even Indira Gandhi's government had realized some of these problems. A number of committees that were appointed during her regime to study these issues reported soon after Mr. Gandhi's rise to power. Based on their recommendations, a number of changes were made in the regulatory environment. Several product groups were relieved of capacity licensing requirements, and in others licensing requirements were eased. "Broad–banding," i.e., allowing licensed capacity to be used for the production of similar products, was introduced. Restrictions on the entry of large business houses into certain industries were relaxed. Attention was paid to minimum economic scale of a plant in licensing capacity. A modified system of value added tax (MODVAT) was introduced to minimize the cascading effect of taxes on input. Restrictions on capital goods imports have been eased to encourage technological modernization. Growth of exports has been facilitated by improved administration of export promotion schemes. Impressive as the list is, its sweep is nonetheless more limited than may be apparent. Large industrial houses and foreign firms do not benefit much from these measures. The priority accorded to the public sector and the reservation of certain product lines to the small–scale sector continue to limit possible efficiency gains. Since several licenses and permissions must usually be obtained before undertaking any new activity, and obtaining them continues to be costly, time–consuming, and difficult, the overall beneficial impact is still limited.

The regulatory system significantly reduced the ability of firms to enter or exit an industry. Firms employing more than 100 workers have to obtain government permission to dismiss workers or to cease operations. Bankruptcy proceedings are long and protracted. The desire to protect employees in their current jobs has often meant that the government took over failing private enterprises. These so–called "sick" enterprises, far from being nurtured back to health, continue to run even greater deficits under public management and thus drain resources from more productive uses. There has been very little change in the restrictions on entry and exit.

The need to improve the efficiency of public sector enterprises, particularly those supplying inputs and services key to improving the efficiency of the industrial sector as a whole, has been recognized. The problem of mounting losses in some of these enterprises, which absorb investable public resources, has been noted as well. A number of government committees that inquired into the operation of public enterprises have made useful recommendations, primarily about autonomy of management and setting clearly defined criteria by which managerial performance can be evaluated. Yet the situation has not improved significantly. For example, compared to an expected total contribution by public enterprises of $29 billion at 1984–85 prices towards the outlay during the Seventh Five–Year Plan (1985–90), the actual contribution during the first three years of the plan is likely to be $9 billion at current prices, which when corrected for inflation will amount to no more than $7.5 billion, i.e., less than a quarter of the targeted amount for five years at 1984–85 prices. The problem continues to be that public enterprises are saddled with several sociopolitical objectives other than economic performance, with no consideration given to assessing whether those objectives could be achieved at a lower social cost through other means. Many, including economists who ought to know better, identify the expansion of the public sector with achievement of "socialism," without considering the possibility that a bloated, inefficient, and corrupt public enterprise drains resources that could be used to alleviate poverty.

The controls on external trade, and particularly the quantitative restrictions on imports, have succeeded in achieving a substantial degree of self–sufficiency in a wide variety of industrial products including capital goods. But this achievement has been bought at a substantial cost in terms of economic efficiency and growth. The indiscriminate way in which domestically produced commodities were protected from foreign competition through policies like the so–called indigenous clearance angle meant that there was no competitive pressure for cost reduction and efficiency. Application of the indigenous clearance angle to imports of capital equipment in the 1960s and 1970s saddled the industrial sector with an obsolete and inferior technology in the production of many vital products. The high cost of domestically produced intermediate inputs inhibited exports of manufactured products and had to be offset through various implicit and explicit subsidies, so that the effective cost of inputs to exporters roughly equalled their international prices. The explicit subsidies for export promotion may have been on the order of 0.4 percent of gross domestic product in 1986–87.

The problems with the regime of controls on the external sector are well known and understood. Both academic and government reports on this issue in the mid–1980s have emphasized the urgent need to encourage exports of commodities in which India would have a comparative cost advantage but for the complex tax–cum–control system on inputs. They have also recognized that the system of quantitative restrictions on imports creates a structure of uncertain and unpredictable incentives for production and needs to be replaced by a system based on tariffs that are set as percentages of the world prices of imports. In such a system, incentives for domestic production will correspond to India's competitive advantage. Some steps have also been taken to implement these recommendations.

It would require a book–length chapter to describe in detail the complex import control and export promotion measures and the changes in them over time. Only a few selected examples will be given here. Imports are broadly categorized into four lists: (1) Open General License (OGL) items, which can be imported without a license provided the importing firm is an "actual user" of the item; (2) imports which are restricted but not banned; (3) banned imports; and (4) imports channelled through public sector agencies. Import policy periodically adds or subtracts items from each of these lists. Obviously, changes in the number of items in each list need not reflect the extent of the changes in the severity of the control system. For example, shifting an item from the restricted to the OGL category may have negligible consequences if there is no available domestic import substitute for it. Although the number of items under OGL has increased substantially in recent years, the extent of 'real' liberalization may be far less than these numbers would suggest. The system still provides producers substantially higher protection and less risk for sales to domestic rather than foreign markets. Incentives provided through export subsidies have not succeeded in reversing this. It is not surprising that the Indian share of world exports has been declining and other countries have gained at India's expense. For example, in 1960 Korea's exports of manufactured goods was negligible, while India exported goods worth over $600 million. But by 1983, Korea exported industrial goods worth over $22 billion compared to India's $5 billion.

In sum, it is clear that a number of steps towards liberalizing the regulatory framework have been taken in recent years by Rajiv Gandhi's government. Yet their real significance is difficult to assess given the continuing complexity of the system. Indeed, if the system can be compared to a set of hoops of varying diameters through which an application for an investment or import license has to pass, liberalization so far has simply increased the diameter of a few non–binding hoops while leaving that of the binding hoop intact! But the continuity of even this hesitant and perhaps anemic liberalization is in jeopardy, primarily because of Mr. Gandhi's political troubles.

A recent news report, since denied (but such denials cannot be taken at face value), describes a note allegedly prepared by officials of the all–powerful secretariat of the prime minister which advocated no less than a reversal of recent liberalization. The note called for nationalization of cotton, jute, and sugar industries; reintroduction of estate duty; sharp increases in excise duties, particularly on the so–called luxury goods, and a lowering of duties on items of mass consumption; restitution of the dominant role of the public sector in national development; tightening curbs on imports and foreign collaboration agreements; decreasing reliance on bilateral assistance from the West and borrowing from multilateral agencies and commercial banks; and strengthening of economic relations with Eastern Europe. Whether or not such a note in fact existed, it is possible that a "leak" may have been deliberately planted to bolster the "progressive" image of the prime minister.

This view is strengthened in light of the resolution that the working committee of Mr. Gandhi's party adopted in April 1987 in the wake of the political scandals and the expulsion of Mr. V. P. Singh and others from the party. This resolution accused the "reactionary forces" within the country of having joined hands with external forces, including multinational corporations, to destabilize India and to overturn its long–established economic policies (presumably the regulatory framework and the emphasis on the public sector). This resolution has not been referred to lately, but it will no doubt be revived if political compulsions call for it.

Conclusion

There can be no doubt that the Indian economy has suffered a severe supply shock because of the drought. While most accounts suggest that emergency drought relief operations are being implemented satisfactorily, there are a few reports that relief resources have been squandered in some areas. It is too soon to assess the short–run and longer–run effects of the drought. For one thing, a reasonably reliable estimate of the autumn harvest and the area sown under winter crops is not available. If the winter crop output is also below normal for the year as a whole, the loss in food output could be as high as 15–20 million metric tons. Without advance imports, public stocks may be too low by the end of the agricultural year on June 30, 1988 to withstand another drought. In some areas, the drought has seriously affected the livestock economy. If the stock of working animals is depleted, agricultural operations next year could be seriously impaired even if the monsoon is bountiful.

Additional agricultural imports, particularly edible oils and sugar, will probably be needed. Even though preliminary data for the period April–September 1987 suggest that exports have increased by nearly 25 percent, and imports by about 15 percent—meaning that the trade deficit narrowed relative to the previous year—the fact that foreign exchange reserves have dropped sharply is disquieting. There is no evidence, despite exhortations and pronouncements, that government nondrought and noninvestment–related expenditures have been contained. Defense expenditures have risen substantially over the last year, and, like the expenses of the Indian Peace Keeping Force (IPKF) in Sri Lanka (estimated at $2.25 million a day), requires substantial foreign exchange. Even with drought relief assistance from the World Bank and other donors, it is likely that the balance of payments situation will deteriorate significantly.

Lack of discipline in public expenditures is evident. In addition to government salary increases incurred to implement the recommendations of the Fourth Pay Commission, the government has recently announced a 'bonus' of 25 days' salary to government servants. Any further expansion of the budget deficit is bound to add to inflationary pressures—by the end of 1987 the annual inflation rate was creeping close to double–digit levels. The cost of servicing the domestic and international debt is reaching heights that cannot be sustained. Gross expenditure on interest on domestic and foreign debt was about 4 percent of gross domestic product in 1985–86. Foreign debt service, as mentioned earlier, costs about 25 percent of earnings from exports of goods and services.

The unfortunate fiscal situation is particularly glaring when reviewed in the context of the Seventh Five–Year Plan. While it is true that almost all plans completed so far failed to achieve their targeted total investment in real terms, and consequently the targets for income growth, there was some expectation that this Plan was going to be different. Indeed, the outgoing Deputy Chairman of the Planning Commission, Dr. Manmohan Singh, announced before leaving office at the end of July 1987 that even if no further deficit financing or additional resources were obtained, 88 percent of the Seventh Plan investment target would be achieved in real terms, the highest proportion on record. Since he made that statement, the drought has intervened. At the mid–term of the Plan it appears that compared to the Rs. 18,000 billion needed for the public sector component at 1984–85 prices, the actual cost for the first three years, and projection for the last two, indicate that the total expenditure may be on the order of Rs. 17,000 billion, which itself is an optimistic estimate.

The gathering fiscal storm is a reflection of the political economy of Indian development. Several interest groups have been bought off by subsidies and fiscal concessions which claim an ever–increasing share of the revenues. Agricultural producers have been lobbying successfully for price supports, subsidies on fertilizers, electricity, diesel fuel, and public supply of irrigation water. They have often succeeded in having their loans—which were given at a subsidized interest rate to begin with—written off. Urban consumers are provided subsidized rations of food grains, sugar, and edible oils. Public sector employees, including those working for public sector banks and enterprises, as well as employees in organized manufacturing, constitute a labor aristocracy whose demands are often granted at the expense of diverting resources from development. Because of the high cost of domestically produced inputs, exporters cannot compete in world markets without subsidies. Indeed, fiscal reform measures proposed by the former finance minister V.P. Singh were in part aimed at raising revenue and controlling the fiscal situation. Left unchecked, deficits may get entrenched, and a Latin American–style structural inflation may result.

If there is no major change in the economic policy environment for the better, the prospects are not sanguine. The old standby, agriculture, which despite fluctuations has so far exhibited a trend growth rate of 2.5

to 3.0 percent, may not continue to grow in the future. By now all irrigated wheat fields have been planted with high–yield varieties. Rice crops, too, have been planted in the areas to which the green revolution could be extended without substantial investment. It is true that there are substantial regional differences in yield per unit of irrigated area for the same crop. To the extent that low yields in some regions are due to factors that can be removed without substantial investment, some growth in national yield can be achieved. Still, it is likely that achieving further gains in yield per unit area, which sustained the growth rate of output in spite of a decline in the growth of cropped area, will necessitate costly investment in irrigation, drainage, and current inputs such as fertilizers and pesticides.

In the industrial sector, much depends on rationalizing and streamlining, if not dismantling, the regulatory system and assuring a reliable and plentiful supply of power, transportation, coal, and other key inputs supplied by the public sector. It is difficult to be optimistic about these. First, past experience suggests that attempts at rationalizing the bureaucratic regulatory framework often expanded the reach and discretionary power of the system. Second, there can be little doubt that if the protective umbrella regulating competition (domestic and foreign) is withdrawn, a number of enterprises will become uncompetitive. To the extent resources invested in such enterprises are not flexibly shifted to other uses at a reasonable cost, at least in the short run, it may be appropriate to initiate a program of gradual reduction in protection. This should be possible if the accepted policy of transforming the protection granted to domestic producers through import quotas, input subsidies, and other channels into a single ad valorem tariff is implemented fully. Then a policy of phased reduction of these tariffs could be announced so that entrepreneurs can plan ahead knowing that protection will be phased out.

Even though unilateral liberalization of foreign trade by phasing out tariffs, subsidies, and quantitative restrictions on exports and imports is in India's interest, there will be less political reluctance to institute such a reform if the external environment for India's exports (actual and potential) is buoyant. Unfortunately, not only has the demand for the exports of developing countries been growing more slowly in the 1980s because of slow growth of incomes in developed countries, protectionist sentiment is also growing. For example, if the outrageously protectionist trade bill is passed by the U.S. Congress in its present form and signed into law, it will be a major blow to the global trading system and to the export prospects of developing countries, including India.

In this context, India's participation in the Uruguay round of the General Agreement on Tariffs and Trade (GATT) negotiations on liberalizing the world trading system are critical. For too long, India and many other developing countries have asked for and obtained special preferences for their exports and exemptions from GATT rules relating to trade restrictions. Granting these preferences and exemptions has enabled the developed countries to get away with special trading arrangements (such as those relating to textiles and apparel) that are far more damaging to developing country interests than the pittance gained from special preferences. India, along with Brazil, is now opposed to the extension of GATT rules to trade in services. This opposition is misguided. India has comparative advantage in labor–intensive services and should negotiate for a bargain in which, in return for extending GATT rules to service trade, the developed countries—particularly the United States—open their countries to importing labor–intensive services. For example, India can "export" labor by Indians working temporarily on a contract basis in some labor–intensive services in the United States.

The possibility that the trends towards economic liberalization will continue and deepen is lessened by the fact that Mr. V. P. Singh, who was dismissed from Mr. Gandhi's cabinet and later expelled from his party, was the architect of a number of the economic policy initiatives. A long–term fiscal policy was formulated under his guidance and announced in December 1985. He sought to give some stability to import–export controls, at least for the medium term. He had also initiated studies of the government's price policy regarding public sector commodities and services. Now that Singh has joined the ranks of the opposition, it is not certain that his initiatives will be followed through. However, the bill recently introduced in Parliament by the new Finance Minister N. D. Tiwari to simplify direct tax laws and to consolidate the changes introduced in the last twenty years is a small but welcome step in the right direction. As pointed out earlier, the fiscal situation is none too happy, and government expenditures not related to growth of the economy are rising unchecked.

Even if the fiscal situation is brought under control, there will be no future for the Indian economy, rosy or otherwise, unless the regulatory framework is radically altered, if not abandoned altogether. But to be able to propose and implement such a change requires political strength to overcome the pulls and pressures of vested interests. Mr. Gandhi, who once seemed to have it, has apparently squandered it. As such, economic liberalization and reform will at best be hesitant rather than rapid, cosmetic and superficial rather than real and thoroughgoing.

Postscript

The financial year 1987–88 (April–March) and agricultural year 1987–88 (July–June) have both ended. Two months have elapsed since the onset of the 1988 summer monsoon.

First, the good news. Fortunately, some, though not all, of the more pessimistic projections in the paper have not come about. The negative effect of the drought on national income and agricultural output in the aggregate have turned out to be modest. Gross domestic product *rose* by about 2 percent in 1987–88 in spite of a *drop* in agricultural output by a little less than 10 percent. The food grain component of agricultural output seems to have fared even better. Compared with the peak output of 152 million tons in 1983–84 and an output of 144 million tons in 1986–87, preliminary data suggest that output in 1987–88 was around 138 million tons, thanks to a record *rabi* harvest of 66.5 million tons. Thus, total output dropped by 4.2 percent compared to 1986–87 and by 9.2 percent compared to the peak. What is more, an 11.4 percent fall in *kharif* output compared to 1986–87 was partially offset by a rise in *rabi* output of 6.4 percent. The general index of industrial production with base 1980–81 rose by about 8 percent in 1987–88, only slightly less than the 8–9 percent achieved in 1986–87. Exports (in U.S. dollar terms) went up by nearly 23 percent in 1987–88 while imports rose only by 8 percent compared to 1986–87, thereby reducing the trade deficit by more than 10 percent. Finally, the 1988 monsoon arrived early. So far normal or excess rainfall has already been recorded in 22 of the 30 meteorological divisions in the country as contrasted with deficient or scanty rainfall in 21 divisions last year.

Now the bad news. In contrast with the budget estimate of Rs. 56.88 billion (or US$4.37 billion), the revised estimate of the government's overall *fiscal* deficit for the year 1987–88 was Rs. 60.80 billion (about 6 percent higher) in spite of the finance minister's assurances that the deficit would not be allowed to exceed the budget estimate. The index of wholesale prices rose by 10.6 percent in 1987–88, while the cost-of-living indices for industrial workers, urban nonmanual employees, and agricultural laborers rose by 9.1 percent, 9.6 percent, and 9.8 percent respectively. Despite the surge in exports and the very modest rise in imports in 1987–88, the balance of payments situation is still tight. During the first quarter of 1988–89, there was an alarming fall in foreign exchange reserves, which stood at Rs. 53.82 billion on July 1, 1988, as compared to Rs. 72.27 billion at the end of March 1988. The stock of food grains in the public distribution system is reported to have been depleted to less than ten million tons by April 1988. Even if there is a bumper harvest in 1988–89, significant imports of food grains at a time when world grain prices are high seem unavoidable, if depleted stocks are to be restored to desirable levels.

The prospects for further economic liberalization seem uncertain at best. On the one hand, the investment limit for exemption from licensing requirements has been raised tenfold to Rs. 500 million from Rs. 50 million, and the scope of concessions given to investment in backward areas has been extended to firms in a segment covered by the Monopolies and Restrictive Trade Practices Act. On the other, the newly appointed finance minister has indicated that he wished to slow down the government's policy of economic liberalization. It is possible that the government is sending such contradictory signals in an effort to please all segments of the public before the widely anticipated general elections. Four opposition parties have recently merged, ostensibly to provide a strong electoral challenge to the ruling party. If the monsoon continues to be better than normal, the *kharif* crop should be bountiful, and it is likely a general election will be called soon afterwards—perhaps in December 1988, a full year ahead of schedule. If this forecast turns out to be correct, no major economic policy initiative can be expected until after the elections. However, fiscally expensive populist measures can be expected. To keep the price of consumption goods in check (at least until the elections), substantial imports of food grains, vegetable oil, sugar, industrial equipment, raw materials, and spares used in the production of consumer durables can be expected. It is likely that the alarming fall in foreign exchange reserves mentioned earlier is in part a reflection of such imports.

August 15, 1988

Sources

Ahluwalia, I., *Industrial Growth in India: Stagnation Since the Mid–Sixties* (New Delhi: Oxford University Press, 1985).

Bardhan, P. K., *The Political Economy of Development in India* (New York: Basil Blackwell Press, 1984).

Bhagwati, J. N. and Desai, P., *Planning for Industrialization: India's Trade and Industrialization Policies 1950–66* (New Delhi: Oxford University Press, 1970).

Bhagwati, J. N. and Srinivasan, T. N., *Foreign Trade Regimes and Economic Development: India* (Columbia University Press, 1975).

Brahmananda, P. R., *Productivity in the Indian Economy: Rising Inputs for Falling Outputs* (Bombay: Himalaya Publishing House, 1986).

Central Statistical Organisation, *National Accounts Statistics 1970–71–1984–85*, New Delhi, January 1987.

Department of Economic Affairs, *Economic Survey, 1986–87*, New Delhi, February 1987.

Fazal, M. A. et. al., *Report of the Expert Committee on Public Sector Management and Performance.* (New Delhi: Government of India, 1982).

Goldar, B. N., *Productivity Growth in Indian Industries* (Bombay: Allied Publishers, 1986).

Hazell, P. R. *Instability in Indian Agriculture, Research Report 30* (Washington DC: International Food Policy Research Institute, May 1982).

Hussain, A., et. al., *Report of the Committee on Trade Policies* (New Delhi: Government of India, 1984).

Jha, L. K., *Report of the Economic Administration Reforms Commission on Government and Public Enterprises* (New Delhi: Government of India, 1985).

Marathe, S.S., *Regulation and Development: India's Policy Experience of Controls Over Industry* (New Delhi: Sage Publications, 1986).

Mehra, S., *Instability in Indian Agriculture in the Context of New Technology* (Washington DC: International Food Policy Research Institute, July 1981).

Narasimham, M., et al., *Report of the Committee to Examine Principles of Possible Shift From Physical to Financial Controls* (New Delhi: Government of India, 1985).

National Academy of Sciences, *Population Growth and Economic Development: Policy Questions* (Washington, DC: National Academy Press, 1986).

National Institute of Public Finance and Policy, *Aspects of the Black Economy in India: Reports and Government Documents* (New Delhi, 1985).

Reserve Bank of India, *Annual Report 1986–87* (Bombay: Reserve Bank of India, September, 1987).

Relevant articles from the following 1987 issues of *Economic and Political Weekly*, Bombay, dated: March 14 and 21, April 11, 18, 25, June 27, August 1, September 26, November 14, 21, December 5, 12, 19, and Annual Number.

India Today, New Delhi, January 15, 1988.

India Abroad, New York, February 12; July 22, 29; August 5, 12, 1988.

Segupta, A., et al., *Report of the Committee to Review Policy for Public Enterprises* (New Delhi: Government of India, 1984).

Sivaraman, B., *Report of the National Committee on the Development of Backward Areas* (New Delhi: Government of India, 1980).

3
India's Foreign Relations: Problems along the Borders

Thomas Perry Thornton

India's foreign policy is shaped by many factors, beginning with the very complexity of the country itself. Perhaps half of India's 850 million people are among the poorest of the earth, living in severely straitened conditions, frequently abject poverty and backwardness. The remainder are a sub–nation of modern, relatively affluent, technologically skilled people generally comparable to a less well–off European country. The elite itself is divided between those who would emphasize growth based on an open market and those concerned with a more socialist pattern of society. While these differences are crucial for India's domestic development, they also underlie the difficulty India has in defining its international role: should it seek to become the leader of the world's underprivileged ("the greatest of the least") or seek its place at the international high table as the least of the greatest?

A force of a different order is the international pressure brought to bear upon India. The greatest impact is from the global competition between the Soviet Union and the United States that plays itself out in South Asia and has substantially altered the regional order in India's neighborhood. During 1987, however, the most important foreign policy issues arose from issues in India's neighborhood itself, deriving mainly from ambiguities left over from the manner of India's creation.

Regional Issues

When India achieved Independence in 1947 it was not as a single nation comprising all of previous British (or, for that matter, Mughal) India. Pakistan, which then included an East as well as a West wing, was carved out of the realm in ways that would ensure conflict. The religiously based separation had been bitter and violent, and the new boundaries were rarely logical, often dividing lands and peoples that had been unified for centuries. In addition, the neighboring new nations of Nepal, Ceylon (later Sri Lanka), and Burma could all have been logically included in a greater India—and feared that they still might be.

India also had to deal with the reality of ethnic spillover along its borders. Bengalis, divided only by religion, populated the Indian state of West Bengal as well as the East wing of Pakistan. When the latter rose against West Pakistani domination in 1971, India could not remain indifferent to their fate, and its army intervened to settle the issue in favor of the Bengalis. Less dramatic but troublesome problems arose from virtually uncontrollable migration between India, Nepal, and Bangladesh. In the south, concern by Tamils over the difficulties of their brethren in Sri Lanka was a major factor in India's most critical foreign problem of 1987.

Another aspect of the new formations in South Asia was the overwhelming preponderance of India. Relations between large and small neighbors can be difficult, and the conditions under which Independence was achieved guaranteed that, with Pakistan at least, they would be extremely difficult indeed. Had India wanted to dominate the region by brute force, it could not have done so for Pakistan was large enough to resist Indian hegemony. Short of that, however, India had to decide whether it wanted to overawe its neighbors and impose its will on them individually, or whether it would seek to win their good will through benevolent cooperation. And, of course, the choice was not solely India's. Each of the smaller neighbors had to decide how to deal with Indian dominance.

Pakistan

From its inception, Pakistan has proved to be the greatest regional problem for India and a major obstacle to India's assertion of a larger global role. Most troubling to India was Pakistan's decision in the 1950s to offset Indian preponderance by looking for support from outside South Asia. It first recruited the United States to its cause and then, in the 1960s, was able to establish close ties with China. The 1965 and 1971 wars between India and Pakistan, the second of which involved the breakup of Pakistan and the creation of Bangladesh, demonstrated the unwillingness of Pakistan's distant friends to come to its aid and established clearly the regional primacy of India. For the rest of the 1970s, it appeared that Pakistan, although unreconciled, would seek its national fulfillment by turning westward for a closer relationship with the Islamic (and increasingly wealthy) Middle East.

The superpowers reentered the equation, however, when the Soviets invaded Afghanistan in late 1979, and the United States declared

Pakistan to be a frontline state against Soviet aggression. President Carter's initial offer of support was spurned by Pakistan, but Reagan's more generous package of military and economic assistance (discussed below) was enough to satisfy the Pakistanis and profoundly disturb the Indians. New Delhi responded by focusing its apprehensions not on the Soviet incursion but on the apparent reestablishment of the U.S.–Pakistani alliance. By the mid-1980s, Indo–Pakistani relations had degenerated into the sadly familiar patterns of the past: claims by each that the other was building up a threatening military capability and interfering in domestic political problems.

Cross–border ethnic problems played their part. Kashmir, the only Muslim–majority state in India, has been in contention between India and Pakistan since Independence. The two countries had fought a war over it in 1948 resulting in a partition favorable to India, and Pakistan's ultimately unsuccessful attempt to redress the situation in 1965 led to war in that year. The Kashmir dispute had appeared to be put to rest in the 1970s, but in the next decade it reentered the political dialogue between India and Pakistan—a recurrent symbol of Pakistan's dissatisfaction with the South Asian order and a continuing problem for India because of the Kashmiris' desire for a distinctive political existence. Although there was fighting in Kashmir in 1987, it was over remote territory and was not directly connected with the ethnic problem; hence it did not threaten the central relationship between India and Pakistan. Kashmir remains, however, a sharply disputed territory: a source of Indo–Pakistani hostility and a constant invitation to conflict.

A more urgent ethnic problem in the 1980s has been the Sikh unrest in the Indian state of Punjab. It is a measure of the Sikhs' dissatisfaction with India that they have sought assistance from Pakistan; in the violence surrounding partition in 1947, Sikhs and Muslims were particularly bitter enemies. India claims that Pakistani assistance is a major contributor to the Sikh problem, but Pakistan denies any involvement. The Pakistanis have, at a minimum, been less than assiduous in preventing Sikhs from finding refuge in Pakistan and purchasing arms there, but Pakistan is not a significant contributor to India's problem in Punjab. New Delhi is nonetheless deeply concerned, and its fears and allegations contributed to the sharp deterioration in Indo–Pakistani relations in the early part of 1986, leading to ever–shriller recriminations in the course of that year.

In this troubled context, Indian military maneuvers along the Punjab border in late 1986, codenamed "Operation Brasstacks," and the deployment of Pakistani forces in response, raised serious concerns that one side or the other was planning a preemptive attack. While matters cooled down at the end of that year, concern flared up again in late

January 1987 as Pakistan overreacted to further Indian maneuvers and the Indians responded by declaring an exceptionally high level of military readiness and, on January 22-24, moving their troops up to the border. Both sides recognized that they had gone dangerously far and set diplomatic machinery in motion to rectify the situation. Drawing on the peculiar shared heritage of the two countries, the late president of Pakistan Zia ul–Haq invited himself to a cricket match in India on February 19, and in the process met with Rajiv Gandhi. By March 2, a comprehensive agreement was reached by the two countries' foreign secretaries that restored the status quo and even provided for some safeguards to prevent such dangerous flare–ups in the future.

Although neither party ever had any intention of initiating hostilities, the Brasstacks contretemps highlighted the volatile nature of the Indo–Pakistani relationship, plagued by profound mistrust and fueled now by huge infusions of modern arms from the Soviet Union and the United States. Leaving aside the unlikely charge, made in the Indian press, that Rajiv Gandhi staged the entire matter as a cover for shifting V.P. Singh from the Finance to the Defense Ministry, it was clear that the Indian government sought to exploit the situation to shore up its imperiled domestic position.

The two countries did come to blows in another sector of the border. In northern Kashmir, the cease–fire line between the two countries was never demarcated since the area involved was the nearly inaccessible Siachen Glacier situated at an altitude of up to 20,000 feet. Undeterred, the armies of India and Pakistan sought to establish a presence in the area and inevitably came into contact and conflict, as early as 1984. During the course of 1987 there was a major increase in fighting; particularly sharp engagements reportedly took place in late September and the casualties reportedly ran into the hundreds. Attempts to ascribe strategic importance to the region are unconvincing and it appears that the two governments have let themselves be driven by the actions of their respective armies as each maneuvered for position against the other. While the fighting at Siachen remains contained, positions on both sides have now hardened, the cost of life has been substantial, and Indo–Pakistani relations have been further poisoned to no apparent purpose.

In addition to military confrontation and conflict, much of 1987 was taken up with verbal skirmishing between India and Pakistan. The two sides had come to blows in early 1965 over the alignment of their border where it meets the Arabian Sea in the Kutch region between the Indian state of Gujarat and the Sind province in Pakistan. That problem was ultimately settled by arbitration; this year it came back in another form since the seaward extension of the border is not clearly defined and there could be considerable amounts of offshore oil involved. At year's end, however, the two sides agreed to handle the matter through negotiation.

A more critical issue between the two countries involves their nuclear programs. Ever since the Indian nuclear test in 1974, Pakistan has been determined to develop its own nuclear capability and by 1987 probably had most, if not all, of the pieces in place to build a few rudimentary nuclear weapons. India, for its part, has conducted no further tests and there is no evidence that it has fabricated weapons. It continues to build up stockpiles of unsafeguarded nuclear material, however, and certainly has the ability to manufacture a number of weapons on very short notice. A nuclear arms race between India and Pakistan thus remains a disturbing possibility.

During 1987 there were no dramatic changes in the situation. A tentative agreement reached by Rajiv Gandhi and Zia ul–Haq in December 1985, that neither would attack the other's nuclear establishments, remained unsigned although press reports suggested that it would soon be in final form. Despite much unhelpful rhetoric, neither side actually took any irreversible step in the direction of a nuclear capability and it remained a strong possibility that each would stop just short of conducting a nuclear test—the "bomb–in–the–basement" option that Israel has found so rewarding. Much of the tension on the nuclear issue during 1987 was, as we shall see later, between Pakistan and the United States. For India, this provided an opportunity to make the nuclear issue a matter of Indo–U.S. relations and avoid addressing it directly in the Pakistan context. Pakistani proposals for negotiations on the South Asian nuclear problem were given short shrift by India. New Delhi claimed that they were simply political ploys on the part of Islamabad that would implicitly equate India and Pakistan—and more credibly, that they failed to take into account the potential Chinese nuclear threat to India.

Even while charges of misbehavior were being hurled and soldiers killed, the two countries continued to maintain a substantial political dialogue. In addition to the late president Zia's visit to India in the heat of the Brasstacks episode, military and civilian consultations took place several times throughout the year. The two sides discussed the problem of securing their border in Punjab against illegal crossings—whether in aid of Sikh insurgents or for smuggling. The meetings of the South Asian Association for Regional Cooperation (SAARC) brought Indians and Pakistanis together at various levels, including a summit in December. None of these meetings dealt effectively with the basic issues in Indo–Pakistani relations, but it is mildly reassuring that dangers of war were kept within bounds while some slight progress was made in forging the kinds of ties that make war less likely.

Sri Lanka

The most dramatic of India's foreign policy involvements in 1987 was in Sri Lanka where the two major ethnic communities have been engaged in a bitter conflict to determine the future shape of that country. In the 1950s, the majority Sinhalese community was swept by a wave of nationalism that worked to the disadvantage of the Tamils, who comprise 12 percent of the island's population. The Tamils responded with demands for greater autonomy, and a few extremists among them called for an independent state (Tamil Eelam). This minority was extremely successful in using classic terrorist techniques to provoke reprisals from the Sinhalese–controlled police and armed forces. The situation became polarized in the 1980s and the extremists gained increasing support from those Tamils who originally had been interested only in negotiating a better deal within the Sri Lankan polity. By 1986, the Sri Lankan government had lost control of the Tamil core area in the north and was using increasingly violent military measures to reassert its position.

The insurgent groups were not completely on their own. The population of the politically important Indian state of Tamil Nadu was sympathetic with the plight of their kinsmen in Sri Lanka, although not necessarily with their political demands. Before her death, Indira Gandhi had given the Sri Lankan Tamil insurgents extensive covert support, partly as a way to gain popularity in Tamil Nadu, but also as a means of bringing pressure to bear on Sri Lankan president J.R. Jayewardene who had moved away from Indian leadership on foreign policy issues, preferring a more pro–Western form of non–alignment, and had sought political ties outside of South Asia.

Rajiv Gandhi took a different approach to the problem. He cut back sharply on support to the Tamil separatists and sought to play a mediatory role between them and the Sri Lankan government. Through 1986 he was unable to make any substantial progress and his political opponents charged that he was being duped by Jayewardene, who continued to increase military pressure on the Tamils with help from outside advisers, including—anathema in New Delhi—Israelis and Pakistanis. By early 1987, government forces were driving ever farther north toward Jaffna, but there was little prospect that the army would be able to restore peace and order. Civilian casualties among the Tamils were heavy, and concern in India was growing rapidly.

During the first half of the year, India issued a series of warnings to Jayewardene against seeking to solve the Tamil problem with brute force and highlighting the plight of the Tamil population around Jaffna. On June 3, a flotilla of Indian Red Cross ships carrying relief supplies for the embattled Tamils sailed towards Jaffna. It was warned off by the Sri Lankan Navy, but on the following day—in a dramatic act unparalleled since the Indian intrusion into East Pakistan in 1971—Colombo was informed that Indian Air Force transports, escorted by fighter aircraft, would fly missions over northern Sri Lanka, dropping token amounts of relief supplies. Objections by Colombo and protests of concern by other South Asian countries were of no avail; Rajiv Gandhi had sent a clear message that India was no longer willing to stand by while events in Sri Lanka went from bad to worse.

Jayewardene got the message. It was further reinforced by the United States, which refused to become involved, leaving him with no alternative to coming to terms with India. Culminating a series of rapid diplomatic moves, Gandhi flew to Colombo on July 29 to sign an agreement that reaffirmed India's support for a united Sri Lanka and cut off support to the Tamil insurgents, but provided for substantial concessions by the Colombo government to the Tamil demands. The key provision was Indian agreement to send troops to Sri Lanka to disarm the rebels and to facilitate the political compromise set forth in the agreement. When Indian forces began to appear the next day, it was widely assumed that tranquility could be restored rapidly and that the terms of the compromise would satisfy all but the most extreme Tamils. The Indian move received widespread international approbation; Rajiv Gandhi was credited with moving decisively and responsibly in settling a situation that had gotten beyond the control of the Sri Lankan government.

The agreement turned out to have some darker sides. First, Gandhi and Jayewardene may have badly misjudged the mood of the Sri Lankan people. Jayewardene, recognizing that his own army was not up to the task, accepted the need for an Indian force to gain control of the situation. Many in Jayewardene's Sinhalese constituency, however, saw the agreement as a sellout to the Tamils and were appalled by the presence of Indian troops in their country. When Gandhi came to Colombo, a Sinhalese member of the naval honor guard broke ranks to club him with a rifle, and Sinhalese groups began to mount acts of terror against the Sri Lankan government. Jayewardene's political position deteriorated and several key Sinhalese politicians refused to support the agreement. Indeed, it was not clear that Jayewardene would be able to implement it even with Indian support.

Prospects dimmed still further when the Tamil extremists refused to cooperate. They surrendered only a token number of their weapons to the Indian Peace Keeping Force (IPKF) and continued to hold Jaffna. In October, the IPKF mounted a major and bloody operation and managed to secure Jaffna and the surrounding region. Even then, however, some of the extremist leaders were able to escape and at the end of the year were mounting a sporadic but ongoing guerrilla campaign in eastern Sri Lanka—this time against Indians more than against Sinhalese. The IPKF moved into the east in force, and by year's end, up to 50,000 Indian troops had been committed to Sri Lanka with the prospect of still larger numbers in 1988.

The Indian forces had sustained well over 300 deaths and the wounded numbered in the thousands. The Sri Lankan government claimed that a political settlement could be implemented in the course of 1988, but few saw much prospect of the IPKF being withdrawn in the near future. Indian opinion, which had originally lauded Gandhi's decisive move, became increasingly concerned with mounting political and human costs; comparisons to American involvement in Vietnam were frequent. Although Gandhi was still able to count on popular support for his actions, his Sri Lankan venture threatened to join the ranks of bold actions on the domestic front (e.g., Assam and Punjab) that were undertaken with good, indeed statesmanlike, intentions, but ended up as political liabilities.

Another dark side to the agreement was evident in an exchange of letters between Gandhi and Jayewardene that formed part of the agreement. It went without saying that if India acted as the responsible leader of South Asia in helping Sri Lanka out of its predicament, Colombo would have to reciprocate by being more sensitive about Indian foreign policy concerns. New Delhi could have conveyed this point subtly, thereby lending strength to the proposition that it was a strong but magnanimous neighbor on whom the other South Asian nations could comfortably rely. Alternatively, it could make a public object lesson of Sri Lanka—a warning to other neighbors that they must hew to India's line and not expect outsiders to help them avoid the reality of Indian predominance. A case can be made for either approach, but India chose the latter. Sri Lanka implicitly agreed to follow the Indian lead in foreign policy and accepted specific Indian demands for a veto over Sri Lankan security relations with outsiders. These were an agreement to stop using non–Indian military advisers (the target was Pakistan and Israel); a promise not to allow any foreign bases in Sri Lanka or to allow non–Indians to operate a petroleum tank farm near the sensitive base at Trincomalee; and a review of U.S. and West German radio broadcasting facilities on Sri Lanka to ensure that these had no military or intelligence functions.

Indian writers—most approving but some critical—saw Indian actions in Sri Lanka as the establishment of an Indian Monroe Doctrine over South Asia. India's neighbors deplored the tone of the agreement and portrayed it as confirmation of their worst fears about India's drive for regional hegemony. In late 1987, Jayewardene began to look for ways to restore some of his domestic political position by proposing that the exchange of letters be converted into a bilateral treaty which would bind India as well as Sri Lanka. This is hardly the vision India has of its role in South Asia, and New Delhi has sidestepped the proposal. Clearly, however, Sri Lanka will not willingly accept its subordinate position as permanent.

South Asian Regional Cooperation

It is not yet clear whether the agreement constitutes a plus or a minus for India as a regional leader. In the fractious atmosphere of South Asia, there is something to be said for an unambiguous statement of India's position. Sri Lanka, however, may not be a useful model for India in dealing with significantly larger countries such as Pakistan or even Bangladesh, which have greater international options.

The Sri Lankan developments set the tone for South Asian regional affairs throughout 1987 and few other regional issues gained prominence. Matters from earlier years dragged on in India's relations with its other neighbors, Nepal, Bangladesh, and Bhutan, especially the disputes between India and Bangladesh over the division of the waters of the Ganges River and the illegal migration of Bangladeshis into neighboring states of Eastern India where they upset delicate ethnic balances and seize economic opportunities that are modest but still prized by the resident Indians. Ethnic Nepalese (Gurkhas) living in the extreme northern part of the Indian state of West Bengal continued to agitate for a separate state of "Gurkhaland"; despite charges that the government of Nepal may be lending aid to the agitation, this remains an internal Indian problem and Indo-Nepalese relations during 1987 remained on an even keel.

The regional organization SAARC marked another year of survival and modest growth. In January a permanent secretariat was established at Kathmandu. In subsequent meetings, agreement on narcotics control measures were reached, panels on cultural and aviation affairs were convened, and the prescribed sequence of meetings at ascending levels—foreign secretaries and foreign ministers in June, and ultimately the annual summit in November, held in Kathmandu—took place.

The foreign ministers' meeting illustrated the strengths and weaknesses of SAARC. Under SAARC's rules, bilateral and contentious matters cannot be raised, but all of the SAARC states obviously sympathized with Sri Lanka and the unilateral Indian relief operations hung like a pall over the meeting. The Sri Lankan foreign minister had originally refused to come but soon realized that Sri Lankan interests would be better served by his presence than his absence. The meeting took place, useful groundwork was laid for the upcoming summit, and the session provided a setting in which the Indians and Sri Lankans not only could, but had to, talk to each other at a time when other communications were frozen into a hostile, rigid formality.

The SAARC summit came after the India–Sri Lankan agreement and the atmosphere was less tense. The participants made useful progress in agreeing to cooperate on the establishment of a regional food grain reserve and in dealing with terrorism. Panels were also set up to study joint cooperation in dealing with natural disasters and threats to the South Asian environment. The summit also provided the opportunity for Gandhi and Pakistani Prime Minister Junejo to discuss the fighting at the Siachen Glacier. They agreed on working–level meetings to defuse the situation and to a demarcation of the disputed maritime boundary at Kutch.

Underneath the surface cordiality, anti–Indian sniping continued. The smaller SAARC nations remained troubled by the Indo–Sri Lankan agreement and the precedent that this might set for India's behavior to them. Matters were hardly helped by the Indian attempt to promote SAARC membership for the Soviet–sponsored regime in Afghanistan, which was opposed by all the other members. SAARC is ill–suited for addressing fundamental political problems and is much more useful for improving atmospherics and bringing people together. Given the touchiness of relations between India and its various neighbors, this is about all that can be expected—that, however, is something quite important in an area so plagued by strife as is South Asia.

Farther Afield

India's principal concerns are in the immediate neighborhood of the South Asian subcontinent, but just beyond its boundaries lie areas that have been important to India historically and continue to pose serious policy problems.

First among these is *China*, which is second in urgency only to Pakistan in New Delhi's security concerns. India has vastly improved its military capabilities since the debacle of the 1962 war and China itself, preoccupied with domestic affairs and under a less aggressive leadership, is a now much less menacing neighbor. Nonetheless, the potential Chinese threat has a critical impact on Indian foreign policy generally:

- India's deep attachment to the Soviet Union grows primarily out of fear of China.
- Concern over China adversely affects other Indian relationships, especially in Southeast Asia, where India supports Vietnam on the Kampuchean issue.
- India's military nuclear program was triggered by the Chinese threat, and New Delhi's refusal to consider atom–free arrangements in South Asia (as well as other nonproliferation proposals) is based at least in part on the realization that China would not be similarly constrained.
- India's unnecessarily overwhelming military posture vis–à–vis Pakistan is justified by the need for sufficient forces to fight a two–front war, should China intervene.

Concern about China is magnified by the fact that Beijing not only has a history of close ties to Pakistan, but in the 1970s also established a strategic relationship with the United States. India is understandably worried that these three countries—two enemies and one whose intentions are questioned—will gang up on India politically, if not militarily. While Americans see this as far–fetched, Indians recall the 1971 war when a similar scenario took place as China lent vocal support to the Pakistani cause and Richard Nixon dispatched a naval task force to threaten India.

At times it has appeared (mainly to outsiders) that India and China are in an inevitable competition for leadership of Asia and that the two countries will remain rivals, at best just short of open hostility. Perhaps this will ultimately be the case, but at present there is little evidence that either side spends much time on such considerations. Territorial disputes are of much more pressing concern. The 1962 war was fought over possession of tracts of territory in the Ladakh region of Kashmir and the area at the extreme east of the India–Tibet border. The war resulted in the reaffirmation of the status quo (China held on to the strategic territory in Ladakh which it did want and withdrew from the territory in the East which it did not) and there has been no substantial change since then. Just as it is probable that, someday, the Kashmir question will be settled between India and Pakistan along the lines of the status quo, there is little doubt that India will come to the parallel conclusion with China. Neither Pakistan nor India is prepared to make the respective concessions required, however, so just like Kashmir, the Sino–Indian border issue remains an obstacle to normalization of relations and a potential flash point for conflict.

In 1987, the issue showed its dangerous potential. In the first months of the year both India and China began to build up their military forces along the eastern sector. Rumors circulated wildly out of New Delhi and Western visitors in Tibet reported large Chinese troop movements toward the border. Both sides made warning noises and in Western capitals there was serious worry that a new war might break out. There was no evident reason why the flare–up took place just when it did, and speculation ranged widely. Some commentators saw the affair as an Indian maneuver to distract domestic opinion from Rajiv Gandhi's increasingly difficult domestic situation, and/or to put a spoke in the process of normalization of relations between the Soviet Union and China. Neither of these explanations is very convincing—although, of course, the Indian government was glad to draw what political advantage it could once the crisis had begun. An alternative set of explanations focused on the Chinese side: that Beijing was tiring of India's refusal to come to a "reasonable" territorial agreement and was showing its displeasure over India's December 1986 grant of formal statehood to Arunachal Pradesh, the disputed area in the east. At the height of the crisis, specific protests and counter–protests were traded on this point. Finally, the flare–up may have been the result of cumulative frictions between forces on the ground and aggressive maneuvering for minor tactical advantages by the Indians in areas where boundaries are vague.

The crisis, if indeed it was one, passed fairly rapidly. Indian defense minister K.C. Pant, en route home from a visit to Korea, held talks in Beijing in early April, and was followed by then–foreign minister N.D. Tiwari in June. Rhetoric was toned down gradually on both sides, and New Delhi was careful not to show partisanship for the anti-Chinese demonstrations that took place in Tibet in the autumn, notwithstanding widespread Indian sympathy for the Tibetans. In November, a Chinese delegation led by the vice foreign minister came to Delhi for the eighth in the long–running series of talks about the border. The atmosphere was less tense than it had been during the preceding round in 1986. The parties agreed to raise the next negotiations from the technical to the political level, but there seems little prospect for rapid movement. Prime Minister Gandhi lacks the political base needed to make the concessions that confront India and it is easier to let matters drift. The flare–up of 1987 showed, however, that a policy of drift also has its costs—beyond those that tensions with China impose on India in terms of military expenditure and loss of flexibility in dealing with other foreign policy issues.

In *Southeast Asia,* Indian support for the Vietnamese regime in Hanoi has multiple rationales, but the underlying one is to prevent Vietnam from coming under Chinese political influence. As long as the United States was involved in Vietnam, support of Hanoi was a fairly popular course of action. In the changed circumstances of the 1980s, however, support for Vietnam—and especially for its puppet regime in Kampuchea—looks like an Indian pay-off of its political debts to Moscow. India is the sole nonaligned nation to recognize the Heng Samrin regime in Phnom Penh—a policy that costs India dearly among its Third World constituency, especially in its relations with the ASEAN nations of Southeast Asia. India pressed on, however, and in January 1987, a delegation led by Tiwari went to Hanoi to work out cooperation on petroleum and natural gas production; Indian technical consultants were also sent to Laos and Kampuchea.

A different policy on Vietnam might not make all that much difference for India. While Southeast Asia was historically an Indian sphere of influence, New Delhi has had little success in promoting its interests there since Independence. Indian officials regularly visit the region (senior officials covered most of the countries in 1987) but economic ties remain thin, and the nations of the region look eastward toward the relatively prosperous Pacific basin rather than toward India, which they regard as an economic sinkhole and too closely tied to the Soviet Union.

Elsewhere in East Asia, Rajiv Gandhi visited Burma, Australia, and Japan during the year, and the foreign minister touched base in Seoul and Tokyo, while the defense minister visited Pyongyang. There was no sign that these visits were anything more than goodwill calls. The travails of Fiji, where an ethnic Indian majority was ousted from power by an indigenous Fijian coup, naturally evoked concern and sympathy, but India was no more able to do anything than was the rest of the world.

There was little Indian activity in *West Asia* in 1987. The Iran–Iraq war is of continuing concern in New Delhi since this is a region of traditional Indian involvement and the source of much of India's oil. Pakistan's strong position in the Gulf region is also a challenge. The Iranians were sharply critical of the killing of Indian Muslims in the communal disturbances at Meerut in May, but India seeks to keep lines open to both sides and would be a potential, though not very likely, mediator should the two sides ever agree that they want help in ending their conflict.

The Indian role in the Arab–Israeli dispute is equally unpromising. Conscious of the need to placate its own Muslim minority and to ensure that the Arabs do not draw too close to Pakistan, India steadfastly supports Arab positions and maintains only token contact with Israel.

Even the kidnapping of an Indian national employed by the American University in Beirut did not shake this support. Increasingly sports–conscious India did waver slightly, however, by agreeing to host the Israeli tennis team in a critical Davis Cup match.

Afghanistan is an area of vital concern to India since ties between the two countries have been close for centuries and the presence of a Soviet military force in Afghanistan has major implications for India's security and political interests. The Soviet invasion triggered the reentry of the United States into South Asian security matters; the presence of a Soviet military force in Afghanistan gives Moscow a role in South Asia that could rival India's; and the implicit Soviet threat to Pakistan is potentially destabilizing for all of South Asia. Overall, the Soviet invasion marked a sharp setback to political trends in South Asia that had been broadly favorable to Indian interests during the 1970s. Yet New Delhi has never officially abandoned the position, enunciated a few days after the Soviet invasion in December 1979, that the Soviets are in Afghanistan by invitation of the Afghan government and that the Soviet involvement must be judged in the context of the involvement of others (i.e., the United States, Pakistan, and China) who are supporting the *mujahidin* resistance forces. While Indians do not hesitate to urge the Soviets privately to leave Afghanistan, the Indian public position remains one of tolerance.

The Indian approach is not solely an expression of gratitude for past services rendered by the Soviet Union. It also reflects an Indian judgement that, undesirable as the present situation is, it is preferable to an Afghanistan under the control of Muslim fundamentalist forces. India, after all, has a much better record in dealing with communists than with Muslims. Even more important, India is less worried about the potential for an extension of the Soviet role in the Subcontinent through Afghanistan than about the reality of Pakistan's alignment with the United States and China, and the rebuilding of Pakistan's military forces during the 1980s. In that sense, New Delhi sees the United States as the greater culprit and target of criticism. India stands almost alone among the nonaligned, and emphatically alone among its South Asian and West Asian neighbors, in its attitudes on the Afghan question. India once again found itself in a small minority in the 1987 United Nations General Assembly vote on Afghanistan. With 123 nations voting against the Soviets, India was one of only 11 abstainers, while 19 (almost all of them Soviet bloc nations) voted to support the Soviets. India also is one of the few nations that extends a hand of friendship to the Soviet puppet regime in Afghanistan. As we have seen, it favors admission of the Najib regime into SAARC, and it also provides various kinds of low–level economic and technical assistance. During the course of the year, the Indian and Afghan foreign ministers exchanged visits and joint Indo–Afghan commissions held economic and technical meetings.

Indians argue that it is better to keep lines open to the Najib government than to leave it with no contacts aside from Moscow. Furthermore, as one of the few countries that has not cut its ties to the Kabul regime, India—by the same logic that underpins U.S. ties to South Africa, for instance—could be in a position to contribute usefully to a resolution of the Afghan problem. The intense activity in late 1987 that followed Gorbachev's moves to extricate the Soviet Union from Afghanistan should have provided a singular opportunity for New Delhi to test the validity of its approach and to justify the substantial political price that it has had to pay for its Afghanistan policy. India, however, seemed to be completely irrelevant in the rapidly shifting situation. Afghanistan is no longer primarily an element of the South Asian equation where India's voice is dominant; its future is likely to be settled in a much larger setting.

The Global Context

Americans think of the global context of international affairs in terms of the U.S.–Soviet competition, with supporting roles to be played by China, Japan, and Western Europe. And that is, of course, the most salient aspect of the global scene for Americans—and others as well, for if things go badly wrong there, what happens elsewhere may not be of much importance. There is, however, another global context that has to do with the nonvetoable activities of the United Nations, the Non–Aligned Movement, the Group of 77 and the various fora that are dominated by the global south. For India, this is a sphere of activity of considerable importance. India sees itself as the natural leader of the global south, and its diplomatic experience and (China aside) size are unequalled in this constituency. It is the forum where India can play its role of "greatest of the least," and it does so with gusto.

Even though India completed its term as chairman of the Non–Aligned Movement in 1986, New Delhi remains a lively focus of international activity. New Delhi hosted the Africa Fund summit in January, and during the year received a steady stream of visitors including the chiefs of government of Malaysia, Vanuatu, Denmark, the Netherlands, Finland, Romania, Angola, and Peru as well as Yasser Arafat of the PLO and the foreign ministers of North Korea, France, and Norway. Indian foreign policy leaders were also peripatetic. The prime minister and foreign minister's travels are noted elsewhere; the ministers of state for external affairs and the foreign secretary were frequently underway to one international meeting or another or to a foreign capital.

The level of activity can be seen in one issue (March 16) of *India News*, published by the Indian embassy in Washington.

- The Minister of External Affairs participated in the extraordinary meeting of the Non–Aligned Coordinating Bureau on the situation in Central America, held in Guyana. In passing, he affirmed India's full support to Argentina on the Falklands/Malvinas issue.
- While in Guyana he met with the President of that country and the two agreed that there should be a meeting of the Indo–Guyana ministerial level joint commission.
- The visit of the president of Pakistan Zia (noted above) was recorded.
- The president of Romania, visiting Delhi, joined Gandhi in a call for a halt to the nuclear arms race.
- The prime minister of Yemen made a brief stop in Delhi en route to Beijing.
- The French foreign minister visited Rajiv Gandhi in Delhi.
- The deputy prime minister of Mauritius also paid a call on Gandhi.
- The foreign minister of North Korea visited his Indian counterpart, N.D. Tiwari.
- Minister of State Natwar Singh visited various capitals in Southeast Asia.
- A Polish parliamentary delegation called on the prime minister.

One can reasonably question the importance to either party of, say, an Indo–Peruvian cultural agreement (reached during President Alan Garcia's visit in January), but symbolism is the stuff of much of international relations. Comings, goings, and signings are important rituals reaffirming India's unique role in the international system and New Delhi's status as the informal capital of the global south. They also add to the legitimacy of the New Delhi government in the eyes of its own people.

There are other areas of global activity that are important to India. One has to do with disarmament and arms control. Although India shows no interest in reducing its own military establishment, it is a principal proponent of arms reduction by the superpowers and is a leading member of the Six Nation group (including also Tanzania, Sweden, Mexico, Greece, and Argentina) that continued in 1987 to lobby both Moscow and Washington to abolish their nuclear arsenals. Less powerful superpowers make for a relatively more powerful India, but concern about general nuclear war preoccupies many Indians just as it does Americans and others. It is a long–standing Indian foreign policy priority. The Soviets gain considerable credit in Delhi by associating themselves rhetorically with Indian demands, especially since the United States is much less receptive.

Another global arena has to do with mobilization of resources. Although foreign aid now plays a much smaller role than it did in the 1950s and 1960s, India is a poor country, and its foreign policy has to take into account the need to secure resources abroad. India is especially active in working with the international lending institutions, pressing for greater trade opportunities and other advantages for the less-developed countries. It is the side of India that most clearly reflects the "second India," the mass of some 700 million very poor people.

Interesting indications of the "first India" and of its upwardly mobile role are its membership in various clubs that usually exclude the less developed. India is one of the few nations that has exploded a nuclear device and has a nascent missile capability. Nineteen eighty-seven provided reminders of Indian capabilities in two less bellicose areas. The Indian Antarctic team completed its eighth year of activity in the south polar region. India has a legitimate interest in the Antarctic on the basis of geography, but its involvement there is even more significant as a symbol of India's claim to great power status. India is a party to the international Antarctic treaty, an instrument that many of the less developed countries see as a tool of the advanced countries. Similarly, in August 1987, India registered with the United Nations as a "pioneer investor" in deep seabed mining; the other enrollees were all economically advanced nations.

Relations with the Soviet Union

India is extremely important for the Soviet Union. It is a near-neighbor of concern strategically and politically, and the Soviets also value it as an access point to the nonaligned world. Almost as important, India is one of the few success stories that the Soviets have in the Third World. Other close friends are either very costly (Cuba, Vietnam) or of little consequence (Yemen, Benin). The Soviet regime needs something substantial to show for its huge investment in the Third World over the past generation, and the attention that the Soviet media devote to India is evidence that the relationship is played this way to the Soviet domestic audience.

There are clouds over the Indo-Soviet relationship. India relies heavily on the Soviet Union for military equipment, but it fears excessive dependence and has diversified part of its arms purchases to Europe and the United States. Although the Soviet Union vies with the United States for the position as India's largest trading partner and is a particularly valued market for Indian manufactured goods, the technological future Rajiv Gandhi sees for his country is bound up with the West. There are relatively few Soviet exports that the Indians want, and trade balances run heavily in India's favor. (In Indian fiscal year 1986–87, exports to the U.S.S.R. totalled 18.7 billion rupees while imports were only 10.7 billion.) Despite grandiose projections of increases in Indo–Soviet trade over the coming years and Soviet efforts to link up with the Indian private sector, trade levels have actually declined for the past two years and it is difficult to see how the projected increases can ever be attained. India's cultural ties are also overwhelmingly with the West, and the tide of Indian emigration is headed in that direction as well.

In the long run problems could be even greater. General Secretary Mikhail Gorbachev's Asian policy design, set forth in his June 1986 Vladivostok speech, looks to improving relations with China, and it is precisely the shared enmity towards China (and to a lesser extent Pakistan, where the Soviets also hope to improve ties) that has provided the primary glue to the Indo–Soviet relationship. As these regional factors decline in importance, the Soviets hope to keep India close by focusing on the bilateral relationship and, to the extent possible, by substituting the United States for China as the common foe of the Soviet Union and India.

The Soviets have much to offer India. Foremost, perhaps, are consistency and esteem. Beginning in the 1950s, continuing through the wars between 1962 and 1971, and through the changes of government in both New Delhi and Moscow over the last decade, the Soviet Union has been a crucial support to India against its enemies. The U.S.S.R. wavered briefly during the Sino–Indian conflict and sought to develop closer ties to Pakistan late in the 1960s, but these were exceptions that tested the rule and found it valid. The two countries have gotten used to dealing with each other on a full range of interests and activities, and the two bureaucracies are generally comfortable with each other. The relationship is taken as a fundamental fact of Indian life and few in India question it publicly.

Similarly, the Soviets are willing to put considerable effort into building up Indian self–esteem and catering to its hunger for recognition as a major world actor. As early as 1960, Khrushchev proposed India as part of a troika to run the United Nations. India was the only Third World country that Brezhnev ever visited, and he went there twice. Under Gorbachev, who is no enthusiast for attachments to the Third World, India and its leader, Rajiv Gandhi, have been inundated with evidence of Soviet concern and esteem, and Soviet propaganda portrays the Indo–Soviet relationship as a major factor for peace and stability in the international arena.

The year 1987 was bracketed by spectaculars in Indo–Soviet relations. As it began, India was still basking in the afterglow of Gorbachev's visit to New Delhi in late 1986. As 1987 ended, it was being treated to a huge Soviet cultural program led off by a November visit by Prime Minister N.I. Ryzhkov. And Soviet attention to India was not lacking in the intervening months.

Military supply is the most important tangible element in Moscow's courtship of India and the expedited delivery of MiG–29s at the beginning of 1987 was evidence of why the Indians prize their security relationship with Moscow so highly. This aircraft was needed quickly to meet a perceived threat from the F–16s that the United States had sold to Pakistan; it had yet to be supplied to Moscow's Warsaw Pact allies, but Moscow rapidly made it available on very favorable terms.

The Gorbachev visit was also followed up in other areas as well: Soviet Academy of Sciences chief G.I. Marchuk and deputy prime minister V.M. Kamentsev appeared during March and April to work out plans for greater technical and economic cooperation. Long–term agricultural and scientific agreements were signed. Anatoly Dobrynin of the Communist Party of the Soviet Union (CPSU) Central Committee visited India in May; the visit focused on bilateral matters but served to highlight the Soviets' attempt to upgrade relations between the CPSU and the Congress Party. Foreign Minister Tiwari visited Moscow in May, and in the following month Prime Minister Gandhi made a trip to Moscow in connection with the cultural festival that India was mounting in the Soviet Union. The rather anodyne declaration that Gorbachev and Gandhi had signed in Delhi in November 1986 became the focus of repeated Soviet commentaries that portrayed it as a new charter for world order. A commemorative meeting was held in Tashkent on the first anniversary of the signing.

The Ryzhkov visit was in a much lower key than the Gorbachev visit had been, but it was an event of considerable dimensions, including calls on all of the senior Indian cabinet ministers. It concluded with the signing of a welter of agreements on economic matters, further amplifying the directions set during the Gorbachev visit and seeking to enmesh broader areas of the Indian economy into the Soviet relationship.

Both sides used 1987 as a year of consolidation, and for the Soviet Union this means specifically a consolidation that will narrow India's options in the economic and technical, as well as the political and military fields. Most observers are confident that India will not let its options be closed off. India holds many of the high cards in the relationship and has shown no little skill in accepting benefits from the Soviets while giving only modestly in return. There is a major difference between India and most other Soviet friends. India is not governed by a Marxist–Leninist regime, nor is it subservient to the U.S.S.R. There are no Soviet bases in India and, as distorted as Indian nonalignment sometimes seems to Americans, India pursues its own foreign policy goals as it sees them. India believes that it can resist Soviet pressures—either through its own considerable capabilities or, in the extreme case, by calling on the United States for support. It is the Soviets, not the Indians, who portray the relationship as a dynamic new factor affecting the course of world history. The Indians are intent on maintaining their nonaligned flexibility and, as we shall see below, the United States was also making efforts to keep the most important of all of India's options a viable one.

In the recently published *The Yogi and the Bear*, however, the Indian journalist S. Nihal Singh raises serious questions about the ability of India to maintain its options under the pressure of the Soviet embrace. Singh is particularly concerned about India's dependence on Soviet military equipment, but also growing dependence of Indian consumer goods manufacturers on the Soviet market, and he points out that all is not well in India's democracy. The Congress party continues to be ineffective and Rajiv Gandhi stumbled badly during 1987.

The Indian press and opposition parties were quick to criticize Gandhi for allowing domestic Indian politics to become (or appear to become) a subject of discussion during his Moscow visit in July. In Moscow, Gandhi condemned outsiders seeking to destabilize India and Gorbachev picked up the theme. Soviet media were assiduous in pointing out what Gandhi had left unstated—that the United States was the culprit. There is no evidence, however, that Gandhi asked Gorbachev to make the Communist Party of India support him against his domestic rivals. The open Indian political system provides some guarantee that Indian policy will not swing too far, especially in the direction of a nation whose system is so antithetical to their own. For many of the Soviets' clients, a particular attraction has been the Leninist model of control that Moscow provides and facilitates through party and police training. Even in the politically dark days of the Indira Gandhi Emergency (1975–77) this was not attractive to India.

It is too early to sound loud alarms about India's ability to maintain its options. India continues to be run by politicians, bureaucrats and diplomats of considerable skill and sophistication. The Soviet Union is indisputably India's most important "foreign relation," but it has been so for nearly two decades and the primacy of the Soviet tie is natural for India—as is its ability to keep that relationship in perspective. The new leaders, Gorbachev and Gandhi, may feel they have much in common but each has many other concerns.

It is not too early, however, to be aware that this relationship continues to grow and is based on many parallel interests. The security assistance, consistency, and esteem that the Soviets bring to India are not paralleled by any Western nation, least of all the United States—nor are they likely to be, given the much greater interest that the Soviets have in India. Those who are interested in seeing India keep its options open—Indians and outsiders—cannot simply assume that Indian non-alignment is forever. An effort has to be made to keep it alive.

Relations with the United States

In 1987, both India and the United States made major efforts to strengthen ties—but each also took actions that were harmful. In a familiar pattern, problems on the American side resulted from global concerns which overrode interests in India. Since the 1950s, the relationship has been overshadowed by U.S. ties to Pakistan. The depth of the shadow has varied considerably, but since the renewal of large–scale U.S. assistance to Pakistan following the Soviet invasion of Afghanistan, it has been the principal factor affecting Washington's image in New Delhi.

In the past year U.S.-Pakistan relations were in particularly sharp focus because the military and economic assistance program was up for renewal. The 1981 program had involved $3.2 billion over five years, and the Reagan Administration proposed to follow this with a $4.02 billion program spread over six years, divided on a 40:60 basis between military and economic aid. India was concerned about the military aspects of the program in general, but specifically with individual weapons systems that would be financed by the program and could be used against India. Foremost of these was the AWACS, an airborne early–warning system that Pakistan needs on its Afghan front but which would also be an important adjunct to Pakistani capabilities in any war with India. The Indian government mounted a major propaganda campaign against the AWACS in the United States. As the year ended, no decision had been made, but this was due less to Indian efforts than to problems that had arisen in Washington's relations with Islamabad over nuclear issues.

In 1987 there was mounting evidence that, despite U.S. opposition, Pakistan was developing its nuclear capability. A person of Pakistani origin was arrested (and later convicted) in Philadelphia for illegally trying to export components for making nuclear weapons. There was evidence that Pakistan was enriching uranium to levels compatible only with a weapons program. The latter would be in direct violation of pledges that Pakistan had made to the United States and the former, under U.S. legislation, could trigger an aid cut–off to Pakistan. The Reagan Administration was able to convince Congress that the importance of Pakistan to the United States in terms of Afghanistan was greater than concern over Pakistan's nuclear program. India, which does not share the American view of the Afghani situation, reacted with outrage to the aid to Pakistan which they see as condoning a Pakistani nuclear program directed against them. To make matters worse, Congressional partisans of Pakistan proposed an arrangement by which any meaningful sanctions against Pakistan would have also resulted in punishment of India. The entire package was ultimately set aside, but the damage to Indo–U.S. relations at the end of the year was severe, offsetting a positive trend that had set in during the second half of the year. The situation illustrates the kind of damage that can be done to that relationship by ill–advised actions in the Congress, where few effective voices are raised in India's cause. In the process, India found a way to avoid hard choices in dealing with Pakistan by shifting attention and blame on Washington.

For its part, the Indian government was demonstrating that its interest in improving relations with the United States was less important than the exigencies of domestic Indian politics. Nineteen eighty–seven was not a good year for Rajiv Gandhi: Punjab was in rebellion, other states were turning against the Congress party, the party itself was in disarray, and a major corruption scandal stopped just short of the prime minister himself. Taking a leaf from his mother's book, Gandhi began to blame these developments on the ubiquitous "foreign hand" that seeks to destabilize India. Little imagination was required to see a red–white–and–blue cuff behind the hand, especially since a private American security firm had played a role in exposing the corruption scandal. Even a joint U.S.–Indian program to develop vaccines was "exposed" as an American plot to use Indians as guinea pigs and to acquire information about India's vulnerabilities to bacteriological warfare!

These allegations trailed off in the latter part of the year and it is questionable whether Gandhi really believes that the United States is engaged in attempts to destabilize India. During his visit to Washington in November, he was again reassured on the point at the highest levels. It is clear, however, that he and many other Indians find it tempting to use the United States as a convenient whipping boy for India's own problems, be they domestic or related to India's problems with its neighbors.

India found itself at odds with the United States (and often in agreement with the Soviet Union) on a variety of international issues. Many of the issues—in particular Israel and South Africa—that agitate the nonaligned are ones where the United States and India have different approaches. This shows up regularly in divergent voting patterns in the United Nations. India is also much closer to Soviet declaratory policy on nuclear arms control than it is to that of the United States. Overall, it is fair to say that Indians see a Soviet Union led by Gorbachev as a more responsible international actor than a United States led by Reagan.

Yet against this background, the two countries still make a major effort to keep their differences in check. Each government has made it clear (and reinforced the point with their skeptical bureaucracies) that they want to strengthen bilateral ties despite, or indeed because of, their global and regional differences. There was an active program of high-level visits in both directions. Under Secretary of State Michael Armacost visited India in August, and although the Indian foreign minister cancelled a visit to Washington as a demonstration of concern about U.S.–Pakistani ties, the Indian Minister of State Natwar Singh came twice and the chiefs of the Indian Navy and Air Force paid visits. The high point was the visit of Rajiv Gandhi to Washington in October, en route home from the Commonwealth meeting held in Canada. Although Gandhi's visit was a low-key affair with little substance, it was of symbolic importance. It provided evidence of his stature as a respected international leader who as a matter of course was welcome to stop by in Washington, and was also a signal of Indian determination to keep lines of communication open and, in the process, balance the several meetings that Gandhi has had with Gorbachev in recent years.

There was solid progress in other areas. India and the United States reached an agreement on cooperation against terrorism, as well as a difficult textile agreement on terms favorable to Indian interests, and there were numerous meetings of Indians and Americans on topics ranging from biotechnology to business. Most important, the United States agreed to share advanced technology more freely with India, which New Delhi sees as the most important test of American good will aside from the U.S.–Pakistani relationship. There had been serious resistance within the U.S. government to the sale of a supercomputer, based on fears of technology leaking to the Soviet Union and possible use in India's nuclear program. The Reagan Administration overrode these concerns as a demonstration of its commitment to a stronger Indo–U.S. relationship. The Administration has also for several years put considerable effort into offering an alternative source for Indian military supplies and in 1985 a Memorandum of Understanding was signed to facilitate Indian imports of items that can be used for military purposes. In both 1986 and 1987, India made approximately 4700 requests under the terms of the memorandum; denials in the two years were a mere 75 and 100, and the total value of material exported was about $500 million in 1986 and $825 million in 1987. Particularly important was the Indo–U.S. agreement to cooperate in the development of a light combat aircraft for India. Agreement had been reached previously on the sale of a General Electric engine for the prototype of the aircraft and further sales of avionics and flight control equipment were concluded in 1987. In addition, the United States agreed to Indian coproduction and prototype sales of a naval turbine engine. These transactions are of important symbolic value and will help India in dealing with specific bottlenecks as they develop their indigenous arms industry. They and other military–related sales represent a striking upward step in the level of Indo–U.S. cooperation in a politically sensitive area. They must be kept in perspective, however, for there is little prospect that the United States can make a major dent in India's heavy dependence on Soviet weaponry, and hopes that the Indo–Soviet relationship can be undermined by Indo–U.S. military cooperation are overly optimistic.

An especially promising support to Indo–U.S. relations is economic. If Gandhi is to lead his nation into the twenty–first century, it will need extensive capital infusions and technological help of the kind that can come only from the West. While the United States is by no means the sole source, it remains the most important one and its attitudes are influential in how others, especially the international lending institutions, deal with India's needs. There was great hope for a burgeoning relationship when Gandhi came to power determined to liberalize the Indian economy. These hopes have dimmed as the realities of Indian economics and, especially, politics have made themselves felt. Successive bad monsoons have hurt India's economy, trade deficits are large, and serious debt repayment problems loom. More welfare–oriented policies are needed for domestic political purposes and, as part of his attempt to woo the leftist parties in India, Gandhi has taken to denouncing the multinational corporations—which must be a main contributor of capital and technology. India will almost inevitably become part of the "economic West," for the Soviets just do not have enough to offer. That is likely to be a considerably longer–term process, however, than had been thought a few years ago.

The United States is India's largest trading partner, and is likely to remain so unless Soviet trade picks up sharply. There are, however, caveats to be noted. First, over 10 percent of that trade involves Indian exports of petroleum to U.S. buyers. India sells this crude petroleum because it lacks the capacity to refine it; subsequently it is reimported. Thus the transaction is not truly a contribution to India's trade balance. Second, despite good performances by a fairly broad range of exports (diamonds, textiles and clothes, raw materials, and manufactured items), and a sharp rise in trade in the period 1979–84, India has been able to do no more than maintain its share of the U.S. trade, and total trade has remained more or less flat since 1984 at about four billion dollars annually. Finally, India could fall afoul of U.S. protectionist sentiment, even though it does not cause major sectoral problems nor, despite running a substantial trade surplus since 1983, is it a significant contributor to the U.S. balance of payments deficit.

The 1980s have seen rapid growth in American economic collaborations and investment in India. About 20 percent of all foreign collaborations are with U.S. firms, and the United States in 1986 provided over 27 percent of all foreign investment in India. (Seen from the other direction, however, this investment is less than 1 percent of U.S. investment abroad.) On the other hand, in the face of a stringent budget in Washington and the Reagan Administration's preference for security–related assistance, the foreign aid allocation for India in U.S. fiscal year 1988 was a paltry $99 million, made up of $24 million in development assistance and $75 million in food aid. This represents a decline from the previous year's figure of $149 million; the most recent high point had been $300 million in the last year of the Carter Administration. In fiscal year 1987, the United States gave less bilateral aid to India than did France, West Germany, Italy, Japan, and the United Kingdom. The aid program is no longer a significant positive factor in Indo–U.S. relations. What remains very important for India is continued access to multilateral lending, where the United States plays a very large role. Pressures there will also be considerable as funds contract and India's gross economic performance statistics suggest that it no longer needs special consideration. Nineteen eighty–seven already saw an attempt in the GATT to drop India from the list of countries deserving special trade preferences (GSP).

In sum, the Indo–U.S. relationship continues to follow a difficult path on which irritants abound and serious policy differences are common. Both sides are committed to avoiding a breakdown, and on the basis of past performance, the chances are good that they can avoid one. Even in the most difficult times there has been a floor below which Indo–U.S. relations have not sunk. There has also been a ceiling in the best of times and it is doubtful whether the relationship can break through it in the next several years. In the near term, regional and global issues will probably remain generally negative factors, although matters could given the Afghanistan settlement that removed a major irritant in Indo–U.S. relations and enabled the United States to approach South Asia more on its own terms than on the basis of global considerations. The more generally positive bilateral trends are still weak (especially on the U.S. side), and it is not certain that current attempts to strengthen them will be successful in offsetting the negative factors.

In these pages last year, it was noted that India's policy options between the United States and the Soviet Union—and *a fortiori* its ability to conduct a nonaligned and independent foreign policy—have been narrowing. If a balance for the Indo–U.S. relationship were drawn for 1987, it would be slightly on the positive side as short–term and mid-term differences have not worsened, and some progress has been made on the bilateral front. In a relationship where annual negative balances often outnumber positive ones, however, the coming years need to show improvements if long–term positive factors are to build the firm foundation for Indo–U.S. relations that is now lacking.

There are important positive trends. Neither side wants to see India committed to the Soviet Union, and that—together with the economic factors—is probably the most important long–term guarantee. Close behind is the fact that some 600,000 Indians now live in the United States. These talented, educated, and politically aware individuals, along with the relatives they have left behind in India, will form an increasingly important bond and a useful lobby in both Washington and New Delhi. Nonetheless, if India is to play the kind of role on the world and regional scene to which it aspires, and if it is to remain, in effect, the only obstacle to Soviet domination of South Asia, both India and the United States must be more concerned with the present state of their short–term relationship.

Conclusion

The responsibility for India's future on the international scene is, however, overwhelmingly India's. Outsiders play only partial roles in determining whether India will join the greatest at the high table or succeed in maintaining its leading position among the least. Their role is even secondary—and rarely helpful—in determining whether India will be able to find a satisfactory arrangement of the South Asian constellation. Indians are glad enough to blame their shortcomings on others; that, however, demeans India's own capabilities and frequently results in problems such as the developing Indo–Pakistan nuclear equation. At a time when Third World nations, working alone or in regional concert, are becoming increasingly the masters of their political destinies, India's role falls well short of its potential. In terms of national power, international recognition and diplomatic skills, India is nearly unique in the Third World. If it is unable to shape its own future, it must first seek the causes in New Delhi, not in Washington or in the stars.

In fact, India's foreign policy record is not all that bad. Like the United States, it has had considerable success in consistently pursuing fundamental policies—nonalignment with a pro–Soviet bent, leadership in Third World councils, primacy in South Asia. Dramatic reorientations of Indian policy are not a realistic prospect, for some price for policy consistency must be paid in the coin of policy inertia.

Also like the United States, however, India is the target of trenchant criticism for maladroitness in foreign policy tactics. A cartoon at midyear showed Gandhi piloting his aircraft through mountainous foreign policy terrain, careening from one collision to another. Large nations tend to get into more difficulties than smaller ones, for they have more wide–ranging involvements and are better able to absorb setbacks. But repeated tactical shortcomings can cumulatively undermine even the largest nation's foreign policy direction.

Looking back over 1987, India was careful in tending its strategic concerns with the nonaligned and the Soviet Union, and the Gandhi visit and other bilateral initiatives were intended to keep the U.S. relationship in balance. Relations with neighbors remained the most problematic arena of Indian activity precisely because regional politics carry such a historical burden and are so entwined with domestic concerns. The year's record with Pakistan and China—like so many before it—is not edifying, even if one grants that Gandhi did not manipulate these crises for domestic political purposes. Catastrophes were avoided, but no progress was made toward relieving the pressures that these relationships put on India in its foreign and domestic policies. The key question centers on the outcome of Gandhi's Sri Lankan undertaking—whether in the long run it will worsen or improve India's regional status, and whether it will in the mid–term be a success in bringing about a settlement at an acceptable cost to India.

Of course 1987 was primarily a year of domestic concerns in India; foreign policy played a distinctly secondary role and it was clear that Rajiv Gandhi was using his foreign relations to shore up his embattled domestic position. Seen from that perspective, his performance was probably a net asset, but ultimately the Sri Lanka outcome will be the bench mark—precisely because it is so closely intertwined with domestic Indian politics.

4
Achieving Security from Within and Without

Raju G.C. Thomas

In 1987, India's security was comparatively strong, though significant external and internal threats to it persist. This has been achieved through a broad and complex buildup of military capabilities, through careful diplomacy, and through the development of policies and organizations to deal with internal separatist movements and other violent conflict. It is not difficult to foresee moves by external or internal challengers that would again test India's security, but there is no reason to doubt the country's capacity to counter them.

India's external security concerns have centered primarily on its neighboring states, Pakistan and China. It has fought three wars with Pakistan in 1947–48, 1965, and 1971, and one with China in 1962. After the war with China, Indian strategy began to assume a dual Sino–Pakistani threat and the need to conduct simultaneously a full-scale war against Pakistan; and a military "holding" operation against China along the Himalayan borders until external diplomacy or military pressure by one or both the superpowers brought about a cease–fire.

The years between the breakup of Pakistan in December 1971 which created the new state of Bangladesh and the Soviet invasion of Afghanistan in December 1979 were a period of strategic transition and transformation. The perception of a dual Sino–Pakistani threat was heightened by the arms buildup in the Islamic Middle East and Pakistan's military ties there, and by the Chinese military involvement in Indochina following American withdrawal from Vietnam.

The Soviet invasion of Afghanistan and its aftermath brought Soviet forces to the Khyber Pass, the traditional route of invaders into the Indian Subcontinent over the last 4000 years. For India, however, the occupation of Afghanistan appeared significant more for the heightened superpower rivalry that it generated in the Subcontinent than for the prospect of a Soviet invasion of Pakistan. Superpower military intrusions into the region have invariably implied a relative loss of Indian power and influence.

Conventional military threats perceived by India must also be examined in light of the high probability of a nuclear arms race between India and China, and, consequently, between India and Pakistan as well. Overt or covert moves by India to counter the growing Chinese nuclear capability produce similar moves by Pakistan against India. Especially since the first Indian atomic test in 1974, Pakistan has been attempting to achieve a nuclear weapons capability. This problem became more acute in the mid-1980s as reports indicated that Pakistan had enriched uranium up to weapons-grade quality. A nuclear arms race between India and Pakistan will radically transform the qualitative nature of the military balance in South Asia with potentially adverse effects for world-wide nuclear nonproliferation efforts.

Of perhaps greater significance for India in more recent years has been the intensification of internal security problems that threaten the stability and unity of the nation. While separatist demands accompanied by guerrilla warfare have occurred in the past among the Naga, Mizo, and Gharo tribal peoples in the northeast of India, the more recent growth of Sikh separatism in the Punjab and the resort to terrorist tactics to achieve an independent Khalistan added a new dimension to India's internal security woes.

Hindu–Muslim riots have increased in frequency, as have the number of caste riots between higher caste Hindus and Harijans (the former "Untouchables") in many parts of India. And Tamil–Sinhalese conflict in neighboring Sri Lanka has taxed the emotions of the 55 million Tamils in Tamil Nadu, forcing the Indian government to intervene in Sri Lanka. Meanwhile, the Kashmir issue remains unresolved—at least in the minds of the Pakistanis. The defense of Kashmir—India's only Muslim majority state—has been complicated by the "Khalistan" separatist movement and Hindu–Muslim conflict, both of which tend to aggravate Indo–Pakistani tensions and add to the security pressures on the Indian government.

External and internal security problems and the interaction of the two have produced new debates in India on how resources ought to be allocated to defense, what strategies ought to be adopted to deal with the changing strategic environment, what type and level of force ought to be used to deal with problems of internal security, and the nature of the relationship that ought to exist between the civilian and military authorities in order to cope with India's security problems. The importance of this last problem arises from the increasing size and role of the regular armed forces and paramilitary forces in maintaining security, and civilian fears of possible military takeovers. This fear is aggravated by periodic government efforts to deal with security crises by bypassing democratic processes through constitutional amendments, actions that ultimately might spell the demise of the Indian democracy.

The success or failure of India's security management cannot be adequately addressed without taking into account the complexity of its people and the divergence of the demands placed on scarce economic and military resources. Adding to these difficulties is the fact that India must manage, and has managed, its domestic and international security problems through the democratic process, which is difficult, time–consuming, and frustrating. But one thing is certain: India is not about to collapse from the external and internal security pressures that it faces.

India's security problems will now be examined under the following themes: (1) the dynamics of the regional and global strategic environments; (2) the effects of a potential nuclear arms race on the region's political and strategic stability; (3) the ethno–social conflict and the resort to various forms of violence by dissatisfied groups; (4) the interaction of external and internal security problems affecting India's relations with its neighbors, especially Pakistan and Sri Lanka; and (5) the alleged erosion of the democratic process in India as the government attempts to respond to its several external and internal security problems. The concluding section will assess (6) American strategic interests and policies in the South Asian region and their effects on Indo–American relations.

The Strategic Environment and External Security

India's external security concerns begin with its neighbors, Pakistan and China, and consequently its strategic posture and defense programs continue to be based on the military capabilities of these two states. Although no wars have been fought with Pakistan and China for over 16 years, and relations with both have improved considerably in recent years, India's arms procurement policies continue as before because the military buildups in Pakistan and China continue unabated.

India's defense strategy has gone through several phases. The period between the 1947–48 Indo–Pakistani war and the 1962 Sino–Indian war was dictated by prime minister Jawaharlal Nehru's idealist vision of world affairs. Defense expenditures were confined to 1 to 2 percent of the Indian GNP. The only major weapons procurement in this period was the purchase of some British and French combat planes and tanks to counter Pakistani acquisitions of American military equipment through its membership of the Southeast Asia Treaty Organization (SEATO) and the Central Treaty Organization (CTO) defense pacts.

Serious Indian defense planning began only after the war with China when efforts were first made to obtain sophisticated weapons from the United States. When these efforts failed, India began to seek greater military cooperation with the Soviet Union. Thus, the period between the 1962 Sino–Indian war and the 1971 Indo–Pakistani war was one of steady Indian military growth. Defense expenditures were maintained at 3 to 4 percent of the GNP and have remained at that level until 1987. Once Pakistan was divided, the resultant Indian military superiority began to be firmly established through steady domestic and overseas weapons procurement policies.

Following the Soviet invasion of Afghanistan, Pakistan acquired large amounts of economic and military aid from the United States that India alleges allowed Pakistan to "leapfrog" its military capabilities. India's concerns have arisen from the Reagan Administration's decision to supply Pakistan with the advanced F–16 *Falcon* fighters, TOW anti–tank missiles, M–198 howitzers, anti–tank aircraft *Stinger* missiles, and, possibly, the proposed sale of the advanced EC–3 Airborne Warning and Control System (AWACS) planes.[1] Indian strategists have perceived these weapons as intended for use against India and not against the Soviet and Afghan Marxist forces in Afghanistan.

The U.S. arming of Pakistan provoked India into first acquiring the French Mirage–2000s and then the Soviet MiG–29 *Fulcrums*. While such purchases are double the 40 American F–16s delivered to Pakistan, India has contended that the French and Soviet planes are technologically inferior to the American planes and that, in any case, India will no longer tolerate a military balance with Pakistan on the Subcontinent. Thus, despite improving Indo–Pakistani relations and the receding importance of the Kashmir dispute, the arms race between the two countries, and perhaps the potential for war, continue as before.

Pakistan has argued that India's military capability is several times greater than that of Pakistan. The Indian Army is more than twice the size of the Pakistani Army (1.1 million to 450,000 men in uniform), the Indian Air Force has almost twice as many combat planes (701 to 381); and the Indian Navy, with its three fleets and one submarine command, is more than three times the strength of the Pakistani Navy with its single naval command at Karachi.[2]

India claims that such an analysis is misleading because India is eight times the size of Pakistan, with land frontiers and a coastline several

---

[1] *The New York Times*, April 10, 1987; and *India Abroad*, June 19, 1987. The decision to supply the AWACs to Pakistan is still pending in the United States.

[2] The figures here are mainly drawn from *The Military Balance, 1987–88*. (London: International Institute for Strategic Studies, 1987).

times greater than Pakistan's, and ultimately faces a dual threat from both Pakistan and China.[3] India argues it needs to maintain a qualitative military balance with Pakistan and China based on the nature of the weapons available, the terrain on which they are deployed, and the fact that wars on the Subcontinent have usually been short. Kashmir, Ladakh, and Arunachal Pradesh—territories claimed by Pakistan and China—are difficult to defend from the Indian side. In procuring aircraft, India emphasizes the qualitative superiority of Pakistan's front-line combat planes, not the total number of combat planes. The criteria for obtaining naval armaments is based on India's long coastline and its growing seaborne trade rather than on countering Pakistan's naval strength alone.

This analysis is reflected in India's military deployments. On the ground, India has sixteen infantry divisions—stationed mainly in south and central India during times of peace—and two armored divisions facing Pakistan's fourteen infantry and two armored divisions (Pakistan has three more infantry divisions on the Afghanistan border). China probably has from ten to thirteen divisions directly facing India's nine mountain (infantry) divisions, with twenty or so additional divisions stationed in its south and southwest regions. About four Indian infantry divisions are deployed in the volatile northeast sector between Bangladesh and Burma.[4]

India perceives the military balance with Pakistan in the air in terms of the qualitative superiority of the 39 F–16 *Falcon* fighter delivered to Pakistan by the United States, over the 40 *Mirage*–2000Hs India initially purchased from France to offset the F–16s. Subsequently the Indian decision to purchase 44 of the Soviet advanced MiG–29 *Fulcrum* fighters gave India superiority in the air, although India claims that the F–16s are still technically superior and that the quantitative leap forward with the MiG–29s was intended to offset Pakistani moves to obtain the Boeing EC–3 AWACS that would neutralize the effectiveness of much of the Indian Air Force.[5] Thus, in the 1980s Pakistan's older French *Mirage*–IIIs and Vs, accompanied by the newer American F–16s, face India's Anglo–French *Jaguars*, French *Mirage*–2000s, Soviet MiG–23s and newer MiG–29s in what now appears to be clear Indian air superiority over Pakistan.

[3] See letter to the editor by S.S. Mukherjee, Press Counselor, Embassy of India, in *The New York Times*, January 23, 1988.

[4] From *The Military Balance, 1987–88*. (London: International Institute for Strategic Studies, 1987).

[5] See views of Selig Harrison in his "Needless Offense to India," in *The New York Times*, November 25, 1986. See also the *Christian Science Monitor*, April 29, 1987.

India has also developed definite naval superiority over Pakistan. Until the mid–1960s, the Indian Navy was neglected, its main weapons systems consisting of aging World War II warships bequeathed by the British when they withdrew from the Subcontinent in 1947. Although there was no apparent increase in the naval threat to India, a modest rearmament program began in the mid–1960s. While the defense buildups of the Indian Army and Air Force were responses to specific threats perceived from Pakistan and China and their strategic ties with other countries, the Indian Navy defense buildup was based on the need to defend India's coastline and seaborne trade. Some naval leaders have even argued for the projection of India as a major sea power in the Indian Ocean from the Cape of Good Hope to the Straits of Malacca, but such grandiose visions have been rejected by the political government. [6]

The modest naval rearmament program that began in the mid–1960s proved fortuitous during the 1971 Indo–Pakistani war when the Indian Navy bottled up the harbors of both West Pakistan and East Pakistan (now Bangladesh). With the formation of Bangladesh, the naval threat from Pakistan has been further reduced, and it would be easy enough for the Indian Navy to blockade Karachi harbor in a future war. But Indian naval growth, although still considerably smaller than that of the other two services, has continued steadily. The Indian Navy has also changed from a British–equipped force to a primarily Soviet–equipped one.[7] By 1987, it included *Kashin*–2 destroyers, F–class submarines, *Petya*–2 frigates, *Osa*–1 and –2 missile boats, and *Nanuchka* corvettes. Some older British vessels such as the aircraft carrier I.N.S. *Vikrant*, a second refurbished British carrier, I.N.S. *Viraat*, added in 1987, one cruiser, and several frigates have remained. However, a new line of *Leander*–class frigates was manufactured in the meantime by Mazagon Docks in Bombay in collaboration with Vickers and Yarrow of Britain. In 1988, in a surprising move, India obtained a nuclear–powered submarine under lease from the Soviet Union, adding a new dimension to the naval military balance in the region. In contrast, the Pakistani Navy consisted of some British destroyers, the Italian *Agosta* and *Daphne* submarines, and several Chinese fast–attack craft, including the *Shanghai*–2 and *Hu Chwan* torpedo and gunboats.

Conventional Indian defense against China has been far more restricted. After its crushing military defeat by China in 1962, India proceeded to raise ten mountain divisions (streamlined now to be nine)

---

[6] Raju G. C. Thomas, "The Indian Navy in the Seventies," *Pacific Affairs*, vol. 48, no. 4, Winter 1975–76, pp. 500–518.

[7] Raju G. C. Thomas, *Indian Security Policy* (Princeton, N.J.: Princeton University Press, 1986) pp. 171–174, 262–264.

to be deployed along the Himalayan borders. These divisions were essentially infantry divisions armed with light arms and mountain guns and acclimatized to function at very high altitudes. The Indian response, therefore, has been to assume that a future war with China would be a repeat of the 1962 one, for which India was very ill–prepared. It is unlikely, of course, that "history would repeat itself" as the Indian government seems to expect. More likely, India has simply acknowledged the futility of a head–on arms race with China and decided to rely on superpower intervention in case of war.

In 1987, sixteen years after the last war was fought on the Subcontinent, Indian military preparations might seem to be based on the worst case scenario, and on conditions prevailing in the 1960s and 1970s. Although India makes no official defense declarations, there has been a change in its policy since the 1971 Indo–Pakistani war. Earlier, India had been satisfied to maintain a policy of "sufficient defense" based on qualitative military balance between itself and Pakistan. Since 1972, India's policy appears to have moved to one of "limited deterrence" based on an overwhelming conventional military superiority in South Asia and a potential nuclear weapons capability that would also deter China. The nuclear deterrent capability against China and Pakistan is still only latent and may be discerned from nuclear energy and space programs that have provided India with the capability to convert to nuclear weapons and missile delivery systems on short notice.

Some analysts argue that whatever the current state of relations between India and these two traditional adversaries, the potential for conflict remains. There are fundamental ideological, territorial, and political differences between India on the one hand, and Pakistan and China on the other, which necessitate military precautions. Advocates of this position would also probably argue that it is better to maintain peace through strength than to tempt Pakistan and China—who still claim the Indian states of Kashmir and Arunachal Pradesh, respectively—into resolving these territorial disputes through force. Wars on the Subcontinent remain a possibility.

Indeed, in March 1987, near–war conditions developed when half a million troops were amassed on either side of the Indo–Pakistani border. The problem began when India chose to conduct its annual military exercise, codenamed "Operation Brasstacks," in the Indian state of Rajasthan bordering Pakistan.[8] The scale of the Indian exercise was much greater than it had been in previous years. Pakistan, fearing a sudden Indian military thrust, countered the presence of Indian troops near its border with similar deployments. By April, troops on either side

[8] See *News India* (New York), January 23; and March 27, 1987.

were withdrawn and tensions reduced with the visit of president Zia ul–Haq to India. Later in the same year, following a dispute over Arunachal Pradesh, India and China deployed troops on either side of the disputed McMahon Line in the northeast of India, producing similar fears and tensions which could be the cause of war in the future.

Nuclear Strategy and Politics

Conventional Indian defense strategy is complicated by the potential of a three–way nuclear arms race between India, China, and Pakistan. India's nuclear dilemma began when China exploded its first atomic bomb in October 1964. The explosion set off a major debate in India as to whether it should embark on a nuclear weapons program to keep pace with China. Advocates of the bomb came mainly from the right–wing pro–Hindu party, the Jan Sangh, as well as from some ruling Congress party members of Parliament and independent defense analysts. The proponents feared that a nuclear threat from China would paralyze the deployment of the new Indian mountain divisions along the Himalayan borders during another Sino–Indian confrontation. To raise conventional forces without raising nuclear forces to offset the Chinese nuclear capabilities would be futile. Subsequently, Chinese threats to intervene during both the 1965 and 1971 Indo–Pakistani wars further strengthened the arguments of the pro–bomb lobby.

In general, stronger arguments were advanced against the bomb than for it. The intensification of the Sino–Soviet rift after 1963 and continued U.S. hostility towards China implied a dual superpower nuclear guarantee on behalf of India against China. Moreover, a nuclear weapons program in India would carry no deterrent value since India would not possess a delivery system that could threaten Chinese cities and industrial centers beyond the range of Indian combat aircraft. (Nuclear deterrence here is assumed to mean the ability of a state to absorb a nuclear attack and retaliate against the population centers of the attacker inflicting unacceptable damage.) The Indian space program was still in a nascent stage and far from providing the country with Intermediate Range Ballistic Missile (IRBM) capability.

The cost of a nuclear arms race with China was also considered to be prohibitive given the unsatisfactory performance of the Indian economy at that time. And a nuclear weapons program in India would surely tempt the Chinese to strike directly at Indian atomic power plants where these weapons were being developed, thus aggravating the Chinese conventional and nuclear threats instead of reducing them. In effect, those against the bomb argued that an Indian nuclear weapons program directed at China would mean less security at a much higher price.

Nonetheless, the Indian government was still unhappy about international pressures to sign the Nuclear Non–Proliferation Treaty (NPT) that was up for signature in 1968 on the grounds that the NPT discriminated between nuclear "haves" and "have–nots": India equated horizontal nuclear proliferation (the spread of nuclear weapons among the existing "have–nots") with vertical nuclear proliferation (the growth of nuclear capability among the existing "haves.")[9] Both were declared equally dangerous to world security since a nuclear war among the "haves" would affect the "have–nots" as well through nuclear fall–out and radiation effects. Conditions could change to weaken the implicit superpower guarantee against China's nuclear threat, making the development of an independent Indian nuclear deterrent imperative on short notice. For these reasons, India did not sign the NPT.

India began to pursue a nuclear strategy which can best be described as "threatening to exercise the option." By not embarking on a nuclear weapons program but constantly threatening to do so, India believed it could put pressure on the existing nuclear weapon powers to reduce and eventually eliminate their nuclear stockpile while pressuring the superpowers to enhance their nuclear guarantees for India against China. This policy was believed to be a happy medium between overreaction (becoming a nuclear weapons power) and underreaction (signing the NPT) to deal with India's perceived nuclear threat.

But regional and global strategic conditions did change after the creation of Bangladesh in 1971. Pakistan assisted the Nixon Administration in establishing diplomatic ties with the Chinese government in Beijing, laying the ground for President Nixon's historic visit to China in February 1972. With this startling development, and in order, perhaps, to reduce the threat of Chinese intervention while India proceeded to settle the Bangladesh issue by force, India signed the Indo–Soviet treaty of Peace and Friendship in August 1971.[10] The treaty contained clauses that called for mutual consultation when either signatory faced an imminent military threat and precluded either state from aiding the adversary of the other under such crises.

At this time there were renewed doubts about the credibility of external nuclear guarantees against China in case of a future war on the Subcontinent. The 1971 Indo–Soviet Treaty may have been sufficient to deal with the crisis at the time but was perceived as inadequate to deter

[9] See Raju G. C. Thomas, "India's Perspective of Nuclear Proliferation in South Asia," in Neil Joeck, ed. *The Strategic Consequences of Nuclear Proliferation* (London: Frank Cas, 1986); and "India, the NPT and Nuclear Proliferation," in the *Wisconsin International Law Journal*, vol. 5, June 1987, pp. 108–129.

[10] The text of the Indo–Soviet Treaty may be found in the *Current Digest of the Soviet Press*, vol. 23, no. 32, September 7, 1971, p. 5.

a future Chinese conventional attack or to prevent veiled Chinese nuclear provisions. Thus, a decision was probably made in early 1972 to proceed with the development and testing of an atomic device.[11]

When the first Indian atomic device was tested in a underground explosion in May 1974, it was called a "peaceful nuclear explosion" intended for mining, dam–building, and road construction in mountainous areas. Greeted with skepticism throughout the world, this claim produced an angry reaction from both Canada and the United States who felt that technology and materials provided for the construction of the heavy water Rajasthan Atomic Power Plant (RAPP) and the light water Tarapur Atomic Power Plant (TAPP) had been diverted for making the atomic device. Strategically, the decision to test the bomb made little sense in 1974 since India's relations with China and Pakistan had improved. In retrospect, it has become clear that Mrs. Indira Gandhi's decision to proceed with the test despite these favorable changes was largely intended to impress a domestic Indian audience in the hope of reviving her sagging popularity.

Although the initial Pakistani decision to acquire nuclear weapons was probably taken after its military defeat in 1971, the 1974 Indian atomic test prompted Pakistan to mount a crash program to acquire nuclear weapons. The then president of Pakistan, Zulfikar Ali Bhutto, declared that Pakistanis would be willing "to eat grass" in order to keep up with India's nuclear capabilities. Although India's nuclear ambitions ceased after the international outcry against its atomic test, Pakistan's relentless pursuit of nuclear weapons, through clandestine means and false assurances to the United States, made it difficult for India to revert to its old policy of maintaining the nuclear weapons option without becoming a nuclear power. Pressures within India to "go nuclear" continue to intensify as evidence of Pakistan's nuclear ambitions increases yearly.

Initially, Pakistani efforts concentrated on acquiring a reprocessing plant from France to be located at Chasma. Under pressure from the Carter Administration, France was persuaded in 1978 not to supply this facility. Subsequently, Pakistan concentrated on assembling a uranium enrichment plant by illegally exporting materials and technology through operators in Western Europe and North America. By mid–1987, news reports indicated that Pakistan had enriched uranium at its plant in Kahuta up to 95 percent, sufficient to make nuclear weapons.

Although reprocessing and enrichment technologies are legitimate parts of a peaceful nuclear energy program, the reprocessing of waste

[11] Some analysis have argued that the Indian and Pakistani commitments to a nuclear weapons program were made before the 1971 Indo–Pakistani war.

nuclear fuel produces the fissile material plutonium which may be used for making bombs; and enrichment capabilities enable a country to enrich natural uranium from the 4 percent necessary for energy use to the 90 percent necessary for bomb production.[12] While India claims that its nuclear energy program aims to fill critical energy needs, it has alleged that the Pakistani program is mainly a cover for nuclear weapons. Even before it embarked on a serious nuclear program, Pakistan focused its efforts on the two points in the nuclear fuel cycle—reprocessing and enrichment—that would enable it to divert material to nuclear weapons production. Confined largely to the Karachi Atomic Nuclear Power Plant (KANUPP) with a capacity of 125 megawatts of electricity, Pakistan's nuclear energy program is negligible. In contrast, India has already established 1800 megawatts of nuclear electricity generating capacity and has, perhaps somewhat unrealistically, planned to generate as much as 10,000 megawatts by the year 2000.

These developments have encouraged the pro–bomb lobby in India which believes that India can and should manage a three–way nuclear arms race against both China and Pakistan. In relation to China, they argue, India's nuclear deterrent posture would resemble that between the United States and the Soviet Union, with both sides possessing rough nuclear equivalence and assured retaliatory capabilities. With a growing IRBM capability derived from its space program, India should be able to retaliate against major cities in the southern half of China. In relation to Pakistan, India's nuclear deterrent posture would resemble that between the Soviet Union and China, where the Soviet Union possesses overwhelming nuclear capabilities and dominates the nuclear relationship.

As of 1988, neither India nor Pakistan has openly pursued a nuclear arms race, but rather a strategy of "mutual brinkmanship" where both threaten to become nuclear weapons states without actually carrying out the threat. The danger is that India's superiority in the region, accompanied by fears that Pakistan will ultimately acquire nuclear weapons, may provoke it into preempting the Pakistanis by embarking on its own nuclear weapons program. Alternatively, India may be provoked into attacking Pakistan's nuclear facilities at Chasma and Kahuta—as Israel attacked Iraq's Osirak nuclear reactor in 1980—despite a 1986 oral agreement not to attack each other's facilities. Meanwhile, the views of those in government who oppose nuclear weapons in principle, or perceive such weapons to be counterproductive for Indian security, continue to prevail.

---

[12] For further elaboration, see Raju G. C. Thomas, "India's Nuclear and Space Programs: Defense or Development," *World Politics*, vol. 38, no. 2, January 1986, p. 315–342.

Internal Security

As India's relations with both Pakistan and China improved in the 1970s, there has been an increase in the level of domestic strife involving various ethnic and economic groups. Correspondingly, the Indian government has increased its deployment of both the regular armed forces and the paramilitary forces to deal with the growing sectarian violence in the country.

Domestic strife in India may be classified first in terms of ultimate objectives, namely secessionist and nonsecessionist movements; and into the type of violence that it involves, namely civilian riots, guerrilla warfare and terrorism. In the northeast of India there have been secessionist movements of varying significance by some Naga, Mizo, and Gharo tribal peoples (mainly Christians converted by Western missionaries) and in Tripura and Manipur. And, of course, there are Sikhs in the Punjab who are conducting a terrorist campaign to secede from India. Many Muslims of Kashmir, and many Tamils, claiming at times to speak for all South Indians, have displayed secessionist sentiments, backed by occasionally anti–central government political movements.

While religion plays an important part in the separatist tendencies among the tribal peoples of the northeast, and for Kashmiri Muslims and Sikhs, Tamil separatist demands for a Dravidastan in the 1950s were linguistic and quasi–racial in character. The Tamils are predominantly Hindu by religion, but they believe themselves to be a separate people with deep historical roots, the main inheritors of the Dravidian language and culture as distinct from the languages and culture of the Indo–Aryan North which are derived from Sanskrit. Early Sikh demands for a separate Punjab state were presented as linguistic demands (especially after Punjabi Hindus declared Hindi as their language instead of Punjabi) until they achieved their goal in 1966, when the new states of Haryana and Punjab were formed. However, more recent Sikh secessionist demands for a Khalistan are based on religion. After the Nagas, Mizos, and Gharos gained internal statehood at various times through the creation of Nagaland, Mizoram and Meghalaya, their separatist demands have all but disappeared.

The threat to internal security posed by movements demanding the recognition of the rights of a linguistically defined people to significant cultural and political autonomy has been met, often after violence and attempted police and military suppression, through political solutions. Although the reorganization of the Indian provinces on a linguistic basis had been a demand of the Congress movement for 25 years before Independence, it took a violent upheaval in Andhra Pradesh in 1953 to achieve reorganization three years later in most of India. After another series of upheavals, separate states of Maharashtra and Gujarat were carved out of the old Bombay state in 1960.

More recently, a movement in the mid–1980s among the Nepali-speaking Gurkhas of the Darjeeling area of West Bengal to create a separate state of Gurkhaland within the Indian Union has, in mid–1988, seemingly been settled with the concession of some autonomy within the state. In Assam between 1982 and 1985 there was severe violence stemming from an effort to expel Muslim Bengali settlers from Bangladesh and Hindu Bengali migrants from the Indian state of West Bengal who had begun to reduce the Assamese–speaking people into a minority in their own state. After an accord with the central government and the consequent electoral victory of the party of the Assam movement, violence has abated.

Thus in 1987, the overt threat to internal security from separatist movements was largely confined to the Punjab. Sikh extremists continued to kill important Hindu and Sikh officials, as well as members of their families, or indeed anybody that opposed their demand for a Khalistan. During 1987, Sikh extremists have turned on moderate Sikhs, killing entire families for alleged collusion with the Indian authorities. The police and paramilitary forces periodically claim that they have killed leading "terrorists" in "armed encounters," which Sikhs claim are usually innocent Sikhs. Killings by Sikh terrorists have gone beyond those officials and politicians that represent the government to random attacks against innocent Hindu and Sikh civilians. In mid–1987 more than 70 Hindu bus passengers were massacred in two separate incidents. Indeed, the assassination in July 1988 of Suhan Singh, the high priest of the Golden Temple—like the assassination in 1985 of Harchand Singh Longwal, the moderate Sikh Akali leader—reflects the intensity of intra–Sikh conflict.

Let us now turn to nonsecessionist internal security threats. There have been armed revolutionary movements in India, most importantly, the immediate post–Independence revolt in the Telengana region of what is now Andhra Pradesh, and the "Naxalite" movement of the late 1960s and early 1970s in West Bengal, Andhra Pradesh, and a few other states. The radical pro–Mao Zedung communists who led the latter movement aimed to seize power through piecemeal armed insurrection. The brief and localized seizures of power they attempted were quickly crushed by armed state and central police, and the Naxalite movement withered away in the 1970s, especially after China under Mao Zedung drew closer to the United States and adopted a less revolutionary line. There was, however, a brief but spectacular incident in Andhra Pradesh in late December 1987. Naxalites seized several high–ranking Indian civil service officers, then demanded and gained the release of several Naxalites languishing in Indian prisons.

The most serious internal violence of a nonsecessionist nature has arisen between Hindus and Muslims. Perennial since before India's Independence, this problem was not solved by the creation of Pakistan in 1947. Most of the prominent Muslim leaders from the areas that remained in India chose to go to Pakistan, leaving the still substantial Muslim minority behind in India without many leaders and confused about their national identity. While there were many Muslims that rose to high office in independent India (e.g., presidents Zakir Hussain and Fakhruddin Ali Ahmed), for the greater part the Muslim masses remained withdrawn and apathetic.

The separation of Bangladesh from Pakistan in December 1971, however, laid to rest the "two–nation theory" of Pakistan's founder, Mohammed Ali Jinnah, who claimed that Hindus and Muslims in the Indian Subcontinent, by virtue of their religions, constituted two separate nations. This theory, which became the basis for the creation of Pakistan, also resolved the doubts regarding Muslim allegiance to India. Thereafter, Muslim political activity and participation in the mainstream of Indian economic and political life increased. But this new Muslim political activity, and probably also the upward economic mobility of Muslims benefitting from jobs in the Middle East after 1973, has produced a growing backlash of Hindu resentment in some parts of India causing religious conflict between Hindus and Muslims to increase.

That this conflict has erupted in rioting is not surprising, since even earlier there had been severe communal carnage, most notably in 1969–70 in Gujarat and Maharashtra. In most cases of Hindu–Muslim conflict, the spark is ignited by a trivial incident—the alleged desecration of a religious shrine, or allegations that a Muslim boy insulted a Hindu girl, or vice versa. Rumor and misinformation quickly spread, resulting in irrational killings of innocent people on both sides. Given the sudden and sporadic nature of such religious riots, the police (predominantly Hindu) are either too late to stop the bloodshed, or sometimes delay ending the conflict where Muslims are getting killed until it is almost over.

Incidents in 1987 illustrate this cycle of violence and the seeming inability of the Indian government to control it. One of the worst cases of communal rioting took place in May 1987 in Meerut, Uttar Pradesh, not far from New Delhi. What made the Meerut riots uniquely disturbing is that the Provincial Armed Constabulary, a paramilitary force under the Home Ministry, opened fire indiscriminately against helpless Muslims, killing more than 40 people and injuring more than 100.

What has become apparent is the Indian government's inability to resolve internal security problems through force. In dealing with secessionist or nonsecessionist movements, the government has often opted for military means rather than addressing the underlying political problems. No doubt, violence in the past led to government concessions establishing the states of Andhra Pradesh, Maharashtra and the Punjabi Suba, but this process of reconciliation has also been characterized by political lethargy and procrastination. However, where demands are secessionist, as among the Nagas, Mizos, and Gharos in the northeast, and Sikhs in the Punjab, the government has been uncompromising. Needless to say, few nations are likely to accede to their own disintegration without a fight. After the creation of Pakistan in 1947, India has been determined to resist further secession at any price and is willing to use force indefinitely to prevent it.

Strictly speaking, internal law and order is expected to be maintained by state governments through the local police armed with batons and *lathis* (long sticks), and the state police armed with rifles.[13] When the central government perceives that the state cannot control the violence, it then introduces paramilitary forces such as the Central Reserve Police Force, the Central Industrial Security Force, the Railway Protection Force, the Defense Security Corps, and the newly constituted National Security Guards. Other than the Railway Protection Force, which reports to the Ministry of Railways, the rest are controlled by the Ministry of Home Affairs. Finally, when paramilitary forces are unable to control the violence, the Indian Army, under the Ministry of Defense, is called in to restore law and order. But this chain of command is not always followed. The central government may resort directly to the paramilitary forces or to the army with or without waiting for the state's request.

Local and state police are often themselves emotionally involved in the conflict, whether it be Hindu–Muslim or linguistic rioting, and tend to aggravate, rather than resolve, the conflict. The use of centrally controlled paramilitary forces may appear more appropriate in the case of communal rioting, but even here their training and professionalism are not always adequate to the task. Moreover, they lack the training or the resources to cope with guerrilla warfare and terrorism. In contrast, the mere introduction of the Indian Army into areas of communal rioting usually produces peace and order without firing a single shot. But army leaders have almost unanimously opposed the use of the regular armed services for internal policing, arguing that the frequent use of the military to deal with communal riots would eventually prove

[13] See Thomas, *Indian Security Policy*, pp. 72–79.

ineffective and weaken the trust that presently exists between the armed services and the people. Even where the army has dealt with guerrilla warfare and terrorism, as in the states of Nagaland, Mizoram, Meghalaya, and the Punjab, the armed services have declared that there can be no ultimate military solutions to these problems. The creation of the elite National Security Guards in 1985 (recruited mainly from soldiers and officers from the Indian Army at the end of their commissions) was intended to deal with this problem of excess use and increasing politicization of the army.

The Interaction of External and Internal Security

Domestic political and military activity in other nations sometimes affects Indian security, and, conversely, internal security problems in India have become entangled with its external security concerns. For example, China's crackdown on the Tibetan revolt in 1959 and the flight to India of thousands of Tibetan refugees, including the Dalai Lama, led to a steady deterioration in Sino–Indian relations, and eventually to war in 1962. Similarly, the Bengali rebellion in East Pakistan in 1971 and the Pakistani military crackdown on secessionists there caused about 10 million refugees to seek refuge in India and ultimately led to war at the end of the year. In Sri Lanka, the Tamil insurgency and separatist movement first produced clandestine support for the Tamils from the Indian state of Tamil Nadu, and later Indian military intervention against the Tamil insurgents to enforce an Indo–Sri Lankan peace accord. In a different mode, the quadrupling of oil prices by the Organization of Petroleum Exporting Countries (OPEC) following the 1973 Arab–Israeli war produced a severe crisis for the Indian economy by 1974–75, contributing to the deterioration in domestic law and order and eventually to the declaration of a state of national emergency on the grounds that India's internal security was threatened.

Separatist movements or other violent struggles within India have often drawn political or military support from abroad. The most significant case is secessionist activity in Kashmir which has been gravely complicated by Pakistani efforts to seize and incorporate that state. Likewise, according to the Indian government, the Khalistan separatist movement in the Punjab has been receiving arms and ammunition from across the border in Pakistan with either official or unofficial sanction. India has also alleged that China and Pakistan (before the secession of East Pakistan) provided weapons to the Naga, Mizo, and Gharo rebels. Hindu–Muslim communal rioting in India invariably brings about Pakistani criticism and anti–Indian propaganda abroad, followed by Indian protests about direct or indirect Pakistani interference in India's internal affairs. And, as noted earlier, the Naxalite movement obtained at least its inspiration from the teachings of Mao Zedung, if not material assistance from China. All of these examples illustrate the degree to which India's internal and external security problems are intertwined.

Ironically, the threat of disintegration of the Indian union may come not only from separatist movements within India aided by adversaries abroad (e.g., Kashmir, Khalistan, Nagaland), but also from separatist movements in neighboring countries that are supported by India. This has not happened, though in 1971 there was some danger that Bengali nationalism in Pakistan, where language and culture overrode religious sentiments, could have spread to the 45 million Bengalis of West Bengal in India. Indeed, the Indian government was apprehensive at the time about the spread of Bengali nationalism in West Bengal, and India's intervention in the civil war was partly the result of pressures applied by West Bengalis.

Similarly, the Tamil separatist movement in Sri Lanka has posed a problem of great concern to the central government in India. Tamil separatism has roots in pre–Independence India, and gained significant strength in the 1940s and 1950s. Ultimately the Dravida Munnetra Kazhagam (DMK) party, giving up its explicitly secessionist program once that had been outlawed by the government of India, came to power in Tamil Nadu in 1967 with a populist program and a commitment to preserve and strengthen Tamil culture and identity.

In 1972, a split occurred in the DMK, and a new party that emphasized reform rather than autonomy was formed.[14] The breakaway All India Anna DMK (named after the founder of the DMK party, Annadurai) led by the south Indian film star, M. G. Ramachandran, later won the state elections in 1977 and has remained in power since. (Ramachandran died in December 1987 and was succeeded in the chief ministership by his wife.) By the late 1970s, an alliance was forged between the Congress (I) Party and the AIADMK, whereby Congress agreed not to contest elections in most of Tamil Nadu—they had little chance of winning there anyway—thus allowing the AIADMK to rule the state without hindrance from the central government. This had consequences later when it came to formulating a policy on sanctuary and the establishment of armed guerrilla training camps for the Sri Lanka Tamils. Meanwhile, the older DMK, led by former chief minister M. Karunanidhi, continued to call for greater autonomy or even independence from India. But it has had less support from the Tamil people and its political base in Tamil Nadu has been considerably eroded.

---

[14] See *India Abroad*, January 1, 1988.

The Tamil secessionist movement in Sri Lanka could provide the spark that ignites the smoldering embers of Tamil separatism in India as well. India's initial policy towards Tamils in Sri Lanka betrays this underlying fear. While the Indian government does not support the creation of an independent Tamil "Eelam" (nation) in Sri Lanka, it did little to prevent the Tamil Nadu state government from allowing its territory to be used as a sanctuary for conducting guerilla warfare and acts of terrorism against the Sinhalese majority. Before the Indo–Sri Lankan Accord of 1987, arms and economic resources were regularly ferried from Tamil Nadu to the insurgents in Sri Lanka across the narrow Palk Straits. The Indian government's dilemma appeared to be how to support the Tamils in Sri Lanka without supporting their independence movement, and how to allow the Tamil Nadu government to support Tamil independence without alienating the Sinhalese–dominated government of Sri Lanka with which India was anxious to cooperate in order to prevent its disintegration.

This ambiguous and contradictory Indian policy created a stalemate between Sri Lankan government forces and Tamil rebels which finally came to a head in 1987. The Sri Lankan government earlier had proceeded to obtain arms and/or military training from India's traditional adversaries, Pakistan and China, and even from the so–called pariah states located on the fringes of the Third World, namely Israel and South Africa. After the Sri Lankan government launched a major military offensive against the Tamil rebels and tightened the economic blockade of the Tamil areas of the northern and eastern provinces, the crisis escalated to the point where the Indian government actively intervened and reached an accord with Sri Lanka. That settlement was short–lived, and India soon found itself fighting the very people—Tamils—whom it had intervened to protect. (For an account of these events, please see "India's Foreign Relations: Problems along the Borders," by Thomas Thornton in this volume.) A year after the accord was reached, the Indian military had replaced the Sri Lankan military in the offensive against the Tamil separatists.

The repercussions of this unusual situation in Sri Lanka have yet to be seen. Meanwhile, the ability of the Indian and Sri Lankan governments to sponsor the moderate Tamil United Liberation Front (TULF) into a leadership role has failed against the continued violence of the LTTE, led by its fiery leader Vellupillai Prabhakharan. And as the Indian military forces step up their offensive against the Tamil rebels, there is danger that the offensive could provoke anger and violence in the Indian state of Tamil Nadu, reviving claims for an independent Dravidastan or a Greater Tamil Nadu that would include the Tamil areas of Sri Lanka.

Security Policy and the Democratic Process

Dealing with an array of external and internal security problems is difficult enough, but having to formulate and execute policy through the democratic process makes matters even more difficult. Perceptions of the nature of internal and external threats, the level and type of resources that need to be allocated to deal with them, and assessments of the government's performance in these matters have been controversial in India since Independence. On the other hand, the conduct of external security policy has elicited less controversy and emotion in Parliament and the attentive public than that of internal security.

While democratic politics affect the conduct of security policy, problems of security also tend to affect the democratic process. Looking back over the last 40 years, it would be legitimate to ask whether there has been a tendency for the democratic process to erode as problems of external, and especially internal, security in India have escalated. Clearly, the government in power must be tempted to circumvent democratic political constraints and procedures in order to deal with persistent security pressures. The passage of the Defense of India Rules (DIR) in 1962 after the war with China first provided the government with sweeping powers to arrest suspected opponents.[15] At that time, many communists were arrested, and during the 1965 Indo–Pakistani war, several Muslims were detained. Such actions were justified on the grounds that those arrested were likely to resort to sabotage—allegations that were never proved.

The 1971 Indo–Pakistani war brought about new legislation known as the Maintenance of Internal Security Act (MISA) which further increased the powers of the government to curb potential opposition and violence in the border regions with Pakistan and China. However, MISA continued to be enforced after the threats from Pakistan and China receded in the 1970s.

In response to an alleged breakdown in internal security, prime minister Indira Gandhi declared a national security emergency in June 1975 under Article 352 of the Indian constitution. During the Emergency, which lasted until March 1977, the fundamental rights of the citizen as stipulated in the constitution were suspended. The internal security powers of the government were further strengthened with the passage of the 42nd Amendment to Article 352, which gave the government the power to detain suspected enemies of the state without explanation or access to legal redress.[16] Although the DIR, MISA and the

---

[15] See Thomas, *Indian Security Policy*, pp. 99–105.

[16] See Henry C. Hart, ed., *Indira Gandhi's India* (Boulder, CO: Westview Press, 1976) p. 18.

42nd Amendment were repealed soon after the Janata party came to power in 1977, the new government also found it difficult not to resort to some of these powers to deal with problems of domestic violence and political disturbances.

The return to power of Indira Gandhi and her Congress Party in January 1980 saw the restoration of some of the repealed national security powers through the passage of the National Security Act (NSA) in December of that year. Unlike the earlier DIR, MISA, and the 42nd Amendment, the NSA included some safeguards such as access to the courts. In response to increasing acts of terrorism by Sikh extremists, these safeguards were watered down in 1984 through the National Security (Second Amendment) Ordinance under which arrests and detentions of suspected Sikh terrorists became more widespread.

The erosion of democratic processes due to security measures is subject to considerable debate in India. There are those who argue that security must take precedence over democratic processes. The breakdown of security and stability, whether from external or internal threats, would make it impossible to conduct orderly democratic government. This particular viewpoint was endorsed during the Emergency by the Indian Supreme Court, which, critics have pointed out, had been substantially altered by Mrs. Gandhi's appointments. In one of the cases of detention without trial heard before the Supreme Court during the Emergency, the court ruled that the fundamental rights under the Indian constitution were rights derived from the state and not rights inherent to the individual, and that the state could rescind an individual's fundamental rights temporarily in order to maintain the state's security and stability.

On the other side of the debate are those who argue that democratic process is the best means of preserving security and stability. The sweeping emergency powers provided for in the Indian constitution are intended to preserve democracy, not to destroy it. As such, the Emergency of 1975–77 was alleged to be a violation of the spirit of the Indian constitution. Indian critics have argued that actions taken by Indira Gandhi's government during that time were intended to preserve the regime and its leader rather than the security of the state. The argument between the advocates of "security first" and those of "democracy first" remains unresolved as widespread arrests and detentions continue in response to Sikh terrorist activities throughout 1987 and early 1988 in the Punjab and surrounding areas.

Potential threats to the Indian democratic system may also be perceived in the growth of the armed services and the paramilitary forces in response to external and internal threats. The wars of 1962, 1965, and 1971 produced a steady growth of the military, which now has about 1.1

million armed personnel in the army, 100,000 in the air force and 50,000 in the navy. Even more spectacular has been the qualitative growth of weapon systems in India, giving the Indian military the power not only to defend the country, but, according to some, an enhanced ability to seize power and establish a military dictatorship. This after all, has been the experience of neighboring Pakistan, Bangladesh, and Burma, as well as of several other Third World countries.

Even if the Indian armed services maintain their professional, apolitical role, the growing paramilitary forces, which are justified as a way of reducing the need to call in the army to deal with internal unrest, may be perceived as a threat to civilian rule and also as contributing to regional factionalism and domestic political disintegration. The state and central government paramilitary forces (including such organizations as the State Armed Police, the Border Security Force, the National Security Guards, the Central Reserve Police Force, the Railway Protection Force and the Home Guards) now number about 750,000 and are armed with light arms and ammunition. Since they are deployed to deal with domestic violence that involves riots, guerrilla warfare, and terrorism on a regular basis, there are fears that these units, lacking the professionalism of the armed services, are likely to become politicized. Violent disturbances within these forces have occurred in the Central Reserve Police Force, the Railway Protection Force, and the Central Industrial Security Force.[17]

It is significant to note that the increasing firepower of the armed services and their frequent deployment for the maintenance of internal security have also been accompanied by an erosion of the military role in the political decision–making process. The limiting of the military's influence in security policy–making may be seen in the changes in the structure of the defense committee system and its decision–making process.

Until the mid–1970s, the main committees in a three–tiered structure consisted of the Defense Committee of the Cabinet (DCC) at the top, the Defense Minister's Committee (DMC) in the middle, and the Chiefs of Staff Committee (CSC) at the bottom.[18] Each of these committees was aided by other intelligence committees and information–gathering bodies. The three committees were intended to provide for the interaction of politically elected representatives at the top level (with the civil service heads and armed services chiefs sitting in on meetings in an advisory role when needed), for the interaction of civil servants at the middle level with the armed services chiefs, and for the interaction of the Chiefs

[17] Thomas, *Indian Security Policy*, p. 84.

[18] Thomas, *Indian Security Policy*, pp. 119–134.

of Staff of the three armed services at the bottom level to coordinate their military policy.

Both the DCC and the DMC were almost exclusively concerned with problems of external security, and the composition of these committees was limited to those elected cabinet ministers or career departmental secretaries concerned with external security. Although the Chiefs of Staff were not formal members of the DCC, they provided advisory inputs to the select cabinet ministers, including those of defense, external affairs, finance, and home affairs, who were involved in formulating defense policy. Similarly, the DMC formally included the minister of defense of cabinet rank and the junior minister of state for defense production, who met with the secretaries of defense, defense production, and the armed services chiefs.

By 1978, the titles and composition of the main committees at the top and middle levels had been changed. The DCC became the Political Affairs Committee of the Cabinet (PACC), and the DMC became the Defense Planning Committee (DPC). Both the new committees were greatly enlarged to take into account new Indian concerns with internal and external security, and the interaction between the two. The PACC was expanded to include all the cabinet ministers as well as other junior ministers of state concerned with the entire array of external and internal security problems. Additionally, given the total concept of security—economic, technological, military, and political—ministers concerned with such areas as economic planning, industry and labor, transportation, and communications were also allowed to participate in the PACC deliberations. Similarly, the newer DPC became top heavy with the heads of the civil service. The committee was chaired by the cabinet secretary and included the secretary to the prime minister, the secretaries of defense, defense production, external affairs, finance, planning, and the three military chiefs.

The Chiefs of Staff of the armed services technically could be invited to participate in the meetings of the PACC. However, because the PACC frequently discussed issues that were non–military in nature, or included politically sensitive internal security issues and party political matters, the armed services chiefs were excluded from its deliberations. And, the disproportionate number of heads of the civil service departments in the DPC tended to overwhelm the input of the three military chiefs. No doubt, the service chiefs on the one hand, and the prime minister or defense minister on the other, could directly approach each other for consultations on an informal basis, but this form of communication would depend considerably on the personality and political style of the ministers.

The decline in the Indian military's input in security policy–making, at the same time that its size and firepower have correspondingly increased, may be deliberately intended to maintain civilian supremacy over the military. Unfortunately, this not only makes security policy–making less informative and professional, but excluding the armed services from the deliberations could increase their frustration and the temptation to seize power in the midst of continuing civilian turmoil. Civilian fears of the military are without basis. The armed services headquarters, for instance, have been vehemently opposed to the deployment of the military to deal with civilian communal violence. They have argued the "the military should not be used against its own people" because that would lead to its politicization and eventual corruption. The Indian armed services remain one of the few integrating forces in an ethnically diverse country and have retained the confidence of the people over the last four decades. But its increasing utilization has begun to create doubts about the neutrality and impartiality of the army, especially among the Sikhs in the Punjab and the tribal peoples of the northeast. The Indian Army's assault on the Sikh's Golden Temple in 1984 produced a mutiny among a few Sikh regiments, the first since Independence.

Civilian fear of the power of the military is also the reason why the army's proposal for a Chief of Defense Staff (CDS) system has not been accepted. The army has contended that India's wider security role needs a decision–making system unifying all three armed services. It has pointed out the lack of military coordination in the conduct of operations during the 1965 and 1971 Indo–Pakistani wars. Unlike the Chiefs of Staff Committee where three independent service chiefs come together periodically for consultations, the proposed CDS would provide for a unified military platform to conduct negotiations with politicians and civil servants, and to conduct military strategy and tactics in the event of war. In order to prevent domination by the Indian Army, which usurps almost 65 percent of the defense budget, the head of the proposed CDS would be appointed on a rotating basis from each of the three armed services. The army has argued that most countries with a large standing military have a CDS or equivalent, e.g., the CDS in Britain and the Joint Chiefs of Staff (JCS) in the United States. However, efforts to establish a CDS system in India remain unsuccessful.

The United States and South Asian Security

Before the Soviet invasion of Afghanistan in 1979, the importance of South Asia in the United States' anti–communist global strategy was secondary. In the early phase of the Cold War, American efforts to draw both India and Pakistan into its worldwide alliance systems succeeded partially when Pakistan accepted the American offer, but only after India had refused to give up its nonalignment policy. As a member of the SEATO (1954) and the CENTO (1955), Pakistan obtained about $1.6 billion in sophisticated arms from the United States that included the F–104 *Starfighter* and F–86 *Sabre* combat aircraft, and the M–47/48 *Patton* tanks. India responded with the purchase of British and French *Hunter, Canberra,* and *Mystere* combat aircraft and the *Centurion* and AMX–10 tanks.

After the outbreak of the war with China, India's nonalignment policy was thrown into doubt. There were some moves to join the Western alliance system and, indeed, India took part in a joint military air exercise with the United States and Britain at that time. India also sought substantial amounts of arms from the United States and Britain to build up its neglected military. As hostilities between India and China continued in 1962, the U.S. government provided India with some light arms, ammunition, and winter clothing for combat at high altitudes. The Kennedy Administration then appeared to be seriously considering further Indian requests for arms until Pakistan strongly protested, claiming that the arms would be used against Pakistan rather than China. At that point, both Britain and the United States insisted that India should first resolve the Kashmir dispute with Pakistan before they would consider the supply of more sophisticated arms such as the F–104 fighter. Since Pakistan would settle for nothing less than the transfer of all of Kashmir held by India, Indo–Pakistani talks under Western supervision failed. The United States did agree, however, to help India build two factories for the production of light arms and ammunition. After the outbreak of the 1965 Indo–Pakistani war, all military assistance to both countries was suspended.

Although India had signed an agreement with the Soviet Union to co-produce the Mig–21 fighter in India three months before the Sino–Indian war of October 1962, the proposed Indo–Soviet military collaboration remained largely minimal or suspended. It was only after Pakistan's use of American weapons against India in the 1965 war (weapons that the United States had assured India were intended for use only against communist aggression), and after the suspension of all American military assistance to the Subcontinent, that India turned to the Soviet Union for major military collaboration. From then on, Indo–Soviet military ties were cemented. Meanwhile, with the American arms embargo affecting Pakistan even more than India, Pakistan turned to communist China for weapons and diplomatic and strategic support. In the 1971 Indo–Pakistani war, Pakistan used the aging American weapons again, although at this point India had obtained substantial Soviet military equipment to offset them.

During the Bangladesh crisis of 1971, Nixon asked Kissinger to "tilt" toward Pakistan in the looming Indo–Pakistani conflict, and secretly ordered the lifting of the arms embargo to the Subcontinent and transferred to Pakistan military spares for the aging American weapons in Pakistan. Moreover, Kissinger is alleged to have warned India that if it chose to go to war against Pakistan to settle the Bangladesh question, the United States would do nothing to assist India if China intervened militarily on the Pakistani side. The Indians responded by signing the Indo–Soviet Treaty of Peace and Friendship in August 1971.

These events shed light on India's hostility towards the United States and its close diplomatic and military ties with the Soviet Union. At different times India did try to achieve a closer military relationship with the United States. Apart from the effort in 1962–63 after the war with China, the pro–West Janata government (1977–79) sought to purchase more weapons such as the F–5 fighter and TOW missiles from the United States. But these efforts failed because of the terms of sale insisted upon by the U.S. Department of Defense. Even the Janata government's efforts to obtain the Swedish *Saab Viggen* combat aircraft in 1979 were vetoed by the Carter Administration on the grounds that the plane had an American Pratt and Whitney engine, and thus its sale would break the prevailing arms embargo to the Subcontinent.

The cycle of the arms race on the Subcontinent was repeated in the 1980s when the Reagan Administration chose to arm Pakistan with sophisticated weapons in response to the Soviet invasion of Afghanistan. Subsequently, India first turned to France for combat aircraft and then to the Soviet Union for a variety of sophisticated weapons including the MiG–29 combat plane. To be sure, U.S. arms sales to Pakistan in the 1980s were rationalized in terms of Indo–Soviet military cooperation and the joint threat perceived to Pakistan. However, there is a tendency on the part of American policymakers to forget that Indo–Soviet military cooperation was and continues to be a response to U.S. arms supplies to Pakistan.

This indirect strategic conflict of interest that has existed between India and the United States has clouded relations between them except for a brief period under the Kennedy Administration, when the United States demonstrated considerable military and economic support for India. However, despite the tensions, there is movement toward military technological cooperation between the two countries. The visit of Prime Minister Rajiv Gandhi to the United States in 1985 produced a Memorandum of Understanding on technological cooperation between the two countries. The visit of a Pentagon delegation to India led by

Defense Secretary Caspar Weinberger in 1986 further consolidated defense technological cooperation. Central to this cooperation was the agreement by the United States to allow the sale of the Cray XMP–14 supercomputer and the General Electric 303 aeroengine for the development of India's proposed Light Combat Aircraft. The long term implications of these efforts remain to be seen, but they appear to be moving in the direction of improved Indo–American relations.

Prospects

As 1988 draws to a close, there are still several security challenges that India must face. Paramount among these are, first, the potential strategic dangers that may arise from a three–way nuclear arms race with Pakistan and China, and all its accompanying international and domestic political and economic consequences; and second, the continued conflict and bloodshed in the Punjab generated by Sikh demands for an independent Khalistan, together with alleged Pakistani aid to the separatists. Neither of these two problems appears to be close to resolution. However, time and again, Indian leaders from Jawaharlal Nehru to Rajiv Gandhi have risen to the occasion to resolve security crises within the democratic parliamentary system. There appears to be little reason to doubt that the security of India will continue to be managed adequately in the future through the same time–tested political processes.

5
Education: Safer Options

Krishna Kumar

In 1987, a new educational policy in its first year of implementation aroused high hopes for advancement. Proposed by Rajiv Gandhi in his first address to the nation in 1985, the plan was discussed in every session of Parliament and became a point of reference throughout the year. It led to the setting up of a new kind of educational institution which is likely to set the tone for Indian education in the coming years.

A call for improved "education" has often been heard in the 150–year history of the Indian educational system. The most radical of all such calls was made in Mahatma Gandhi's proposal for *nai talim* (new education). It was part of his greater plan for India's development along the lines of a new social order, which featured uplifting the oppressed castes, village–based decision making, and guaranteed employment. Gandhi's plan for educational change under *nai talim* reflected these goals mainly by linking education with production. The link was to be established by creating a place in the elementary school curriculum for the skills and knowledge associated with the laboring classes of Indian society. Gandhi's proposal was unprovocatively worded, referring to local provision of learning materials and the pedagogical advantages of manual work, but no amount of Gandhian subtlety could save his plan from the urban intelligentsia's contempt. The scheme was phased out in the early 1960s with the same speed with which it had been launched a decade earlier.

When Rajiv Gandhi spoke in 1985 about his intention to create a new educational policy, he was not referring to the Gandhian *nai talim*. Between the early 1960s and the early 1980s, India had in many ways been transformed. Central to this transformation has been the growth of market economy and its penetration into the countryside. Because of the continued growth of population and illiteracy, the growth in the market economy has not "solved" the problems of poverty and unemployment as many commentators on India in the 1960s had assumed it would. It has helped an urban *nouveau riche* class to grow and to assume influence in India's cultural and political life disproportionate to its size. In the countryside, the market economy assisted the rich farmer, the beneficiary of the Green Revolution. Increased productivity and the new state-supported credit facilities have enabled these farmers to participate in the consumption-based cultural patterns of the urban rich, giving their demands new weight in the current political scene. The rise of these two classes alone would be enough to transform socio-cultural life; an added impetus has come from the dramatic expansion of electronic media technology such as television and video cassette recorders. Through advertising, the media industry has become a significant aspect of India's current political economy and culture. Nehru's conviction that Indian culture could never accept acquisitiveness for its own sake has become as irrelevant now as the worry of modernization theorists of the 1960s that India lacked an achievement-oriented ethic.

The expansion of India's market economy has meant stiffer competition with foreign and multinational companies. This competition has been exacerbated by the fairly rapid erosion in the 1980s of the Indian state's traditional role of protecting native industry. Indeed, the state is under pressure from the urban *nouveau riche* to import all the Western props of the "good life." One way in which Indian industrialists have responded to the new permissive policy is by collaborating with foreign companies. This collaboration has begun to alter the demands that industry makes on the more successful graduates of the Indian educational system. Indigenization of foreign technology is still a part of the political rhetoric, but in fact Indian engineers end up working as managers in foreign companies. New establishments are looking for young men and women who are reliable and dedicated rather than innovative, talented, and independent. This kind of demand has begun to elicit from the educational system the response it finds easiest to give—one emphasizing old values like "discipline," "character," and "leadership."

Another aspect of the growth in the market economy and the accompanying rise of the new electronic media is that, to many people, the old perception of illiteracy as India's major educational problem no more rings true. Proponents of electronic media openly claim that illiteracy is no longer a barrier to development. The fact that Indian democracy has survived numerous crises has led to a similar feeling among critics, including the Western media. It is also true that neither Indian industry nor wealthy farmers feel the need for a larger literate labor force. The association between illiteracy and cheap labor (including child and female labor) persists. And now with the opening of the Indian economy to foreign companies and their advanced (labor-thin) technology, the possibility that industrial development will demand and absorb a substantial literate labor force has dwindled. This does not mean that adult literacy will be dropped from the state's well–worn educational rhetoric. It merely means that work on this front is even less likely to be taken up with passion today than it was in the first decade after Independence, when it was considered a "moral" issue, or in the second, when it was a part of the Green Revolution strategy.

Finally, the distribution of equal educational opportunity was a major focus of educational policy in the first two decades after Independence. Its most clear expression was in the policy of protective discrimination for the Scheduled Castes and Tribes. Expansion of schooling facilities and provision of scholarships for children belonging to these groups were the ways in which the government could persuasively claim some success. The fact remains, however, that increased school enrollment from these groups did not translate into substantially greater participation in higher education. Rather, what little share of higher learning and white collar jobs they acquired led to a disproportionate amount of anger among youth of urban middle class. Their feeling that "injustice" was being done to them (for their merit was being pushed aside to acknowledge someone else's caste background) was further compounded by the "backward caste" movement in several states. The backward castes are not "untouchables"; they are largely peasant and craftsman castes whose educational and economic "backwardness" has translated into far stronger political currency than the more entrenched "backwardness" of the Scheduled Castes and Tribes. Over the last ten years, resentment against the reservation policy has grown rapidly. Although politics will not allow the state to dismantle the policy, it cannot ensure that the policy will be implemented with enthusiasm and attention to detail.

Birth of The New Policy

In his first address to the nation in January 1985, Prime Minister Rajiv Gandhi gave more time to education than was ever before given to it in a post–election speech. He mentioned three aspects of educational reform as priorities. First, he proposed opening of a "model" school, or pace–setting institution, in every district. Second, he wanted to disassociate degrees from jobs. Third, he wanted modern communication technology to be used extensively in education.

Soon after assuming office, he asked the minister of education to begin formulating a new educational policy. As a first step, a report called "The Challenge of Education—a Policy Perspective" was published in August 1985. By the standards of state discourse on education in India, it was a new kind of document. It carried a sharp critique of the educational system, and an unhesitating acknowledgement of many of the state's failures. The purpose, it was pointed out, was to start a national debate on education. A debate in seminars, newspapers, and magazines did follow. In the meanwhile, the minister of education was removed, and the ministry itself was amalgamated in a larger Ministry of Human Resource Development. In May 1986, the new ministry released the "National Education Policy," and three months later, a "Programme of Action."

Indeed, the government went about formulating a policy on education with unprecedented speed and focus. From January 1985 to May 1986, education was on center stage as a national concern—no small feat for a country like India where daily events so often have such emotive force that long-range issues get pushed out of public attention. Education, in any case, was never before treated with so much interest and patronage from the highest office. This unusual treatment created the impression that there was no lack of political will for educational reform. Extra funds, too, were repeatedly said to be available. As a result, the new educational policy aroused high hopes in 1987 and became a focal point in key events during the year.

The major event of this kind was the strike by university and college teachers throughout the country. The strike announcement in August came as no surprise since university teachers' organizations had made it clear months earlier that they were angry over provisions in the new policy pertaining to the employment of teachers. The main point of controversy was the weight given to length of service for promotion. Technically, the "merit promotion scheme" which teachers were bent on saving and the government was equally bent on ending was not directly addressed in the new policy. The government, however, took shelter behind the policy to resist the teachers' demand to keep the old scheme, which favored seniority. The government argued that the new policy allowed for upward mobility strictly on grounds of merit, not seniority. The teachers' argument was that the new standards for determining merit were bureaucratic and would inevitably erode academic autonomy. After a display of remarkable unity and stamina by the teachers in August and September, the strike came to a sudden end in early October without achieving the gains of earlier university teachers' strikes. Worse still, the settlement aroused bitterness among many teachers towards the union leaders who had handled the negotiations with the government. The new educational policy prevailed, but at the cost of disillusioning many teachers about the government's supposedly "positive" attitude towards their profession.

The strike provides a glimpse of a central problem of the educational system. The conflict between university teachers and the state points to the problem of power, and specifically to its distribution among different sectors of the intelligentsia. The teaching profession as a whole has no share in the state's power structure. Except for the presence of several highly acclaimed economists and other experts who serve on state committees, teachers are absent from decision making in state activities. Nor is there a link between universities and industries which would permit teachers to be involved in the country's economic life. The position of teachers contrasts sharply with that of civil servants who are no better educated than teachers but who distinctly feel they are running the nation. The bureaucrat's influence over education itself was proved in the new educational policy debate. This contrast fostered a sense of alienation and opposition among teachers towards the state.

The sense of alienation and its consequences can be seen most sharply at the school level. The teacher's power at this level is limited to the extent that he has no right to structure the curriculum or to choose learning materials. In terms of salary and social status, his position is far weaker than that of the college or university teacher, whose own salary and status are not particularly high. Despite a vast network of nearly four million members, school teachers lack a sense of professional identity, and professional standards are weak. In many states, school teachers' associations actively support opposition parties. Though neither the political nor the cultural roles of the village teacher have been carefully analyzed, we can tell something about these roles from the widespread contempt for teachers' politicization. The alienation of the school teacher and his enfeeblement by the bureaucracy result in politicization and lack of concern for self–fulfillment in the classroom.

These aspects of the ethos *within* the educational system are rarely acknowledged as obstacles to reform, but they certainly are. Acknowledging them would imply the possibility of change in the relationship between teachers and the state. The new policy gave no indication of government interest in any change. Nor does the recently published report of the Teacher's Commission appointed by Indira Gandhi in 1982. While the commission's report emphasized welfare measures, the new policy stresses discipline and quality control. It is clear that the government would like education to remain a quasi–civil service, rather than to become a professionalized system. Instead of permitting spheres of professional autonomy to emerge in areas like health and education, the state prefers to try reforms that are consistent with the prevailing distribution of power. These measures are necessarily limited to maintaining norms and controls. The new educational policy revolves around such measures, and it is no surprise that the policy was received so poorly by India's teaching community.

Setting up new institutions comprises the other major strategy outlined in the new educational policy. At the school level, the policy features the starting of *Navodaya Vidyalayas* ("new rise schools") and District Institutes of Education and Training. In higher education, the policy offers an "open" university network and Academic Staff Colleges. Building these institutions and implementing tougher measures for maintaining norms are the principal "new" elements in the policy.

Elementary Education

At the elementary level, the government has indicated its plans to enlarge the nonformal educational sector (NFE), that is, formal instruction outside the schoolroom or later in life than "normal" (e.g., adult education, or correspondence courses). The new plan "assumes that NFE can result in provision of education comparable in quality with formal schooling." In a literal sense, this statement says little, for the quality of formal schooling at the elementary level is poor throughout the country. Nonetheless, the statement is significant in that it equates nonformal education and proper, primary education (now known as "formal" education).

Nonformal education has been a marginal activity, mainly involving voluntary development groups, with the government's role confined mostly to funding. The government was directly involved in nonformal education in a few states, but mostly with illiterate adults rather than children. For children, primary schooling was not questioned as the main strategy for achieving universal literacy. This is how the directive principle mentioned in the Constitution—that the state will endeavor to provide free and compulsory education to all children aged six to fourteen years—was interpreted. Against this background, the new thrust on nonformal education, especially the perception that it is equivalent to primary school education, was a major shift in policy.

There is no doubt that nonformal education is attractive to the government as an acceptable alternative to primary schooling. Most important, it is cheaper. Nonformal teachers are not recognized as professional teachers. They are treated as temporary workers much like staff hired for child care and women's development projects. The new policy allows for a 30–day training for nonformal instructors, most of whom are expected to be local women. Such meager training suggests that the government does not expect nonformal teaching to have the status or pay scales needed if it is to attract career–oriented professionals. In fact, in 1987, women who had been employed for years in some

60,000 *Anganwadis* (day care centers) unsuccessfully demanded higher salaries and permanent pay scales.

Nonformal education has the gloss of a "new" concept even though it has been around for twenty years. In international aid circles, it is seen as a fashionable area for investment, a perception which contrasts with that of primary schools as a lost cause. No more do Western countries and international aid organizations consider building primary schools or equipping them with pedagogical materials a worthwhile task. Instead, international aid for educational projects in India is flowing into the nonformal sector. At present, only one British–aided project is concerned with primary school improvement. The likelihood of raising large scale international funds for nonformal education has undoubtedly upgraded its status in the Indian educational system.

Before examining the implications of granting nonformal education equivalency to primary schooling, it is important to look at why primary schools are fighting a losing battle. The curriculum remains archaic, rarely going beyond mechanical reading, arithmetic, and writing drills, and is taught mainly through old methods such as recitation by poorly trained teachers who, as "government servants," are subject to transfer and nonteaching requirements, such as monitoring the polls during elections.

Not only has the quality of primary schooling failed to show improvement, but even the expansion of primary schooling facilities has not given results. At the time of Independence 40 years ago, India had 141,000 primary schools; today there are more than 500,000. The government's claim that every Indian child lives within walking distance of a primary school is now true in most parts of the country. The hard fact remains, though, that this proliferation of schools has had little impact. In 1981, only 36.2 percent of the total population was literate; at Independence the figure was approximately 16.2 percent. Given the growth in the population from 361 million to 684 million in this period, the advance is only slight.

And, although there is no doubt that initial enrollments in primary school (i.e., to grade one) have increased, the rate of retention has remained very poor. On the average, only 37 out of every 100 children who enroll in first grade stay through grade five. In less developed states, the dropout rate is even higher, despite the policy of automatic promotion at the end of each grade. Consequently, more children are out of school today than 20 years ago—for the simple reason that while the dropout rate did not decline, the population continued to grow.

India's famous educational planner, the late J.P. Naik, commented in 1977 that "the crisis in elementary education which has persisted throughout the post–Independence period has only deepened over the past 12 years." His words are even truer today. Even though enrollment statistics now show that more than 90 percent of children aged six to eleven are in school, these statistics are poor and unreliable. First, there are serious problems related to age–grade matching, which means that the figures for this age group include a substantial proportion of children over age eleven. Secondly, enrollment is almost certainly inflated by teachers who are under official pressure to show that every eligible child is on the school register. Indeed, the disparity between the department of education's statistics and those of the census is quite serious. If census figures are accurate, the picture of enrollment in this group would appear to be dismal, especially in rural areas. Village girls have been particularly affected; only one–third of this population is currently enrolled in primary schools.

Consequently, a consensus has grown among planners in the last few years that achieving universal elementary education will require special attention toward rural girls. The fact that they are required to look after younger siblings has been cited by several studies as the reason why girls do not attend school, and the new policy promises to provide village day care to enable them to do so. So far, little progress has been made. But even establishing widespread day care may not have as radical an impact on primary school enrollment as planners expect. Although it is true that girls who do not attend school often look after siblings, this does not necessarily mean that they do not attend school *because* they have siblings to look after.

An outsider visiting the average Indian primary school is likely to be struck by the bareness of the school, the lack of teaching aids, the archaic nature of the curriculum, and the absence of basic amenities for children. The last All India Educational Survey revealed that 53 percent of primary schools lacked a permanent building, 71 percent had no library, 53 percent had no play space, 40 percent had no blackboards, 59 percent lacked a drinking water facility, and 85 percent had no lavatory. These are national figures; the situation of the least developed states like Bihar, Orissa, Uttar Pradesh, Rajasthan, and Madhya Pradesh is worse. It is not hard to understand why children do not go to school.

An "Operation Blackboard" was announced in the new policy to improve the material conditions of primary schools. More than one year later, the "operation" has barely begun in Gujarat, which is not even one of the "backward" states. The government has promised to provide basic amenities in phases during the next few years. And, each primary school is to have at least two teachers, including one woman. While this is surely an important step, its impact on enrollment and the dropout rate will probably not be dramatic since it will not be accompanied by an increase in the primary school teachers' power and status. For better training of primary teachers, the government intends to establish a new institute in each district. Better–equipped teachers with improved facilities could translate into improved teaching, provided the teachers achieve a greater sense of freedom and a higher morale than they now have. Planners have failed to recognize that teachers who wish to enforce compulsory attendance face serious resistance by economically dominant village families. As P. Acharya pointed out in his study of illiteracy in Bengal, keeping poor children out of school is a vested interest of the rich farmer. Teachers who make an effort to attract children to school have a great political problem on their hands; solving it would require granting them higher status and power within the government's hierarchy.

Navodaya Vidyalayas

At the post–primary level, the government has launched a flashy scheme involving a special school in each district. Initially called "model" schools after the reference made in the prime minister's first post–election speech, they are now called *Navodaya Vidyalayas* (NV), or literally, "new rise schools." The change in the name had to do with the considerable criticism that the scheme received during pre–policy discussions in which the government stressed the following points: the program was to provide a "good" school in the countryside and to nurture talented children by providing them with special opportunities. A third point referred to the "pace–setting" character of the model school. Now that 200 NVs have started functioning, we have a basis on which to analyze these claims. The speed with which the scheme has been implemented, indicated by the number of NVs started within the last year, does show that the government attaches great significance to it.

Geographically, NVs are located in the countryside, although many are in the vicinity of a district town. They provide for 80 seats in grade six. Admission is made on the basis of rigorous national selection tests prepared by the National Council of Educational Research and Training (NCERT). Any resident child of the district who has passed grade five can compete for admission to an NV, but 80 percent of the places are reserved for rural children. A percentage of NV places is reserved for both rural and urban children from the Scheduled Castes and the Scheduled Tribes.

Financially, the NV scheme is better provided for than any other in the history of school education in India. The Seventh Five–Year Plan earmarked a sum of Rs. 5 billion to meet capital costs of setting up a NV in each district. To remove bureaucratic hurdles and delays, the government set up a registered society in New Delhi to handle funds and select teachers. NV teachers will be better paid than others and will be provided housing facilities. Once admitted, students will have all tuition and living expenses (NVs will be boarding schools) covered by the central government. NV schools have library and laboratory facilities and classroom equipment far beyond what ordinary schools have. Evidently, NVs will be "pace–setting," but not in the customary sense of establishing an example that others might follow if they cared to.

The rationale behind the NV scheme can be questioned in terms of who they are likely to serve. The government's claim that NVs are for the lower strata of rural society is unconvincing. By the government's own acknowledgement, dropout rates for primary schooling are higher in the countryside, and most children who leave school before completing grade five belong to the lowest socio–economic strata. These children are not eligible for taking the admission test for NV. Indeed, one can reasonably expect the selection procedure to be monopolized by the upper strata of rural society—the richer farmers whose political power is now a force to reckon with in all parts of the country. The NV scheme is one of the gestures the government has made in response to the dissatisfaction expressed by the richer peasantry over its economic policies.

Within the educational system, the NV scheme represents an acknowledgement that the state of general education is so poor that substantial improvement may only be possible in little islands. In terms of the norms envisaged by the Secondary Education Commission (1953) and the Education Commission (1966), today's secondary schools have long been neglected. The material conditions of the schools can at best improve marginally with the modest investments the government has proposed. The new policy talks about generating community support for school maintenance, but presents no tangible plan in this direction. By starting the well–equipped NVs, the government has made a counter–gesture, suggesting that it has *all* the money to invest where it wants to.

During the policy debate, critics of the NV scheme—including high level government officials—pointed out the school's inevitably elite character and the unreliability of testing as a means to spot talent. The social implications of "merit"–based selection on such a large scale were also pointed out. The government, however, went ahead, and now that NVs have been built, one can see why. There is no sign of public resentment, and NV admission tests are being taken by thousands of children in the districts where they have been set up. Private coaching classes to help candidates prepare have shot up in many districts. Educated as well as uneducated parents perceive testing as a fair procedure for selection of children. Their faith in meritocracy has been nurtured for more than a century by the public examination system which was the mainstay of colonial employment policy, and of social order under chronic high unemployment. Teachers have also received the NV scheme without resentment, and there is a visible craze for NV positions. In this poorly paid profession, NVs have introduced a fresh avenue for upward mobility. At present, only ordinary school teachers seem to be feeling the negative effects of the scheme. Demoralized as they are, they now have reason to view their students as the "NV–rejected" lot.

In the context of India's national politics, the NV scheme marks a significant step toward the dilution of the autonomy that provincial governments have enjoyed in school education. The NV network will be funded and managed from Delhi, and will undoubtedly push a uniform curriculum. A "national curriculum framework" was proposed separately by the NCERT during the policy debate. Interestingly enough, the states ruled by opposition parties have not shown discomfort with the NVs or the idea of a national curriculum. The only objection that the governments of West Bengal and Tamil Nadu expressed over the plan had to do with the suspicion that the curriculum would be used to impose the Hindi language. The fact that even states controlled by leftist parties did not find much fault with the meritocratic ideology reflected in the NV plan shows the range of support for this ideology in India. As for the other states, the main attraction of the plan is that it is a financial "gift" from the central government. No state can afford to forego the "gift" which others will gladly accept.

Vocational Education

Institutions that train strictly for a vocation form a very small part of the secondary educational system, and their distribution by region is unbalanced. Of the nearly 359 polytechnic schools in the country, two thirds are in West Bengal, Uttar Pradesh, Karnataka, and Andhra Pradesh. They offer diploma courses lasting two to four years. In addition, the Industrial Training Institutes train skilled workers and craftsmen in engineering as well as non–engineering trades. A third group of institutions, specialized schools, offers courses in subjects ranging from nursing to the fine arts. In all, the vocational sector has some 5,000 institutions, with an enrollment of slightly more than 700,000. Compared to the total number of general secondary schools—more than 188,000 with an enrollment of about 40 million students—this is a small sector indeed. The reasons for its underdevelopment are not hard to guess. Vocational learning lacks status within the educational system, and the careers to which it leads without exception involve working in subordinate positions. This is true even when the vocational school graduate knows more than the university graduate. This perception of vocational training may be universal, but in a country like India where subordination in workplaces has strong vestiges of feudalism, and where manual abilities lack sanction both in the wider culture as well as in modern educated society, the problem becomes very serious indeed.

Administrators and planners since the mid–nineteenth century have longed for and tried to create a "vocational bias" in the school curriculum, especially at the secondary level, but such attempts have been consistently unsuccessful. The latest to be introduced was a course subject named "Socially Useful Productive Work" (SUPW), consisting of "purposive and meaningful manual work resulting in either goods or services which are useful to the community." Ten years of implementation of the SUPW idea have proved yet again that most schools have neither the infrastructure nor the inclination to take seriously any kind of activity–based learning. The fact that examination and achievement continue to be tied to book–based learning also discourages programs like the SUPW or the "work experience" which preceded it.

The creation of a district "vocational" stream at the senior secondary level has also been tried since the mid–1970s in the context of the new "10+2" pattern of secondary education, a twelve–year course which replaced the eleven–year plan in most states. But even the states that implemented this pattern, which involved funneling students into vocational classes after the tenth year in school, failed to enforce it in any substantial proportion of schools. Of the total number of higher secondary schools in India, less than 3 percent offer a purely vocational course during the two final years of study, and only about 2.5 percent of the total student population at this level enroll in these courses. This is indeed a far cry from the recommendation made by the Education Commission (popularly known as the Kothari Commission) in the mid–1960s that 50 percent of senior secondary students ought to be absorbed in the vocational stream. The new educational policy places its target at a modest 10 percent by the end of this decade.

The chances of vocational courses becoming a viable option for senior secondary students are likely to remain dim for two major reasons. First, no major expansion of skilled labor employment is on the horizon. Second, what scope there is in the economy to absorb skilled labor remains largely irrelevant to the secondary school for the simple reason that the school's capacity to produce readily employable hands is not an established fact. Rather, the school continues to be seen in India as the route to office jobs. With increasing stringency at the tenth grade examination, reflected in a shockingly low passing rate, and the erosion of basic school facilities, students are likely to cling to academic (rather than vocational) courses as the only practical option. Pre–secondary education also prepares them to see academic learning as "true" knowledge.

In technical education, the new policy's major promise was to give statutory authority to the All India Council for Technical Education (AICTE). The government fulfilled this promise last year. In its new incarnation, the AICTE has the power to accredit, and to discredit, poor quality institutions. Although undoubtedly an important development, it is still too hard to say how much impact AICTE will have on the mushrooming of private, poor quality institutions, including engineering colleges, in several parts of the country. The majority of such institutions are started with political backing, and inevitably achieve substantial commercial profits. The essential criteria for admission is the student's capacity to pay, not merit. If the AICTE does indeed discredit such institutions and improve the functioning of others, it will have accomplished something unusual in the history of private education. So far the effect of accreditation agencies on the functioning of institutions, including those run directly by the state, has been rather modest.

But even more stringent measures would not necessarily mean a dramatic improvement in technical education. A backlog of attention to key problems will continue to hurt this sector. One is the low status and salaries of teachers. Leaving aside prestigious institutions such as the Indian Institutes of Technology, the general run of advanced institutions offer poor salaries and working conditions to their staff. Research and development receive low priority, and links with industry are nearly nonexistent. Despite the creativity that a handful of high–status institutes like the National Institute of Design have demonstrated, the input of technical education to India's industrial advancement is far from satisfactory.

Colleges and Universities

On the face of it, higher education ought to be the most "manageable" sector of the Indian educational system. It is not unduly huge, considering that less than 7 percent of the relevant age–group population goes to college. The breakdown of the different kinds of institutions that comprise India's post–secondary system is as follows:

Table 5.1

Universities	119
Institutions deemed to be universities	16
Undergraduate colleges	4,005
Junior/Intermediate colleges (mostly in Uttar and Andhra Pradesh)	4,060
Engineering colleges	198
Medical colleges	117
Teacher training colleges	367

This network employs some 200,000 teachers who teach about 3 million students in all. Compared to the elementary or secondary school systems, the picture is brighter. As in most developing countries, India's per student investment in higher education is a lot closer to what the developed countries spend than its investment in school education.

Despite the growth of population and the ongoing expansion of school education, enrollment in higher education has ceased to grow rapidly since the mid–1970s. Enrollment in colleges and universities grew at a rapid pace during the first two decades of Independence. During the 1950s, the overall annual growth rate in higher education enrollment was 12 percent, and during the 1960s it was 14 percent. Then, during the 1970s, the growth rate declined sharply from 9.5 percent in the beginning of the decade to 1.2 percent towards the end. The University Grants Commission (UGC) report for 1979–80 says that the growth rate "seems to have stabilized at the level of 2.3 percent per annum, which is fortuitously in close correspondence with the average rate of growth of the national economy." One can endorse such a pleasant view of the matter only if one chooses to not to take an overall view of the educational system.

There seems to be no doubt that the decline has come about mainly as a result of a sharp rise in the rate of failure at the secondary level. The addition of a public examination at the end of grade ten has enhanced the secondary school's capacity for eliminating students. We can estimate this capacity from the 1986 results of the examination in Madhya Pradesh in which only 56,000 out of 250,000 students who took the exam passed it. This was the first year of the tenth grade public examination in Madhya Pradesh; in several other states it had been administered earlier. The percentage of passing grades at both the tenth and twelfth grade examinations in several states has been astoundingly low in the recent years.

Over the last decade, higher education has suffered everything from widespread malpractices in examinations to the "political" appointment of senior college and university administrators. One element of the decline in norms is the conflict between teachers and government discussed above. That conflict may well be at the root of the concerns and remedies which the new educational policy presents for higher education, rather than the large numbers of students which is customarily cited as the main problem of higher education.

The treatment which teachers received during the August strike could have been a product of circumstance rather than design, but it does appear to be consistent with the new policy's emphasis on a "data-based system" of teacher evaluation, enforcement of attendance rules and the "nonnegotiability" of certain "norms of performance." The point that career advancement will be tied to an evaluation of performance is precisely the sort of idea that enraged the teacher's organizations and led to the August strike. The teachers cannot believe that any fair assessment of performance is likely under the prevailing circumstances. They were also opposed to a national recruitment test which the government wants to introduce for appointment of teachers. A national test for selection of doctoral research fellows has already been introduced, much to the chagrin of teachers' organizations and several eminent scholars.

Another device to tighten administrative control of teachers, though ostensibly to enhance quality, is giving some 400 colleges the status of "autonomous colleges." This will allow them to frame their own curricula and give degrees, thus departing from the practice of "affiliation" to a university under which most colleges in India now function. Teachers' organizations are afraid that the freedom to develop curricula will be more than offset by the power that "autonomous" status will give to the private management of many colleges.

Another new step taken in 1987 is the establishment of Academic Staff Colleges to train new college teachers. Here again, the government is at odds with the teachers' organizations. The government feels that new recruits to college teaching need training as much as school teachers do. Teachers find this insulting, and interpret it as yet another inch cut in the scarce cloth of their professional autonomy and status. More irksome to them is the plan's proposal that the newly set up Indira Gandhi National Open University (IGNOU) will have the responsibility, among others, for developing a full training course for college teachers.

Indira Gandhi National Open University

One of the first "open" universities in the country, IGNOU was set up by Parliament and will be funded directly by the central government rather than through the University Grants Commission which serves as a fiscal channel for other universities. IGNOU is expected to use and develop modern electronic media for educational communication, rather than relying on correspondence courses. Since television and radio are the central government's monopolies, it makes sense for IGNOU to have a direct accountability to the government. It is likely that IGNOU will be given rights to use a separate TV channel that the government is about to start. IGNOU is almost certain to become the model for other "open" universities planned in some states. It will also have its own regional centers throughout the country.

It is too early to discern what impact the IGNOU experiment will have on higher education in general. It is clear, though, that the government is expecting the experiment to have a wide impact. To begin with, the "open" university idea promises to absorb some of the general undergraduate students who would otherwise enroll in college. The Bachelor of Arts, Bachelor of Science, and Bachelor of Communication degree programs account for more than 80 percent of university student population in India. Most of this population attends colleges that are affiliated to a university, which means they are subject to the syllabus and examination set up by the university. Though the number of students is no longer growing, most college classrooms are crowded, and facilities such as libraries are feeling the crunch. Like correspondence courses in recent years, the "open" university system is expected to ease some of the physical pressure off the colleges.

A major challenge for IGNOU will be to develop a new examination system that has credibility in the market. The notion of examinations as the main function of a university is a colonial legacy which has persisted in independent India. A big, social event involving several thousand students, an Indian examination is an annual show, demanding stupendous memorization, literary skills such as composing essays, and stamina for competition. The system is routinely criticized for discouraging creative abilities, but persists. It has defeated many well thought out reforms in several universities. My own assessment is that it persists because it has proved a worthy instrument signifying, if not always dispensing, justice in a society with a deep–rooted, oppressive caste system, a pervasive culture of patronage, and a parallel subsystem of elite private schooling. The fact remains, though, that the examination system is one place where reformist voices in higher education have always converged, irrespective of their politics. For IGNOU to develop a modern system of evaluation and to ensure market acceptance for such a system would take an enormous act of political support and institutional solidarity. Yet the political support it has may hinder the growth of institutional solidarity. Other initiatives of this kind, most prominently NCERT, which was set up in the early 1960s, became bureaucratic in no time, losing both the will and the capacity for innovation, even without having to deal directly with the public and the market as IGNOU has to.

Conclusion

Taken as a whole, the new policy shows that the government has gone for safer options. These options mainly comprise new institutions. They are "safer" because they do not affect the structure of the educational system. Structural characteristics that were recognized in the report, "The Challenge of Education," as impediments to progress have been largely ignored. For instance, the strongly selective character of the primary system, reflected in the high drop out rate, has received no specific attention. Indirect, mild correctives like "Operation Blackboard" and nonformal education are supposed to address the problem. The fact that the most ambitious aspect of the new policy, the *Navodaya Vidyalaya*, was targeted at grade six rather than grade one does tell us clearly that the government did not consider primary schooling an area fit for change. Had a radical measure been adopted to enhance the retention capacity of primary schools, it would certainly have meant an enormous buildup of the eligible population for secondary education. This would have greatly increased the pressure on the overall educational system, and probably would have forced the system to provide for diversity in curriculum and testing. The new policy shows that the government does want diversity in the secondary level curriculum, but only within its present, lean size.

There are other, more general reasons why India, like many other Third World countries, continues to neglect its children's education. A major reason is that children's education, like health, continues to be essentially a welfare activity. The state is under no pressure to treat children as a serious responsibility; indeed, not even the communist parties have shown any particular anxiety on matters like child labor and malnutrition. High levels of child mortality prevail throughout the country, and malnutrition in its acute forms still afflicts a sizeable proportion of the child population. These conditions continue to feed entrenched perceptions that childhood is a precarious stage not worth taking seriously. The name of the new Ministry of Human Resource Development, which covers education, was supposed to indicate a departure from this line of traditional thought. Obviously, a real departure would take more than naming a ministry.

Structural relationships between secondary and higher education have also been neglected. The very modest goal for vocationalization indicates this. There is no sign that vocational courses are being introduced on a large scale in higher education. There is no reason to expect that the textbook–oriented character of higher education will change in the years to come, or that the examination system will actually be leavened by new grading procedures indicated in the new policy. The fact that the examination system is the agency responsible for keeping the higher education clientele in check is a good enough reason for it to last. It will perhaps be reformed in fringe areas such as specialized institutions, elite schools, and career jobs. It is in places like these that we may see some initiatives taken for the sake of improvement, while the general educational system continues to be geared to maintaining social order.

6
Science, Technology, and India's Aspirations

William Blanpied

> It is an inherent obligation of a great country like India with its traditions of scholarship and original thinking and its great cultural heritage, to participate fully in the march of science, which is probably mankind's greatest enterprise today.
>
> Government of India
> Science Policy Resolution, 1958

> As a result of three decades of planning, and the Scientific Policy Resolution of 1958, we now have a strong agricultural and industrial base and a scientific manpower impressive in quality, numbers and range of skills. Given clear-cut objectives and the necessary support, our science has shown its capacity to solve problems.
>
> Government of India
> Technology Policy Resolution, 1983

A Historic Faith and Commitment

In March 1987 Prime Minister Rajiv Gandhi, who once studied engineering in England and who, like his grandfather and mother, also holds the cabinet portfolio as minister for science and technology, proposed that India's allocations for research and development for the forthcoming fiscal year be increased by almost 50 percent over the 1985 level, thus taking an important step in making good his commitment to provide more generous financial resources to the country's science and technology establishment. Since the central government dominates research and development (R&D), the 1987 increase provided a seeming vote of confidence for science in India. Not surprisingly, most of the increased budget allocations were focused on areas that the government's economic planners have pinpointed as essential to India's industrialization, such as nuclear energy, space, biotechnology, electronics, and nonconventional energy sources.

By coincidence, in March 1987 a U.S. government–sponsored workshop convened in suburban Washington, D.C., to explore areas in which more purposeful Indo–U.S. scientific cooperation could be achieved. Participants, consisting primarily of U.S. scientists with first–hand knowledge of the work of their Indian colleagues along with a few expatriate Indians, cited specialties in physics, chemistry, materials science, microelectronics, and biotechnology as areas in which Indian scientists are conducting work of consistently high quality by international standards. Since many of the specialties cited underlie the economically important technologies favored by India's 1987 R&D budget, the casual observer might conclude that India's investments in science are almost certain to result in substantial benefits for the country. But that is not necessarily the case. Whereas the achievements of individual Indian scientists and groups of scientists working at premier institutions throughout the country have been long internationally recognized, the relevance of those achievements to the country's long–term social and economic aspirations remains uncertain.

India's faith in and commitment to science as a key to economic and social development are almost legendary. Indeed, the Indian government was probably the first in the world to make that faith and commitment a matter of official policy. In 1958, at the urging of then prime minister Jawaharlal Nehru, India adopted a Science Policy Resolution which opens:

> The key to national prosperity, apart from the spirit of the people, lies, in the modern age, in the effective combination of three factors, technology, raw materials and capital, of which the first is perhaps the most important....But technology can only grow out of the study of science and its applications.

There is now ample evidence that the connection between scientific research and national prosperity is not as straightforward or automatic as it was thought to be 30 or 40 years ago. While it is clear that scientific research undergirds advances in virtually every area associated with social and economic progress, the precise causal relations between research and tangible benefits are tenuous, difficult to trace even in retrospect, and virtually impossible to predict in advance. This is particularly true for basic research, usually defined as research to increase fundamental knowledge about phenomena and processes occurring in nature, as opposed to applied research which uses scientific knowledge to explore possible new applications. It is even more true in the case of technology, which can be defined as the application of human skills, experience, knowledge, and "know–how" to the solution of broad social and economic problems.

Both applied research and technology would be hampered without a continual flow of basic research results. Yet there is no assurance that maintenance of basic research capabilities in a particular country leads automatically to high–quality applied research and technology of particular relevance to that country's needs. Scientific knowledge, whether domestic or imported, is critical to a wide range of technologies. But so are economic understanding, capital investments, management and administrative skills, and a technologically literate work force.

Thus, while the problem of selecting priorities for investment in scientific research is scarcely unique to India, it takes on added dimensions—even an added poignancy—when viewed in the context of the country's long standing faith in, and commitment to, science as a key to development.

Achievements and Dilemmas

India's achievements in adapting and implementing a variety of science–based technologies have been notable. India was the first country outside the industrialized world to design and construct a general purpose satellite, INSAT–2, which was orbited by a U.S. launcher in 1982 and has both remote sensing and communications capabilities. The latter are being used as the basis for two innovative pilot programs, each with significant social implications. The first is designed to test the feasibility of satellite–based domestic telecommunications. The second is to bring educational television to three remote regions that previously had little contact with modern technology. India plans to become self–sufficient in space technology by having its own operational launching capabilities by the early 1990s.

Significant achievements have also been made in the field of nuclear technology. Immediately after Independence, the Cambridge–educated physicist Homi Bhabha (1909–61) convinced prime minister Jawaharlal Nehru that India should invest in developing new and largely untested nuclear technologies as a means for rapid electrification of the country. Thanks in part to Bhabha's vision and organizational abilities, India now has a highly regarded research and development infrastructure underlying its nuclear power program that has been contributing to the country's increase in per capita consumption of electric power by more than a factor of ten during the past 40 years. The program also underlies the government's confident projection of an additional tenfold increase by the year 2000.

Although less spectacular than its advances in space and nuclear technology, India's achievements in applied agricultural science and medicine, particularly preventive medicine and health–care delivery, have no doubt had a more profound and widespread effect. Once subject to devastating, unpredictable famines, the country not only feeds itself but has become a net agricultural exporter, while the average life expectancy has increased from 27 to 57 years since Independence.

Paradoxically, each of these achievements can be matched by a counter example indicating limitations on the ability of science to have a significant social and economic impact.

- Although India was the first country outside the industrialized world to design and construct a general purpose satellite, the bullock cart remains the country's principal means of transportation.
- Although India's nuclear power program has contributed to an increase in the available per capita electric power supply by more than a factor of ten since Independence, animal dung and wood remain its principal sources of fuel. Moreover, the economic viability of the country's nuclear–based electrification program is questionable.
- Although advances in preventive medicine have almost doubled the population's average life expectancy during the past 40 years, diseases which are virtually unknown in the West, such as leprosy and filariasis, continue to exact a heavy toll.
- Although the "green revolution" has enabled India to become a net exporter of agricultural products, a large fraction of its population still suffers from diseases directly attributable to malnutrition.

This essay will provide an overview of the state of science in India 30 years after the government's 1958 Science Policy Resolution and 40 years after Independence, particularly in the context of the country's professed social and economic objectives. There has been a distinct shift in India's economic objectives during the past decade, and thus in the ways its economic planners look at the country's scientific resources. Up to the mid–1970s, India had to be concerned primarily with problems endemic to rural poverty, and its scientific priorities therefore emphasized applications in the fields of agriculture and health. Today the emphasis is on gearing up the industrial sector to the economic demands of the twenty–first century. But the problems of linking science with improvements in agriculture and health are vastly different from those of linking it with industrial productivity. A central question is the extent to which India will succeed in establishing those links that are vital to its domestic prosperity, as well as its aspirations to serve as an example for other developing nations and to assume what it regards as its rightful status as a major Asian nation.

After pointing to the specific current emphasis on science and technology in the current Seventh Five–Year Plan, this essay provides an overview of the country's current investments and priority allocations in R&D compared to investments in other countries, particularly the United States. This is followed by a description of the system that those investments are meant to support. Against this background, structural problems inherent in India's research and development system, including underinvestment by private industry and the decline and isolation of the university research system, will be noted. Broad issues of scientific quality and relevance with which India's political and scientific leadership continue to grapple will be raised, touching upon the current domestic and international political contexts in which those issues are being addressed. Finally, the essay will underline the dilemmas and opportunities for science as India seeks to position itself for what it regards as a rightful international leadership role in the twenty–first century.

Role of the Government

The central government dominates Indian science and technology to a far greater extent than in the United States or most industrialized countries, playing three distinct though related roles. First, it sets overall planning goals for the public sector (including both central and state government agencies) as well as the private sector. Second, it provides the bulk of the funds for R&D, and finally, it controls and in many cases operates most of the country's best research institutions, employing the great majority of its scientists, engineers, and technicians. India's constitution reserves certain specific powers to the governments of its states. However, with the partial exception of agriculture, the central government dominates science and technology in the country. Education is an area in which the central and state governments share responsibility, but for scientific and technical education, the center remains the pacesetter.

Planning and Priorities

During the early 1930s, the distinguished physicist Meghnad Saha (1894–1956), a professor at Allahabad University who won international recognition a decade earlier for his research in theoretical astrophysics, became an outspoken champion of national economic and scientific planning. He continued to press his views through various fora, including editorials in the journal *Science and Culture*, which he founded in 1935 and edited until shortly before his death. In 1939, Saha became a charter member of the planning committee of the Indian National Congress chaired by then Congress president Jawaharlal Nehru. Following Independence in 1947, that committee was institutionalized as the Government of India's Planning Commission, which is responsible to the prime minister through the cabinet.

The commission's most visible products are the five–year economic plans. Each of these plans (1) establishes overall national economic objectives consistent with the broad pre–Independence Congress platform of economic growth, modernization, and social justice; (2) assesses progress in each of several economic sectors during the previous five–year plan period; and (3) assigns goals and allocates minimum, baseline financial resources to each sector for the forthcoming period. Following the precedent established by Saha's membership on the pre–Independence planning committee and the government's first planning commission, an eminent scientist traditionally sits on the commission. The current scientific incumbent is the respected physicist M.G.K. Menon, a protégé of Homi Bhabha who was formerly Director of the Tata Institute for Fundamental Research in Bombay and is currently science adviser to the prime minister.

Continued confidence in science and technology as keys to development and economic growth infuse the rhetoric of the two volumes that comprise India's Seventh Five–Year Plan for the period 1985–90. The first volume discusses overall goals and assesses performance during the Sixth Plan period. The second is comprised of detailed analyses of ten economic sectors, one of which is designated as the "science and technology sector." Even though that sector received only 2.4 percent of the plan's total baseline budget for the five–year period, the centrality of science itself looms considerably larger in the plan's rhetoric and its assessment of priority issues. For example, substantial specific references to science policy issues appear throughout the analyses of three sectors that, taken together, account for 80 percent of the plan's financial allocations: energy, industry and minerals, and social services, the third of which includes education.

The overall tone of the Seventh Five–Year Plan is guardedly optimistic. Volume I opens with the assertion:

> There is now fairly convincing evidence that since 1974–75 . . . . the Indian economy has moved to a higher growth path . . . . The progress made by the country in the recent years suggests that, given clarity of

objectives and disciplined management of development programmes, poverty eradication is an attainable goal.

That is, India can no longer regard itself—or be regarded—as simply a poor country for which eradication of poverty and its associated evils remains the overarching goal. Rather, the country must now assume responsibilities incumbent upon a major regional power with rich human resources. The plan stresses that most of the infrastructure the country requires to resolve its still severe developmental problems and to play a more prominent role in the global economy is now in place. To that end, the plan envisions an accelerated growth rate and increased productivity in the agricultural sector, and in particular in the industrial sector.

Within that context, the three principal economic goals for the 1985–90 period are to accelerate the growth of food grain production; increase employment opportunities; and raise productivity. The plan proceeds to link the latter two goals and relate them explicitly to subsidiary science and technology policy objectives:

> . . . the objective is to expand employment opportunities consistent with increases in productivity. . . . [T]he expansion of small scale and medium industries would add significantly to the growth of productive employment opportunities. Promotional measures designed to improve the access of this sector to modern technology, supply of inputs, credit and risk capital would help to enhance its productivity and competitiveness. Taking all these factors into account, the Seventh Plan provides for a faster industrial growth than during the Sixth Plan.

A high priority must be improving the quality of the infrastructure in all sectors and on using those elements more effectively for the benefit of the nation and its people. The nation's science and technology infrastructure is singled out as among its most important:

> For achieving self–reliant growth and for making the economy immune to external shocks, domestic technological capabilities are of strategic importance. To strengthen the country's scientific and technological base, a two–pronged strategy has to be pursued, namely, (i) to enhance domestic technological capabilities in the strategic sectors of the economy . . . and (ii) to initiate research and development efforts in frontier areas of science and technology to enable the country to play a significant role in the world technology market.

National Investments in Research and Development

Budget allocations contained in the five–year plans are regarded as baseline targets, and annual allocations for specific sectors may exceed those targets, depending on the importance they are accorded by the government. To date, investments in science and technology during the Seventh–Plan period have been approximately 50 percent higher than what would have been anticipated on the basis of the plan's target figures alone.

During 1985 (the latest year for which complete data are available), combined public– and private–sector investments for R&D in India totalled 18.14 billion rupees, the equivalent of about U.S. $1.5 billion at the prevailing official exchange rate. Of those investments, 15.35 billion rupees, or 84.6 percent, was devoted to nondefense purposes.

There has been a good deal of generally inconclusive debate about the significance of using official rates of exchange for cross–national comparisons, particularly between industrialized and less developed countries where conditions for research are so vastly different. For example, scientific labor costs are certainly less expensive in India than in the United States. However, a good deal of the scientific instrumentation required for high–quality research in frontier areas needs to be imported and is therefore more costly. On balance, 18 billion rupees can probably "purchase" considerably more science in India than can $1.5 billion in the United States. But even if India's R&D investments could purchase ten times as much science (which is dubious), they would still have to be regarded as small by international standards. By comparison, in 1985 total national (i.e., public plus private sector) R&D investments in the United States totaled $106.6 billion, of which $74.6 billion, or 70 percent, were for nondefense purposes.

How great an increase in its R&D investments could India make? Not much. Measured in terms of its own economy, the country's current investments are quite respectable. India's 18.14 billion rupee R&D expenditures during 1985 represented 0.96 percent of its gross national product (GNP), and its nondefense R&D about 0.84 percent of GNP, which was 1,884.6 billion rupees (U.S. $157 billion). Significantly, the former ratio has increased steadily from a level of about 0.6 percent in 1980. In view of the respectable increases in government R&D investments in 1987, total national investments are now in excess of 1 percent.

A ratio of R&D expenditures to GNP slightly in excess of 1 percent also prevails for Brazil and Yugoslavia, for example, and probably for China, although the data from China are somewhat unreliable. In the United States and Japan, the comparable ratio is currently about 2.7 percent. However, the ratio of U.S. nondefense R&D investments to

GNP is about 1.8 percent, or slightly more than twice the comparable ratio for India.

In short, like other less developed countries, India is faced with a difficult dilemma: strong science and technology capabilities are clearly essential to the achievement of economic and social goals. Yet investments in R&D are constrained by the size of the economy itself and by other demands made explicit in the Seventh Five–Year Plan, such as the need to protect the economy against fluctuations in international oil prices and irregular monsoons, and the continuing costs of rural development, all of which are considerably larger relative to India's GNP than in the industrialized countries. Yet more effective utilization of science and technology remains essential to address such demands.

On the basis of other official documents and reading between the lines of the Seventh Five–Year Plan, it is clear that India's official planners are well aware that structural limitations in the country's science and technology infrastructure limit their effectiveness. An examination of those limitations and possible remedies requires an understanding of how India's science and technology system is organized. That system can be characterized by three related qualitative differences from the analogous U.S. system:

- First, whereas in the United States industrial, university, and government research facilities play important complementary and often cooperative roles, with a few notable exceptions virtually all significant R&D in India is conducted in facilities under the direct control of the central government.
- Second, whereas in the United States (and most other industrialized countries, including newly industrialized countries such as Korea and Taiwan), private industry provides significant support for R&D both in its own laboratories and (particularly in the United States) in universities, in India private sector investments remain relatively small.
- Third, whereas in the United States basic research is conducted primarily by universities or major laboratories associated with and managed by universities, Indian universities, with a few notable exceptions, have declined in importance and generally remain isolated from the national R&D effort.

Research Agencies and Facilities

Seven agencies (which official government documents refer to as science and technology departments) account for approximately half of the central government's R&D budget. Among these, the Departments of Atomic Energy, Space, and Electronics either operate or oversee most of the best R&D facilities in the country.[1] The other four agencies—the Departments of Science and Technology, Ocean Development, Environment, and Biotechnology—are within the cabinet–level Ministry of Science and Technology, a portfolio held by Prime Minister Gandhi. The other half of the central government's R&D budget is divided approximately equally among three research councils (the Council for Scientific and Industrial Research, the Indian Council for Agricultural Research, and the Indian Council for Medical Research), and 24 so–called Non–Science and Technology Agencies scattered among various ministries in which science plays a relatively minor role. These include the Department of Education (whose fiscal year 1985 R&D budget was 24.9 million rupees) and the University Grants Commission, both of which support university research.[2]

The Department of Atomic Energy, whose R&D budget is almost triple that of any other, is without a doubt the premier nondefense science agency in India. That it retains its favored status despite serious questions about the economic viability of the country's nuclear–based power system merely sharpens the question of the relevancy of India's premier scientific establishments to its economy. The department owes its inception and sustained reputation for scientific excellence to the now almost legendary Homi Bhabha who, in 1944, began to press the twofold argument that (1) generation of electricity through nuclear fission would permit India to leapfrog over older, conventional power generation technologies, and (2) first–rate basic research facilities were required as a springboard to self–sufficient industrial development, particularly in the nuclear power field. The Tata Institute of Fundamental Research (TIFR) was established in Bombay in 1945 with Bhabha as director, and the Department of Atomic Energy was established in 1954 with Bhabha as secretary. R&D institutions under the department's aegis in addition to TIFR include the Bhabha Atomic Research Center (BARC) at Trombay, which engages in a wide range of basic and applied nuclear research, the High Altitude Research Laboratory at Gulmarg, the Nuclear Research Laboratory at Srinagar, the Variable Energy Cyclotron

[1] Defense–related research, which accounts for approximately 15 percent of the R&D budget, will not be considered here, in part because access to information is restricted and in part because it is not linked to economic or developmental goals. Facilities for that research are, however, reputed to be excellent.

[2] The science technology sector as defined by the five–year plans includes both the seven science and technology departments and the three research councils, but excludes the 24 so–called non–science and technology agencies.

Centre, and, lastly, the Saha Institute of Nuclear Physics at Calcutta.

In addition to maintaining world-class R&D facilities in nuclear physics, the Department of Atomic Energy was largely responsible for initiating and nurturing research programs that were later spun off to two new agencies: the Department of Electronics, established in 1970, and the Department of Space, established in 1971. The latter has pioneered the experimental use of satellites for domestic communication, remote sensing, and rural education. Although all operating Indian satellites were placed in orbit by either a U.S. or Soviet launcher, India plans to have its own independent launching capabilities in the early 1990s. Notable scientific research facilities under the aegis of the Department of Space include the National Remote Sensing Agency at Secunderabad, the Physical Research Laboratory at Ahmedabad, and the Vikram Sarabhai Space Centre at Trivandrum.

Of the remaining four officially designated science and technology departments, all except the Department of Science and Technology (DST, established in 1971), were established too recently to have made much of an impact on India's overall science and technology enterprise. DST has wide-ranging responsibilities, even though its annual budget is currently only about 7 percent of the government's total R&D budget. In particular, it is responsible for research in newly emerging fields and in areas that are not under the jurisdiction of other agencies. DST coordinates all international science and technology relations and plays a role in encouraging and supporting scientific activities in the states and in supporting the development of technologies that are particularly relevant to the rural areas. Finally, it finances several semiautonomous research facilities, the most notable being the highly regarded Raman Research Institute in Bangalore, founded in 1948 by Chandrasekhara Venkata (C.V.) Raman, India's first Nobel laureate.

Of India's three research councils, the Council of Scientific and Industrial Research (CSIR) and the Indian Council of Agricultural Research (ICAR) have each been receiving approximately 10 percent of the central government's R&D budget, and the Indian Council of Medical Research (ICMR) has received approximately 2 percent. CSIR is the most prominent of the research councils in terms of the number of facilities under its jurisdiction, its presumed importance to industrialization, and in the controversy that continues to surround it. The council was established on a British model in 1942 in the expectation that it would oversee applied research and undertake pilot development projects as a basis for commercial exploitation by private industry. At present, the CSIR complex consists of 44 institutions, some of which conduct applied research whose quality is judged to be good, including the Central Electrochemical Research Institute at Karaidudi, the Central Electronics Engineering Research Institute at Pilani, the Central Scientific Instruments Organisation at Chandigarh, the Centre for Cellular and Molecular Biology at Hyderabad, the National Botanical Research Institute at Lucknow, the National Chemical Laboratory at Pune, the National Institute of Oceanography at Goa, and the National Physical Laboratory at Delhi.

Role of Non–Governmental Sectors

Despite the fact that a good deal of the scientific work carried out at many CSIR facilities is credible in its own right, there has been a long–standing controversy about CSIR's effectiveness in conducting research of value to Indian industry. CSIR's response to such charges is that private industry has shown little interest in supporting or adapting indigenously–created innovations in applied research and technology, preferring instead to purchase or license foreign technologies. Although the relative merits of these charges and countercharges are difficult to disentangle, CSIR's problems are at least symptomatic of India's inability to make effective use of its existing science and technology resources for economic and particularly industrial development.

Industrial Research

Private–sector investments *are* small relative to those of the public sector. In 1985, the central government supported 77 percent of all the R&D performed in India, while private sources accounted for only 13 percent (state governments accounted for the remaining 10 percent, with their expenditures focused on applied agricultural research). In contrast, in the United States private industry supports slightly more than half of all R&D activities, and in Japan, approximately 80 percent. Although India's private–sector investments in R&D have increased steadily during the 1980s, they have remained virtually static relative to government expenditures.

Total R&D investments in industry have increased more rapidly than those in the agricultural and service sectors, accounting for 25 percent of the 1985 national total. However, roughly half of the 1985 industrial sector investments were accounted for by public–sector enterprises. Moreover, private–sector investments remain highly concentrated with four industrial groups—electricals and electronics, chemicals, drugs and pharmaceuticals, and industrial machinery—which accounted for almost half of the total. In contrast, three industrial groups essential to the agricultural and industrial sectors—telecommunications, fuels, and fertilizer—accounted for a combined total of less than 2 percent of total private–sector R&D investments in 1985. The lack of appreciable private–sector investments in telecommunications R&D is particularly disquieting in view of the government's heavy investments in a satellite–based communications infrastructure. India has little hope of becoming more competitive in the information–based international economy without becoming familiar with the fundamentals of rapidly changing communications technologies.

The reluctance of India's private sector to invest more substantially in R&D can be understood in part by recognizing that such investments, intended to provide the basis for new products or to improve processing efficiency, almost always require several years to yield visible marginal profits. Indeed, the time lag between marginal increases in R&D investments and visible marginal profits is U.S. industry's standard response to criticism that it is underinvesting in R&D relative to Japanese industry. The problem is compounded in India by a relative lack of experience in conducting and adapting industrially related research either at in–house facilities or under contract at university laboratories. For that reason, the time required for indigenous research to achieve tangible profits is more protracted in India than in the United States. Finally, since Indian industry has traditionally relied on a large domestic market and has been largely shielded from foreign competition by protectionist government policies, it has had little incentive to pursue R&D–based innovations.

The Seventh Five–Year Plan recognizes several structural weaknesses in the country's R&D, particularly in the industrial sector. The plan notes that despite a promising start during the Sixth–Plan period (1980–85), "there is a substantial technological gap [in the industrial sector] that needs to be closed." It stresses that since ". . . a new phase of industrialization has now commenced . . . marked by greater emphasis on technical progress and productive efficiency," the private sector will have to expand its role in the national economy. In order to encourage that expansion, the government will provide appropriate stimuli to enable Indian industry not only to readjust, reequip, and retool for accelerated growth, but also to fan out into new areas, for example in applications of computers and electronics to production processes, and improvements in fuel efficiency and in the use of new materials. However, private industry will have to shoulder most of the responsibility ". . . to upgrade technology and management, attain economies of scale, pursue greater value–adding activities, and selectively launch an export drive." Moreover, Indian industry can no longer count on the same measure of protection from foreign competition. For, as the plan emphasizes, such protection has given rise in the past to "high–cost manufacturing, which is inhibiting both the expansion of the domestic market and the more rapid development of exports."

While emphasizing the need for a more responsible, forward–looking attitude on the part of the private sector, the plan also concedes that ". . . at least for the remainder of the century, the public sector . . . will be a pace–setter and will encourage emerging new high technology industries. . ."

The plan also points to public sector inefficiencies as a serious impediment to the goals of the plan, noting if the public sector is to perform its "historic task," it has to undergo "basic structural changes to conform to the plan priorities of efficiency and productivity."

University Research

The Seventh Five–Year Plan envisions that "research within the university system will get due emphasis and be coordinated with national research efforts under the Science and Technology programme." It also stresses the need for an increase in the quality of university research, its integration into the national research system, and improvements and modernization of scientific and technical education. However, it is vague about the specific steps to be taken.

Indian universities, where the first creditable modern science was conducted outside of Europe and the United States, have declined in importance as contributors to the country's research enterprise. This decline can be attributed in part to the structure of the university system, in part to the fact that most universities are supported by the states rather than the central government, and in part to the explosive growth in the number of institutions of higher education in India during the past 40 years.

The first three European–style universities in India were established in 1857 at Calcutta, Bombay, and Madras. Modeled after the University of London, they were intended primarily as examining bodies rather than teaching or research institutions. Their principal functions were to set the curriculum for and administer examinations at a widespread, diffuse network of affiliated colleges. The virtual absence of innovation and creativity in the country's higher education system has often been attributed to the persistence of this model.

India's first post–graduate school of science, established at the University of Calcutta in 1914 on the initiative of several members of the local Indian community, became the first center in Asia where sustained, internationally recognized research was conducted by non–Western scientists. For example, C.V. Raman was awarded the Nobel

Prize in Physics in 1931 for research conducted in Calcutta during the time he served as the Palit Professor of Physics at the university.

The premier institution for scientific research and education in pre-Independence India was the Indian Institute of Science in Bangalore, in what was then the princely state of Mysore, established in 1909 as a private institution by the Bombay industrialist Sir Jamshediji Tata, whose grandson provided Homi Bhabha with the initial funds to establish the Tata Institute of Fundamental Research. The Indian Institute of Science was the first unitary university in India, i.e. the first to unify teaching, examination, and research functions under a single administration and at a single site. It served as an important model for the five Indian Institutes of Technology at Delhi, Bombay, Madras, Kanpur, and Kharagpur, established by the central government in the late 1950s and early 1960s.

During the decade preceding Independence in 1947, a handful of scientists under the leadership of Meghnad Saha attempted to establish a national research system based on the expanding university system, but failed due to insufficient funds and a pronounced lack of interest and support on the part of the colonial government's educational bureaucracy. Despite that failure, individuals and occasional groups still managed to conduct internationally recognized research.

There are now over 120 universities in India, all but a handful of which are controlled by state governments and function both as examining bodies on the pre-Independence model and, at the post-graduate level, as instructional bodies. Most are at best bit players within the national research system. For example, Indian government statistics do not consider scientific degree holders who teach in colleges, universities, and related institutions as being employed in R&D organizations. In most instances, that omission reflects the actual state of affairs. For while many Indian universities that offer the Ph.D. degree in a scientific field maintain experimental research facilities, little of their work is even close to being internationally competitive. In fact, virtually all internationally-recognized university research in India is carried out in one of three categories of institution: national universities under direct control of the central government, including Delhi University, Nehru University in Delhi, and Benares Hindu University; government-supported centers of advanced study in specific fields; and the Indian Institute of Science and the five Indian Institutes of Technology, supported by the central government's Department of Education but managed separately from the regular university system.

The Questions of Quality and Relevance

The decline or, perhaps more precisely, the dilution of the Indian university research system should be viewed in the context of larger questions regarding the quality of scientific research and its relevance both to international science and to the country's developmental and economic objectives.

The Quality Gap

For at least 50 years, foreign observers have been aware of the high caliber of the scientific contributions of individual Indians and, more recently, have acknowledged the sustained quality of the research conducted at a handful of Indian institutions. Predictably, perhaps, participants in the March 1987 Washington, D.C., workshop on Indo–U.S. scientific cooperation confirmed the assessments of numerous predecessors. Indian centers cited for scientific excellence at the workshop included the Tata Institute of Fundamental Research and the Bhabha Atomic Research Center in Bombay, the Physical Research Laboratory in Ahmedabad, the National Chemical Laboratory in Pune, the National Physical Laboratory in Delhi, the Indian Institute of Science and the Raman Research Institute in Bangalore, at least four of the five Indian Institutes of Technology, and the Universities of Delhi, Bombay, Calcutta, and Madras.

The fact that these institutions were praised in virtually all scientific fields explored at the workshop did credit to the breadth of the institutions. At the same time it was somewhat disquieting, suggesting that the layer of scientific quality in India is very thin indeed. Departments or centers for advanced study at universities such as Chandigarh, Hyderabad, and Rajasthan (at Jaipur) occasionally made the good–to–excellent list in one or two fields. However, the consensus among workshop participants was that research conducted in their specialties in virtually all other institutions is at best uninteresting because it focuses on problems that are no longer of international interest, and at worst is of inferior or even shoddy quality.

Equally disturbing was the consensus that even research conducted at many of the acknowledged premier laboratories is often not as good as it should be given the caliber of the scientists involved. Workshop participants attributed this to a number of causes, one of the most important being the scarcity of modern scientific instrumentation even in many of the best laboratories. Indeed, the lack of good facilities is no doubt one reason why so many talented Indian scientists concentrate on theoretical rather than experimental science, despite the fact that the latter is more directly and immediately applicable to industrial development. That Indians are more culturally inclined toward theory may well be a myth, in view of the fact that many expatriates have made excellent contributions to experimental science.

Relevance: Agriculture and Health

Given the uneven quality of scientific research in India, it is fair to ask what visible difference the government's considerable R&D investments have made to the country's economic development and its industrial economy and, more to the point, what impact they are likely to have in the future. The Seventh Five–Year Plan itself raises and partially answers that question in stating that ". . . despite considerable investments, science and technology have so far not made commensurate impact on programmes of development of the economic sector." It also emphasizes the need for improvements in the quality of research at government facilities, introduction of additional research facilities in the industrial and agricultural sectors, and reviews of research management on a continuing basis to assure better integration of science and technology into those sectors. However, those needs will not be easily met.

Certainly, as suggested above, India has done remarkably well in adapting science–based technologies in several areas, including agriculture, health, space, and nuclear power. However, while not denying the magnitude of these accomplishments, it should be stressed that they have resulted primarily from applications of research and/or the adaptation of technologies developed outside India.

Agriculture is a case in point. The "green revolution," which provided the country with the means both to feed itself and to become a net–exporter of agricultural products, occurred largely because the country made use of new strains of rice and wheat developed at internationally supported agricultural research institutes outside India. Indian scientists were heavily involved in the research, and certainly the new genetic strains could not have been introduced successfully without an enormous commitment and effort on the part of scientists at agricultural stations throughout the country. Still, basic research conducted in India itself has yet to have any appreciable, direct impact on Indian agriculture.

Similar observations apply to health, where dramatic advances have been made in reducing infant mortality, improving sanitation, introducing primary health care facilities in rural areas, and eliminating or bringing under control a variety of epidemic diseases long since conquered in the West. However, while the achievements of Indian medical scientists and auxiliary personnel have been magnificent, they have not resulted from basic research conducted in India.

Appreciable additional increases in agricultural productivity will most probably require improvements in plants indigenous to India itself, and will thus have to rely more heavily on indigenous research capabilities. Similarly, significant improvements in health will require greater reliance on indigenous scientific resources. For example, India, like most tropical countries, continues to be plagued by a variety of parasitic diseases. Because these diseases are virtually unknown in nontropical countries, few Western scientists have studied them closely. The resultant gap in understanding lays a particular burden on the scientific resources of relatively advanced tropical countries such as India.

The means required for a successful attack on problems in agriculture and health may be at hand. Spectacular worldwide research advances in biotechnology have provided the potential for new technologies across a broad spectrum, including agriculture and medicine. Experts agree that additional, more impressive advances in understanding living organisms will be forthcoming. Indian scientists have contributed to research underlying biotechnology, particularly in plant genetics. Given adequate support, they are almost certainly capable of doing more, as specialists at the March 1987 workshop agreed. However, one vital question not addressed at the workshop was how closer links can be established between India's government and university research systems and its productive sector, thus permitting exploitation of some of the achievements of India's scientists—in this case its biological scientists.

Relevance: Industrialization

This question is even more significant when posed with respect to areas other than agriculture and health. For it may be that in these areas only marginal institutional changes will be required to link high–quality research in universities to the existing infrastructure for infusing advances in science and technology throughout the country. But in areas such as energy and communications that are important both to further increase living standards and to the industrial economy, the situation is very different. Obviously, India's aspirations to compete in export markets, particularly in Asia, will be heavily dependent on its ability to exploit its own (as well as foreign) scientific resources for purposes that are not directly related to basic human needs, and the requisite infrastructure is largely lacking.

The character of India's nuclear and space programs underlines the problem of exploiting science for industrial, as opposed to strictly developmental, purposes. Even though nuclear power has helped bring electricity to rural areas and the experimental satellite INSAT–2 has delivered educational television to selected villages, neither program was designed to address basic human needs in agriculture and health. Rather, nuclear power is intended primarily as a means to electrify the country and thus provide a necessary prerequisite for increased industrialization, while the space program is intended to provide remote sensing and weather–monitoring capabilities as well as a means for improved domestic and international communications.

In view of the very large capital investments involved, it is appropriate for the central government to have taken the initiative and retain control over both programs. But it is not obvious that either can provide a model or a stimulus for improved productivity throughout the industrial sector.

Despite the fact that nuclear power has made substantial contributions to increasing per capita availability of electricity throughout the country, the economic viability of the enterprise itself is questionable. Nor do even its most fervent advocates claim that nuclear power can provide sufficient nonelectrical energy to meet rural fuel requirements. At present, those needs are being sustained mainly by burning wood or animal dung, and widespread burning of wood continues to further rapid deforestation of the country. A number of technologies derived from physics and chemistry (e.g., solar energy) or biotechnology (e.g., alcohol production from agricultural waste) are available for adaptation to the multiple, small–scale energy needs of rural areas, and Indian scientists are fully capable of adapting them to local conditions. India does not lack the scientific capabilities to develop usable, nonconventional energy sources, but rather enterprises that are willing and able to provide the means to do so.

A similar though more pronounced situation prevails in the communications field, which India desperately needs to upgrade if it is to function as a modern, competitive industrial state. The Seventh Five–Year Plan recognizes the promise of domestic satellite–based communications technologies to achieve economic and social goals and stresses the need for adapting of existing technologies in the fields of electronics, computers, and space. But much of this adaptation will have to be accomplished in the private sector.

In the United States, private enterprise seized upon the availability of government–funded communication satellites to upgrade, diversify, and broaden existing communications capabilities. No analogous initiative has been undertaken by the Indian private sector, in part because the government may have been overly zealous in reserving the communications field for itself. Nor has there been any clear recognition by private industry of the desirability of investing in other promising areas of R&D that underlie modern communications, such as lasers, solid–state physics, or microchip development, fields in which Indian university scientists are making creditable contributions. The Seventh Five–Year Plan recognizes that these capabilities need to be exploited to develop competitive research capabilities in "solid–state electronics, lasers, integral optics, and telecommunications systems based on digital electronics." Based on those resources, ". . . attempts will have to be made during the prospective plan period to start and develop a number of high technology industries, such as advanced machine tools, electronics, fibre optics, lasers, and biotechnology." But the fact that the plan talks about attempts rather than actuality is itself an admission of structural inhibitions in Indian R&D.

It would be presumptuous for a foreign observer to offer detailed prescriptions for improving India's system for supporting and exploiting the capabilities of its scientists. However, it is now widely acknowledged that overcentralization of planning and control of a country's scientific enterprise often stifles innovation and creativity. As a case in point, the decentralization of control and decision making over scientific enterprise has been one of the cornerstones in the political and economic reforms of the People's Republic of China during the past decade. Likewise, General Secretary Mikhail Gorbachev's proposed reforms include a roughly analogous though less far–reaching decentralization in the Soviet Union. It will be instructive to see what lessons, if any, India draws from these examples, or whether administrative decentralization, should it occur, will provide any appreciable stimulus to India's many small, nongovernmental science and technology–related institutions.

Utilization of Scientific Personnel

India is aware of the problems associated with the weak or nonexistent links between its research sector (particularly in its best universities) and its industrial sector. The inadequacy of those links is a recurring theme in official policy documents, as earlier citations from the Seventh Five–Year Plan indicate. The Council of Scientific and Industrial Research (CSIR) was established in 1942 expressly to stimulate industrial research, and the five Indian Institutes of Technology (IITs) were established and handsomely endowed a little more than a decade after Independence in part to provide the high–quality education required for a modern industrial nation. But until recently, there has been no particular motivation for private industry to link itself more closely with either the CSIR institutions or the IITs.

Recent government encouragement for small–scale consulting organizations which are intended to act as a bridge between industry and the country's research institutions may improve matters. There are now over 100 consultancies, employing approximately 20,000 scientists and engineers either full or part time. The best of these are based in or associated with premier universities, including—prominently—the IITs. Government sources indicate that the IITs are deriving appreciable income from their consulting work so in that sense at least they appear to be successful. Whether their activities will make substantial impact on Indian industry remains to be seen.

These organizations could conceivably help to decentralize, diversify, and rejuvenate the Indian R&D system. They could also provide an outlet for the talents of large numbers of underutilized scientists and engineers. India is fond of boasting that it has the world's third largest science, engineering, and technical community, exceeded only by those of the United States and the Soviet Union. In 1985, India estimated this group to include 2.2 million professionals, an increase of almost 100 percent in fifteen years. However, a relatively small proportion actually engage in R&D–related activities within the country. In 1985, according to these same government statistics, only 77,000 of the 2.2 million, or fewer than 4 percent, were actually engaged in R&D work (68 percent employed by the central government, 18 percent by private industry, and 14 percent by state governments). An additional 140,000 were listed as being in administrative and auxiliary positions related to R&D.

What of the remaining trained personnel who neither emigrate nor are acknowledged by government statistics as being engaged in R&D–related activities? Many probably teach and even attempt to conduct research in colleges and universities throughout India, and continue to subscribe to the value system that even the quest for trivial knowledge within the narrow confines of an academic discipline is a more worthy endeavor than the application of existing knowledge to the solution of specific, socially–defined problems. M.G.K. Menon, currently science adviser to Prime Minister Gandhi, has noted the unfortunate tendency among scientists to define basic research as any research that is not obviously applied, rather than more correctly as research of internationally competitive quality that attempts to advance the frontiers of knowledge. Yet because the value system that places a high premium on "pure" research is so deeply ingrained among many Indian (and Western) academics, large numbers of talented, dedicated Indians devote their careers to essentially rote data collection that makes little or no contribution to international science and is at best peripheral to India's social and economic needs. That their efforts are often well meant and even heroic cannot obscure the fact that they are most frequently wasted.

What happened to the rest? Many of those who can, emigrate. During the 1985–86 academic year, there were approximately 16,000 Indian students in all fields studying at U.S. academic institutions, an increase of 10 percent over the previous year. Indian students now make up the fourth largest continent of foreign students in the United States, and it is estimated that between 70 and 90 percent of them remain in the United States after completing their training. Although distributions by discipline are not readily available, employment opportunities in the United States suggest that a sizable majority of those who remain are scientists and engineers, many of whom are making significant contributions to U.S. science. Many also maintain close working relations with their colleagues at home and in that way contribute indirectly to the development of science in India.

A desirable tonic for the Indian R&D system could be one that offered reasonable incentives (including a measure of prestige) to those scientists outside the first–rate universities whose talents could be directed toward applied research aimed at solving local problems; that provided adequate facilities for applied pursuits; and that, like the pilot consulting organizations, helped forge links with potential local users. However, establishing an effective system and allowing it to develop with a minimum of bureaucratic interference would entail risks not only for the government, but for private industry, the universities, and the individuals involved. Unfortunately, there seems to be little willingness to take calculated risks in India today.

Basic Research in Less Developed Countries

The issues of quality and relevance point to a fundamental question that India's political and scientific leadership have grappled with since before Independence, namely, how much basic research ought to be conducted and supported. The continuing debate over that question is epitomized in the careers of Meghnad Saha and Homi Bhabha, both of whose international reputations had been established prior to World War II.

Saha, whose first internationally recognized contributions to theoretical astrophysics were made while he was a junior faculty member at the University College of Science at Calcutta in the early 1920s, turned his attention to national planning during the 1930s while a professor at Allahabad University. He pressed his advocacy even more vigorously from the time of his return to Calcutta University until his death in 1956. Saha argued, in effect, that within national planning, India's scientific priorities ought to be focused on establishing an infrastructure and an associated research agenda to attack development problems. Saha did not question the value of basic research, which he continued to pursue and to encourage his better students to pursue. Rather, he argued that basic research ought to be a means to specific, well–defined ends rather than an end in itself.

Bhabha, who established his reputation in theoretical nuclear physics in Europe during the 1930s, advocated a more Western–oriented, free–market approach to the support, conduct, and utilization of scientific research. That is, he advanced the argument familiar in the United States and Western Europe that if sufficient numbers of vigorous, high–quality basic research centers existed, then the productive sector (by which Bhabha meant primarily the industrial sector) would have a continuous supply of the scientific results required for innovation and modernization. Bhabha recognized that a more substantial foundation for industrialization needed to be established, and for that reason successfully advocated a nuclear–electric generating program linked closely with a first–class center for basic research.

As it happened, Bhabha won the short–term battle, but the war is still being waged. During his lifetime, organizations under Bhabha's direct administrative control—the Tata Institute for Fundamental Research and the Department of Atomic Energy—performed as he had predicted, and in large measure still do. But as his protégé M.G.K. Menon has sadly acknowledged, the expectation that strong basic research centers would automatically spur creative industrial development has not been fulfilled. Nor is much of what passes for basic research in most universities of much value.

Still, the need for basic research in less developed countries is undeniable, for two related reasons. First, since basic research is judged by internationally established criteria, it must be of a high quality in order to be competitive. Therefore, a strong basic research enterprise, by providing a high standard, tends to raise the quality for the applied research and development work that must underlie both the application of indigenously produced scientific results and the adaptation of foreign technologies to a country's particular conditions. Bhabha used this argument in 1944 in his successful proposal to establish what was to become the Tata Institute of Fundamental Research, no doubt the premier basic research center in India, and probably in the less developed world:

> If much of the applied research done in India today is disappointing and of very inferior quality, it is entirely due to the absence of a sufficient

> number of outstanding *pure* research workers who could set the standards for good research [emphasis in the original].

In some cases justification for supporting basic research as a springboard for viable technologies has reaped considerable dividends for India, as in the cases of nuclear power and agriculture. Certainly those who spearheaded India's achievements in health and agriculture must have had a broad grasp of, as well as access to, foreign work in their respective areas.

However, one problem with the springboard justification (which is hardly unique to India) is the difficulty of distinguishing, in advance, between scientific fields that are likely to underlie promising technologies from those that are peripheral to future economic and social needs. The usual counter response is that a country must therefore maintain strength across the entire spectrum of basic research fields. But that is an exceedingly difficult option for a country like India with severe financial constraints on its ability to invest broadly in R&D.

The second justification often given for supporting basic research in less developed countries is that the breadth, rigor, and international standards characterized by training in those disciplines gives practioners unique qualifications for assessing detailed needs in applied research and development. According to this justification, for example, people trained to conduct basic research (regardless of their subsequent careers) represent an elite cadre well–equipped to determine the feasibility of developing indigenous technologies in their specialty areas, as well as to determine which technologies ought to be imported and how they ought to be adapted for indigenous needs.

The Seventh Five–Year Plan accepts these arguments, at least partially, by reiterating the "critical role of technological competence in determining the long–term growth prospects for the economy." It goes on to admit the necessity of adapting and absorbing key foreign technologies in both industry and agriculture, but in a manner "interlinked with facilities for research and development so as to promote technological self–reliance to the maximum extent possible." Clearly the country must place a high premium on people with the training and competence to manage that difficult assignment.

However, while training in basic research may, in fact, be essential to produce an elite cadre attuned to specific technological needs and priorities, it does not follow that experience in conducting basic research inevitably produces such a cadre. The applicability of the training argument is dubious in view of the hopeless inadequacy of basic research facilities at most Indian institutions, particularly at universities, where most scientific training takes place. Certainly postgraduate students who are educated to believe that rote data collection can be regarded as internationally competitive basic research, or senior scientists who spend the better part of their careers conducting research with inferior, dated apparatus on problems that no longer interest their Western colleagues, are unlikely candidates to make informed assessments of a country's priorities in applied research and development.

The question India needs to address is not whether the country ought to encourage and support basic research, but rather how much basic research it should support, where, and at what levels. An important corollary question is how to refocus the talents of those individuals and institutions whose basic research aspirations cannot be encouraged toward more productive applied undertakings. All conceivable justifications for basic research presuppose that it will be conducted by highly capable, motivated people who have the means to conduct it properly. For those reasons it makes no sense to expect trained, capable scientists to conduct internationally competitive research with wholly inadequate facilities. Nor is it fair or in the best interests of the country to endow people who have less than first–rate abilities with research opportunities that are denied to the very best.

The Seventh Five–Year Plan admits, by implication, that Indian scientists often have not received the requisite sustained support and guidance from the government that might allow them to have a greater impact on the economy. At the same time, it serves notice that scientists will be expected to focus on coherent, clear–cut objectives in exchange for more adequate support. In particular, they should be given the opportunity to begin to implement ". . . a set of science and technology missions in which domestic technological capabilities would be fully developed to achieve well–defined goals." Exactly what those goals are and whether the government is prepared to pursue them effectively is not clear.

The Domestic and International Political Environment

Their value as economic tools aside, India's five–year plans are noteworthy for their candor in admitting deficiencies in performance, overall and within each economic sector, in assessing probable causes, and in pointing to specific structural problems.

The Domestic Political Environment

The foregoing sections have highlighted the factors underlying deficiencies in Indian science and technology as addressed implicitly and explicitly by the Seventh Five–Year Plan: (1) excessive dominance of the central government bureaucracy in all aspects of the science and technology system, including planning and policy–making as well as the support and conduct of R&D; (2) insufficient participation by the private sector either in supporting and conducting research or in making use of existing technological innovations; (3) the decline of the university research system as a viable component of the national effort; (4) weak or nonexistent links among the government, industrial, and university research sectors; and (5) inefficiencies and an absence of quality control in all sectors.

The Seventh Five–Year Plan became effective at about the time that Rajiv Gandhi succeeded his mother as prime minister. The new prime minister, who studied engineering in England and who (it was confidently predicted) would view government from a technocratic rather than a bureaucratic or political perspective, announced his intention to demand greater efficiency in government operations, including R&D, as well as a more visible commitment to economic and social goals on the part of the country's scientists. In particular, his government made it clear that future budget allocations for scientific facilities under its direct control would be determined on the basis of past performance and future potential within the context of those goals.

In exchange for demanding greater efficiency and accountability, Rajiv Gandhi's government promised to provide more generous financial resources to the country's best scientific institutions and also to improve the overall environment for research. The substantial increases in the R&D budget proposed in March 1987 and allocation to areas underlying high–technology capabilities are consistent with that policy. The government also has liberalized import restrictions on essential scientific instrumentation, including computers, the lack of which has been identified as a serious factor behind the disappointing performance of many otherwise first–rate Indian scientific institutions.

In addition Prime Minister Gandhi has sought to broaden and rejuvenate the government's planning and priority–setting processes by replacing (in 1986) an internal, cabinet–level scientific advisory committee with a nongovernmental one. That committee is responsible directly to the prime minister and is comprised of six distinguished industry and university scientists and chaired by C.N.R. Rao, an internationally recognized chemist who is director of the Indian Institute of Science. At the same time the prime minister confirmed the appointment of M.G.K. Menon as his personal science adviser, thus strengthening Menon's position within the planning commission.

Most of Rajiv Gandhi's science policy initiatives, taken during 1985 and 1986, were applauded by scientists at the premier institutions. However, during 1987 it began to be clear that as in so many other important national areas, what had been initially regarded as Rajiv's fresh, technocratic, and allegedly nonpolitical style would not instantly resolve all problems inherent in India's science and technology system. More seriously, doubts began to emerge about whether his government understood and had the long–term interests of Indian science at heart.

For example, during 1987 respected and generally sympathetic members of the government's scientific establishment charged that on at least two policy decisions, the government was acting in a hasty, high–handed manner. The first had to do with the prime minister's decision to appoint as director of the Bhabha Atomic Research Center an engineer rather than the physicist who was overwhelmingly the scientific community's preferred candidate. The second had to do with the government's interpretation of recommendations by an independent government committee on improving the effectiveness of CSIR. Critics both within and without CSIR alleged that the prime minister and his advisers had seized on several recommendations that could undermine the most effective of the CSIR facilities, while ignoring others that went to the heart of the council's inability to forge meaningful links with private industry.

In short, the record of Rajiv Gandhi's government with regard to science policy was mixed in 1987, as it was in so many areas. Nonetheless, he still appears to enjoy broad support from the best of India's scientists.

The International Political Environment

At the international level, Prime Minister Gandhi, following the lead taken by his mother during her last three years, moved to reestablish firm scientific ties with the West, particularly the United States. India's scientific and political leadership have long regarded international cooperation as essential both for augmenting the country's limited resources and for helping to strengthen its science and technology infrastructure. Significantly, the Western scientific value system that places a high premium on open communication and free international exchange has been integral to the country's scientific culture from the outset, in part because modern scientific ideas and institutions emerged in India during the long period of British tutelage.

One result has been the generally lukewarm response by Indian scientists to repeated government attempts during Mrs. Gandhi's years to encourage more substantial scientific exchanges with the Soviet Union. Although Rajiv Gandhi's government initially exhibited a pronounced preference for exchange with the West on the grounds that it would be more beneficial to India, the possibility of upgraded cooperation with the Soviet Union was raised during General Secretary Gorbachev's January 1987 visit to Delhi.

Prior to 1970, India and the United States had enjoyed an extensive, long–standing, and generally fruitful record of scientific cooperation. However, during the 1970s scientific relations between the two countries became hostage to generally cool political relations occasioned by the Nixon Administration's notorious tilt toward Pakistan during the 1971 war with Bangladesh. Prime minister Indira Gandhi's state visit to Washington in 1982 signaled an end to that era. On that occasion, she and President Reagan established a new Indo–U.S. Science and Technology Initiative for the support of substantial cooperation in areas of mutual benefit to the two countries, subsequently identified as specific problems in the fields of health, agriculture, monsoon research, and solid–state science and engineering. The agreement to pursue that initiative was extended and expanded during Rajiv Gandhi's 1986 visit to Washington.

Because many of India's political and scientific leaders formed close associations with British colleagues as students in England, cooperation with that country remains important even though the amount of financial support derived thereby is relatively small. However, the United States has supplanted England as the favored country for advanced study by Indian scientists and engineers, many of whom remain in this country. Their close links with their colleagues at home are an important component of Indo–U.S. scientific cooperation. The obvious importance of this network to India, coupled with the observation that India is unable to make optimum use of its scientific talent, mitigates accusations of "brain drain" that were formerly leveled against the United States. Indeed, several of India's scientific and political leaders, including Prime Minister Gandhi, have referred to the expatriate contingent as a brain bank rather than as a "brain drain."

India's Role in Multilateral Scientific Affairs

Large numbers of Indian scientists are prominent in the scientific programs of official intergovernmental multilateral organizations such as United Nations Educational, Scientific, and Cultural Organization, the Food and Agricultural Organization, the World Health Organization, and the International Atomic Energy Agency, and India has consistently supported their involvement with those organizations. India's prominence and influence in these organizations far outweigh those of any other Asian country, including Japan or China; they are probably greater than that of any other nation, save the United States, the Soviet Union, and the Western European countries. The visibility of

Indian scientists in the nongovernmental International Council of Scientific Unions, comprised of the National Academies of Science of 77 nations, provides one important measure of the high level of international respect those scientists enjoy. That organization elected M.G.K. Menon as its president at its biennial meeting in Bern in September 1986.

India's strong participation in multilateral scientific affairs is more than symbolic. One of former prime minister Nehru's enduring dreams was that the Third World nations could collectively exert a positive influence on global affairs, and that India had a moral obligation to take the lead in that direction. Although Nehru's larger vision of a beneficent world order mediated by the less developed nations failed to materialize, India still maintains aspirations for leadership among those nations. That is particularly true in multilateral scientific affairs where India is struggling to define its responsibilities as one of the most advanced of the less developed countries, with the most experienced, sophisticated, and internationally regarded scientific community.

For example, there is within the British Commonwealth a science unit that meets annually to discuss problems of common interest. India has emerged as a leader of this group and is trying to define an effective role as a link between the wealthier members of the Commonwealth and, in particular, the African countries. In addition, beginning with the Sixth Five–Year Plan period (1980–85) India has been actively encouraging the country's scientists and engineers to undertake technical assistance projects in poorer countries. Many such projects are planned and carried out by private consulting organizations, with partial financial support by the government. India also provides full financial support for ICSU's Committee on Science and Technology for Development, housed at the Indian Institute of Technology at Madras, and has constructed meeting and visitors facilities there to provide an international center for programs to further the development of scientific resources, including educational resources, for use throughout the Third World.

Opportunities and Dilemmas

Economic necessity as well as national pride compel India to place heavy reliance on its scientific endowments as it seeks a more prominent international role with respect to the industrialized countries of the West, the poorer countries of the South, and of course, the newly prominent giants of the East. India's intellectual and political leadership are painfully aware that the country's mixed record in applying technology to economic development has been overshadowed not only by the spectacular performance of Japan, but also by Korea and Taiwan whose scientific and economic potential was generally dismissed two decades ago. And, of course, the vast though largely unexploited potential of China looms large among India's scientific policymakers as both an example to emulate and a threat to avoid.

The ambiguous status of Indian science with respect to East Asia was epitomized by the second Asia–Pacific Physics Conference held in Bangalore in January 1986. The presence of large, distinguished delegations from Japan and the People's Republic of China was a clear indication that those two countries regard Indian physics as a factor to be reckoned with.

Near thc close of the conference, the Nobel Laureate C.N. Yang, who has resided in the United States for 40 years and is noted for his quiet personal wisdom as well as his evident scientific achievements, recounted his first trip to India late in 1945, when he was in transit to the University of Chicago for graduate study from a China devastated by decades of civil strife, foreign occupation, and war. During a two–month stay in India, Yang was hosted by the Institute for Nuclear Physics at Calcutta University through the courtesy of Meghnad Saha with whom his professor in China had once studied. Calcutta was Yang's first exposure to genuine world–class physics. Among the handful of Asian centers of excellence in scientific research in 1945, most—in fact probably all—were in India, including the Institute for Nuclear Physics at Calcutta and the Indian Institute of Science at Bangalore. Certainly there were no such centers in China or Japan.

Today the situation is vastly different. China now has several recognized world–class research centers and several more that promise to join that class. Japan's scientific capabilities and its skill at exploiting both domestic and foreign capabilities are, of course, the envy of the entire world. Korea is beginning to be recognized for its scientific accomplishments in a few selected fields, as are Thailand and, to some extent, Taiwan. Of course it is naive to expect that science alone can be a panacea for all economic and social problems. Still, as the cases of Japan and Korea indicate, scientific resources, if properly integrated with other economic sectors, can lead to spectacular economic growth. Given the relatively small investments India has been able to make in R&D, it is remarkable that the country's scientific institutions and its individual scientists have accomplished as much as they have. Still, as the East Asian examples suggest, there remains the nagging sense that it could have done more.

India cannot be regarded as a typical less developed country. On the contrary, it has aspired to leadership in the Third World, particularly in the uses of science and technology for development. Indeed as noted earlier, its political and scientific leadership recognized the importance of science well before the country attained political independence in

1947. In that sense, India's success in adapting world science and technology for its own purposes could well be a measure of the potential for science and technology in much of the rest of the world.

Unlike most of the world's less developed countries, the political leadership of independent India has (with a short lapse in the mid–1970s) been firmly and consistently committed to science and technology, particularly basic science. As such, it presents the anomalous case of a poor country with a sophisticated scientific community that can lay legitimate claim to membership—and a voice in—the international scientific community. Other countries (most notably China and perhaps Brazil) can lay similar claims. In the future, world science—and U.S. science—will have to take account of those claims.

This essay has explored the effectiveness of Indian science in contributing to the country's social and economic goals. Yet the question of how and why science, and particularly basic research, ought to be supported is complicated by the fact that India—virtually alone among Asian countries—subscribes to an additional, nontangible justification for science. That justification, which is rarely voiced in public by those who seek financial support for science on the grounds that it is vital to economic growth, is that science is every bit a part of culture as music, painting, or literature, and that therefore a humane society must necessarily encourage the conduct of basic research. Many gifted individuals devote their lives to science because they regard the pursuit of knowledge as a supreme human endeavor, and that is the principal reason why societies as diverse as those in the United States, Europe, the Soviet Union, Japan, and the People's Republic of China support disciplines such as pure mathematics, astronomy, and high–energy physics that almost certainly will never yield any direct, tangible benefits.

Yet few countries have been so explicit and open as India in subscribing to the cultural justification. The 1958 Science Policy Resolution is perhaps unprecedented as an official policy document in its articulation of that justification:

> It is an inherent obligation of a great country like India with its traditions of scholarship and original thinking and its great cultural heritage, to participate fully in the march of science, which is probably mankind's greatest enterprise today.

No Westerner should presume to suggest that India is too poor to encourage the best of its scientists to pursue the expansion of human understanding for its own sake.

That the depth of India's commitment to modern science on both cultural and tangible grounds exceeds that of any other less developed country and perhaps any other Asian country may not be surprising in view of the fact that that commitment dates from the country's long period of British rule.[3] Yet India's scientific community, and its political leadership, are still trying hard to make it both on "Western" terms and on their own. Its scientific community (and again during the past few years its political leadership) look to the West, particularly the United States, for leadership and encouragement. At the same time they are striving to provide leadership, and an example, to the world's poorer nations. India presents a fascinating case study of the potential and the limitations of science for fostering development within a single economy. Increasingly, India's relations with both richer and poorer countries are likely to be an important source of information on the relative importance (or lack of importance) of modern science in international affairs.

---

[3] Of course India's cultural commitment to science, like China's, predates Western influences by many centuries. One remarkable aspect of India's commitment to *modern* sciences in the 19th and 20th centuries is that it came about despite the official indifference and often the hostility of the colonial government.

Suggestions for Further Reading

Politics: Ambiguity, Disillusionment, and Ferment

Hardgrave, Robert L. Jr., and Kochanek, Stanley. *India: Government and Politics in a Developing Nation.* New York: Harcourt Brace Jovanovich, 1986.

Kohli, Atul, ed. *India's Democracy: An Analysis of Changing State–Society Relations.* Princeton, NJ: Princeton University Press, 1987.

Rudolph, Lloyd I., and Rudolph, Susanne H. *In Pursuit of Lakshmi: The Political Economy of the Indian State.* Chicago: University of Chicago Press, 1987.

The Economy: Stresses, Strains, and Opportunities

Papanek, George F., and Lucas, Robert E. B., eds. *The Indian Economy: Recent Development and Future Prospects.* Boulder, CO: Westview Press, 1988.

Ahluwalia, Isher J. *Industrial Growth in India.* Delhi, India: Oxford University Press, 1985.

Bardhan, Pranab. *The Political Economy of Development in India.* New York: Oxford University Press, 1984.

Bhagwati, J.N. and Srinivasan, T.N. *Foreign Trade Regimes and Economic Development: India.* New York: Columbia University Press, 1975.

Dernberger, Robert F., and Eckaus, Richard S. *Financing Asian Development 2: China and India.* Lanham MD: University Press of America and The Asia Society, 1988.

India's Foreign Relations: Problems along the Borders

Barnds, William J. *India, Pakistan and the Great Powers.* New York: Praeger, 1972.

Hardgrave, Robert. *India Under Pressure: Prospects for Political Stability.* Boulder, CO: Westview Press, 1985.

Mansingh, Surjit. *India's Search for Power: Indira Gandhi's Foreign Policy, 1966–82.* New Delhi and Beverly Hills, CA: Sage, 1984.

Singh, S. Nihal. *The Yogi & the Bear: The Story of Indo–Soviet Relations.* Riverdale, MD: The Riverdale Co., 1986.

Achieving Security from Within and Without

Cohen, Stephen P., ed., *The Security of South Asia: American and Asian Perspectives.* Urbana, IL: University of Illinois Press, 1987.

Ganguly, Sumit. *The Origins of War in South Asia.* Boulder, CO: Westview Press, 1986.

Thomas, Raju G.C. *The Defence of India: A Budgetary Perspective of Strategy and Politics.* New Delhi: The MacMillan Co. of India, 1978.

Thomas, Raju G.C. *Indian Security Policy.* Princeton, NJ: Princeton University Press, 1986.

Education: Safer Options

Altbach, Philip et al. *Education in South Asia: A Select Annotated Bibliography.* New York: Garland Publishing, Inc., 1987.

Karlekar, Malvika. "Education and Inequality," in *Equality and Inequality: Theory and Practice,* Andre Beteille, ed. New Delhi: Oxford University Press, 1983.

Kumar, Krishna. "Educational Recovery," *Seminar* (New Delhi), Annual Number, January 1986.

Naik, J.P. *Equality, Quality and Quantity: The Elusive Triangle in Indian Education.* New Delhi: Allied, 1973.

Science, Technology, and India's Aspirations

Alexander, Jane, ed. *Research Partners Half a World Apart.* Washington, DC: National Science Foundation, 1986.

Anderson, Robert S., Brass, Paul R., et al. *Science, Politics, and the Agricultural Revolution in Asia.* Boulder, CO: Westview Press, 1982.

Blanpied, William A. "India's Scientific Development," *Pacific Affairs*, vol. 50 (Spring 1977), pp. 91-98.

Morgan, Robert P. *Science and Technology for Development*. New York: Pergamon Press, 1979.

1987—A Chronology

JANUARY

9 On a visit to Washington, D.C., India's Foreign Secretary A.P. Venkateswaran, worried by the U.S. sale of AWACS to Pakistan, stresses that a continued supply of arms to Pakistan would create a dangerous and unstable situation and trigger an arms race.

15 **In a virtually unprecedented action, President Zail Singh rejects the Indian Post Office Amendment Bill, which would have authorized the government to intercept mailed articles, and offers suggestions for change.**

18 **While making friendly overtures on the political front, Pakistan masses troops in near combat readiness on its border from Kashmir to Rajasthan.** Pakistani officials claim the move is in reaction to the current exercise by Indian troops in Rajasthan, code-named "Brasstacks." India, however, says it informed Pakistan in advance of Operation Brasstacks.

19 Continuing violence in the Punjab is marked by the killing of the secretary general of the Punjab Congress (I) party. While ruling out the imposition of President's Rule, Gandhi accuses Chief Minister Barnala on January 20 of being slack in handling terrorist problems and of some Punjab ministers being involved with extremists.

20 **At a general press conference, Rajiv Gandhi insultingly announces the retirement of Foreign Secretary A.P. Venkateswaran.** He is succeeded by K.P.S. Menon, India's ambassador in Beijing. **The move further feeds building resentment in the bureaucracy against the prime minister.** Venkateswaran, a respected, efficient, and dynamic 36–year veteran of the diplomatic corps, had strongly objected to the government's Sri Lankan policy and to the curtailment of the foreign office's role in border negotiations with Pakistan.

22 In a fresh attempt to resolve the Gurkhaland issue, Congress invites the GNLF leader for talks but only in reference to the question of citizenship of Nepalis living in India. The GNLF leader agrees, on January 28, to peaceful solution of the Gurkha problem.

23 **The Indian Army and Air Force are put on alert and the Punjab border is sealed. Simultaneously, India proposes to Pakistan a mutual de-escalation and a withdrawal of troops to original positions.** On January 25, India extends a formal invitation for secretary level talks. Two rounds of intensive talks begin on January 31. Gandhi declares that the security and integrity of India will be "defended at all costs," but says India will never take any step to trigger a war. On February 4, India and Pakistan sign the first agreement to de–escalate the situation and they agree to pull back forces in Jammu–Kashmir area.

24 Finance Minister V.P. Singh is appointed defense minister.

AFRICA Fund Summit opens with Rajiv Gandhi as chairman. The fund, which consists of nine non-aligned nations, calls for the international community to mobilize resources for helping the victims of the South African apartheid regime. Members pledge $70 million to the fund. India contributes $40 million.

The Babri Masjid Action Committee withdraws call to Muslims to boycott Republic Day celebrations following appeal by President Zail Singh and other leaders. There are no demonstrations on January 26, Republic Day.

28 A Pakistani weekly breaks the news that Pakistan is capable of building a nuclear bomb within a few months. Pakistani troops build up on Jammu–Kashmir border. On January 29, outgoing U.S. Ambassador to Pakistan Deane Hinton hints that Pakistan is going forward with a nuclear program.

FEBRUARY

9 In Punjab, the crisis in the leading political party, the Akali Dal (Longowal), deepens. Chief Minister Surjit Singh Barnala is declared *Tankhaiya,* guilty of religious misconduct, by Sikh high priests and on February 11 is excommunicated from the Sikh community or *panth.* On February 15, Barnala expels twelve prominent leaders from membership in the Akali Dal (L).

18 **The Mizo National Front wins a victory over Congress (I) in assembly elections. The Union Territory of Mizoram is declared India's twenty–third state on February 19.** Mizoram is in the northeastern part of India bordering Burma.

21 Pakistani president Zia ul–Haq arrives in India for a three–day visit to discuss military de–escalation on the India–Pakistan border. After attending a cricket match on February 22, Zia offers India a package which would commit the two countries to renunciation of any support for separatist movements in either country.

The Misra Commission of inquiry, in a two-volume report, absolves the Congress (I) of the charge of organizing violence in Delhi in the wake of the assassination of prime minister Indira Gandhi on October 31, 1984. Opposition groups and civil rights activists denounce the report as a whitewash.

MARCH

2 **India and Pakistan sign an agreement to pull out nearly 70 percent of their troops deployed close to the border.** This follows the February 4 agreement in which India and Pakistan had already withdrawn 150,000 troops from the Ravi–Chenab corridor. The Punjab border is to remain sealed and the Indian triennial military exercise "Brasstacks" is to go on unhindered.

Differences between the president and the prime minister surface and rock Parliament. The national daily *Indian Express* publishes a letter from President Singh to the prime minister accusing Gandhi of not respecting the constitution and failing in his duty to regularly brief the president on issues of national importance.

22 **In a critical political test for Gandhi and the ruling party, 50 million voters go to the polls in West Bengal, Kerala, and Jammu and Kashmir to elect new state assemblies.** In West Bengal, the CPI(M)–led Left Front gets two–thirds majority; in Kerala, the CPI(M) returns to power after a five–year absence and in Jammu and Kashmir, the alliance between the National Conference (F) and Congress (I) gains a majority with Farooq Abdullah chosen to head the coalition. The ruling party's defeat is expected to erode Congress (I) strength in the upcoming Haryana elections and its influence in the Hindi heartland.

31 Debate in Lok Sabha centers on V.P. Singh's highly controversial hiring of a U.S. agency, the Fairfax Group, for the investigation of Indian nationals having illegal funds abroad in violation of the Foreign Exchange Regulation Act (FERA). In protest, the entire opposition stages a walkout from the Lok Sabha on April 2. Gandhi announces, on April 3, that a Supreme Court judge is to be appointed to investigate.

APRIL

9 **Creating a furor in Congress (I) and adding to the infighting within the ruling party, V.P. Singh orders an inquiry into kickbacks allegedly received by Indians in the Rs. 11 billion (1,100 crore) arms deal with the Swedish manufacturing firm Bofors.** Coming on the heels of the Fairfax affair and further adding to the pressures on the Rajiv Gandhi government, National Swedish Radio discloses that a Rs. 300 million commission was received by an Indian agent in the deal with Bofors in April 1986 for the supply of 155mm Howitzer field guns.

10 Sri Lanka promises to end the fuel embargo and restore telecommunications to Jaffna if the nine–day ceasefire, from April 11 to 20, is successful. The ceasefire is revoked on April 17, after 107 Sinhalese are gunned down by LTTE (Liberation Tigers of Tamil Eelam) guerrillas. India condemns the massacre.

12 **Under attack for his publicized and controversial inquiry into the Fairfax and Bofors affairs, Defense Minister Vishwanath Pratap Singh resigns.**

22 In light of the continuous violence and killing in the Punjab, Gandhi tells Punjab Chief Minister Surjit Singh Barnala to restore law and order in the state. On April 26, Gandhi warns Barnala to take action against ministers supporting terrorists and those interfering in administration of law and order.

24 In a triumph for the Reagan Administration, the U.S. Senate Foreign Relations Committee approves the bill for renewed aid to Pakistan, placing few controls on Pakistan's nuclear program, and rejects an amendment to limit military assistance to Pakistan and to restrict the sale of a supercomputer to India.

25 Citing lack of government credibility, six chief ministers of opposition–ruled states hold their first meeting with the objective of creating a national alternative to Congress (I).

29 Swedish government orders independent inquiry into Bofors deal after India asks Sweden to help in the investigation.

MAY

2 With the Bofors crisis still rocking the central government, tensions between the prime minister and the president increase in the controversy over Article 78 of the Constitution, especially the right of the president to be informed in all state matters. Gandhi maintains that paramount interests of state can be withheld from the president and refuses to share information about Bofors with President Zail Singh. Fears spread that the president can and will dismiss the government for violation of the constitution.

11 **President's Rule is imposed on the Punjab and approved by Parliament on the 12th.** Gandhi, citing the sharp increase in terrorist killings, refers to the move as a short term measure "necessitated by the sharp deterioration of law and order." The decision highlights the government's contrary stand on the Punjab. Gandhi had openly supported the Barnala government until the end of April. Critics see the tough move as one of political expediency as Haryana, the neighboring and predominantly Hindu state, will go to the polls in five weeks.

24 **Five days of devastating communal riots between Hindus and Muslims in Meerut, 70 km from Delhi, claim 111 lives, and over 1,000 are injured.** More than 13,000 army troops are called in to stem the violence in a community which is 60 percent Hindu and 40 percent Muslim. In one of the worst cases of police brutality in India, the Provincial Armed Constabulary (PAC) massacred over 50 civilians on May 23. Critics of the government blame the rising tide of communalism in politics.

30 **Statehood is conferred on the Union territory of Goa.**

JUNE

3 **Indian boats, carrying food and medical supplies for a beleaguered Jaffna, are prevented from landing by the Sri Lankan Navy. India condemns Sri Lanka's action.** Sri Lanka complains to the United Nations of a "potential external threat" to its sovereignty. **On June 4 and 5, Indian Air Force planes drop supplies on Jaffna. India justifies the act as a humanitarian necessity.**

7 Gandhi asserts that President's Rule will continue in the Punjab as long as terrorism exists in the state.

18 **Congress (I) suffers a massive defeat in the politically crucial Haryana assembly elections.** The Lok Dal (B)–Bharatiya Janata Party alliance led by Devi Lal wins more than four–fifths of the seats in the 90–member Haryana assembly in a heavy voter turnout. As in Andhra Pradesh, a regional party wins on the platform of regional identity. Following in the footsteps of defense deal scandals, the crushing election defeat highlights the dramatic reversal in the fortunes of Congress (I) and casts serious doubt on Gandhi's leadership abilities.

21 Former Supreme Court justice V.R. Krishna Iyer is chosen by the opposition to contest the presidential elections.

23 In a meeting in Paris chaired by the World Bank, the Aid-India Consortium increases aid by $1 billion to $5.4 billion.

JULY

2 Gandhi begins a two-day visit to Moscow to inaugurate the festival of India. Discussions center on Pakistan and China in light of the recent thaw in Sino–Soviet relations and U.S. arms sales to Pakistan. India and the USSR sign on July 3 a long term comprehensive agreement for cooperation in science and technology, including joint ventures.

9 A near–total strike in North Indian cities in protest of the mass killings of 76 bus passengers by Sikh extremists in Haryana is marked by mob violence and arson.

13 **Congress (I) candidate R. Venkataraman wins the ninth presidential election.**

15 **Former defense minister V.P. Singh, former internal security minister Arun Nehru and other prominent Congress (I) members of Parliament launch campaign against corruption and communalism.**

Three former union ministers, Arun Nehru, V.C. Shukla and Arif Mohammad Khan, are expelled from Congress (I) for "anti-party" activities.

17 **Amitabh Bachchan, film star and close friend of Rajiv Gandhi, resigns from Lok Sabha over accusations that both he and his brother Ajitabh were involved in Bofors kickbacks.**

21 A two–day–old doctors' strike, which has crippled health services all over India, is declared illegal under the essential services maintenance act.

24 The leader of the LTTE, V. Prabhakaran, arrives in Delhi for talks with Rajiv Gandhi regarding a cease-fire between Tamil militant groups and the Sri Lankan forces. A few days later, Tamil militants agree to the peace accord.

28 **Sri Lankan peace accord signed by Rajiv Gandhi and J.R. Jayewardene in Colombo. The accord would bring about the reconciliation to a strife–torn island after five years of ethnic conflict.** Four Sri Lankan ministers, including Prime Minister Premadasa, boycott the signing. A curfew is clamped down on Colombo because of demonstrations.

AUGUST

3 Deadlock in Parliament over Bofors continues as the government rejects the main demands of the opposition.

5 The LTTE arms surrender begins. In a symbolic gesture, Vilupillai Prabhakaran, the LTTE leader, stays away.

17 Congress (I) and opposition leaders reach a consensus on a vice presidential candidate. They choose the Governor of Maharashtra, Dr. Shankar Dayal Sharma, who is elected without opposition on August 21.

28 **Monsoon showers that had remained weak for most of June and July finally arrive, slightly alleviating the drought that has devastated 21 states ranging from Kerala to Himachal Pradesh, and from Gujarat to Orissa.** In Orissa alone, the drought has claimed over 400 lives since April. The government releases Rs. 2.26 Billion (226 crore) in relief funds. On September 11, the government announces austerity measures to redeploy Rs. 6.5 billion to fight drought and on September 19, additional taxes of Rs. 5.5 billion are imposed for drought and flood relief.

SEPTEMBER

1 The offices of the newspaper the *Indian Express* are raided all over the country by the Directorate of Revenue Intelligence. Zail Singh calls the move "ill-advised," and the editor of the paper accuses the government of infringing on the freedom of the press. Rajiv Gandhi claims he was not aware of the raids.

4 In an age-old rite of *sati,* an act in which the widow burns on her husband's funeral pyre, 18-year-old Roop Kunwar burns as 4,000 villagers watch. The funeral ceremony on September 16 in Deorala—just 50 km from the Rajasthani capital of Jaipur—attracts

over 250,000 people. Although *sati* is banned under Indian law, no police interfere.

15 Internecine fighting between Tamil militant groups in Sri Lanka claims over 100 lives in Batticaloa (eastern Sri Lanka). Indian troops intervene and additional troops are sent to the island on September 16.

OCTOBER

1 Rajasthan's chief minister issues an ordinance against the glorification of *sati,* which provides for a death penalty for those aiding or abetting *sati* and imprisonment or fine to the widow who attempts to commit the act. The ordinance provokes defiant pro–*sati* demonstrations, some 70,000 strong.

2 **On the birthdate of Mahatma Gandhi, V.P. Singh launches a new forum—the Jan Morcha—to concentrate on creating a mass movement on "value–based" politics.** Stressing that it is not a political party, Singh's aim is to create a "strong, secular, united, democratic, self reliant, and non-aligned India."

3 The Indian Army becomes openly involved in a full–scale war with the LTTE as over 1,000 IPKF reinforcement troops are sent to Trincomalee district in eastern Sri Lanka. On October 5, twelve of seventeen captured LTTE leaders and activists, who were about to be handed over to the Sri Lankan government authorities, commit suicide by swallowing cyanide capsules; an angered LTTE massacres 150 civilians and soldiers in retaliation on October 7.

India and Sri Lanka reaffirm their determination to implement the peace accord as the 10,000 strong IPKF moves in on LTTE strongholds on Jaffna. Over 130 people are killed on October 11 as Indian troops surround and lay siege to curfew–bound Jaffna.

8 The Indian government announces that the Indian Army has repulsed the fourth attack by Pakistan on the Siachen Glacier, inflicting a total of 150 casualties

(Indian Army estimate for September 23, 24, and 25 attacks).

9 The United States and India sign an agreement on the purchase of a Cray supercomputer to be used for monsoon research and agricultural studies.

19 **Jaffna city falls to Indian forces after 10 days of heavy fighting.** Since the beginning of the offensive on October 10, Indian troops have suffered 215 dead and over 700 wounded. On October 25, Indian troops capture LTTE headquarters in Jaffna.

28 Hundreds of journalists and newspaper workers attempt to cross picket lines and break a fortnight-old strike at the Delhi edition of the English language daily, the *Indian Express.* Police brutally beat picketers. No dailies appear in Delhi on October 29 in a one-day token strike protesting police brutality.

NOVEMBER

2 **The third summit of the South Asian Association for Regional Cooperation (SAARC) opens in Kathmandu, Nepal.** The six participating nations—India, Pakistan, Sri Lanka, Nepal, Bhutan, Bangladesh, and the Maldives—sign a new regional convention on terrorism on November 3.

9 A bomb blast in Colombo kills 50 and injures over 100. The continued violence is aimed at undermining the Indo–Sri Lankan accord and the Jayewardene government.

19 **Congress (I) triumphs, getting an absolute majority in the legislative assembly elections in Nagaland. Hokishe Sema is elected chief minister.**

DECEMBER

6 **MiG–29s, a high technology interceptor aircraft, are inducted into the Indian Air Force.**

9 The Thakkar–Natarajan Commission report on the hiring of the Fairfax Group is presented to Parliament. The report comes out with few additional facts on an issue that had threatened the Gandhi government. It concludes that no money was paid to Fairfax or given by Fairfax. (But it finds that the engagement of the Fairfax group to investigate foreign exchange violations was not consistent with the security of India.)

V.P. Singh and opposition leaders see report as a political statement and say sole purpose of commission was to exonerate and shield Gandhi.

17 **Bhopal District Court orders the Union Carbide Corporation to pay Rs. 3.5 billion (Rs. 350 crore) as interim compensation to victims of the December 1984 gas tragedy.**

24 Death of Tamil Nadu chief minister and leader of the AIADMK, M.G. Ramachandran.

28 Armed Naxalites ambush and kidnap eight Andhra Pradesh officials and demand the release of eight extremists.

Glossary

Abdullah, Farooq. Chief Minister of Jammu and Kashmir and leader of the *National Conference (F)* party. Son of the late Kashmiri leader Sheikh Abdullah, Farooq led his party in coalition with *Congress (I)* in the March 1987 state assembly elections.

Akali Dal. The major party of the Sikhs for 40 years, it governed the state of Punjab until May 1987 when *President's Rule* was imposed. Now split into the Akali Dal (L), led by Surjit Singh *Barnala,* and the *United Akali Dal.*

Aksai Chin. High desert plateau of Kashmir that is claimed by India but has been controlled by China since the 1962 Sino–India war. Disagreement over China's occupation of this area, which links Tibet to China's Xinjiang province, is a major obstacle to improvement of Sino–Indian relations.

All India Anna Dravida Munnetra Kazhagam (AIADMK). Former ruling party in the state of Tamil Nadu, ousted by imposition of *President's Rule* in January 1988 following the death in December 1987 of its founder, *M.G. Ramachandran.*

All India Sikh Students Federation (AISSF). Militant Sikh student group.

Anti–Defection Bill. Bill passed by Rajiv Gandhi's government in 1985 forbidding members of Parliament and state assemblies from changing their party affiliation without standing for election. A person expelled from a party does not lose his or her seat.

Arunachal Pradesh. Formerly the Northeast Frontier Area, this region's status was changed from union territory to state in December 1986. China's claims to sovereignty over much of this region makes it a key element in the Sino–Indian border dispute.

Asom Gana Parishad (AGP). Ruling party in the northeastern state of Assam representing the interests of native Assamese. It was formed just before the December 1985 elections from members of the pro–Assamese All Assam Gana Sangram Parishad (AAGSP) and the All Assam Students Union (AASU).

Assam Accord. Agreement signed by Rajiv Gandhi, the AASU, and the AAGSP in August 1985 to end six years of violent student agitation against immigrants to the state from neighboring Bangladesh. Under the agreement, all migrants who arrived since March 1971 were to be expelled, and those who arrived since 1967 were to be deleted from the electoral rolls.

Bachchan, Amitabh. India's foremost film star and a personal friend of Prime Minister Gandhi, he resigned his seat in Parliament when the Bofors scandal touched him and his brother Ajitabh.

Backward Classes. Classes recognized by the Constitution as disadvantaged and allowed remedial treatment. In practice, backward classes have been defined in terms of caste membership.

Badal, Parkash Singh. Leader of a dissident faction of the *Akali Dal* which broke off after an April 1986 raid on the *Golden Temple* by government commandos. He had previously been a supporter of the *Punjab Accord.* He was arrested for sedition in December 1986.

Bandh. Protest through general strike or closure.

Barnala, Surjit Singh. Chief minister of the state of Punjab government from October 1985 to May 1987. His inability to control violence in Punjab and dissension in the ruling *Akali Dal* Party led to his removal from office through imposition of *President's Rule.*

Bharatiya Janata Party (BJP). Party formed from elements of the *Jan Sangh* party, with support mainly in northern India. Its attempts to broaden its social base by taking a more secular course has cost it valuable *Rashtriya Swayamsevak Sangh* support.

Bhindranwale, Jarnail Singh. Sikh priest and principal leader of the militant Sikh separatists in the early 1980s. He was killed in the *Golden Temple* during the 1984 *Operation Bluestar.*

Bofors. Swedish armaments company alleged to have paid commissions to middlemen, in violation of its agreement with the Government of India, to secure a Rs. 1.1 billion contract to supply 155mm howitzer field guns.

Chandigarh. Joint capital of the states of Punjab and Haryana. The transfer of Chandigarh to Punjab under the *Punjab Accord* was scheduled for January 1986 but has been indefinitely postponed.

Chandrashekar. Starting as a "Young Turk" of the *Congress (I)* party under Mrs. Gandhi before the *Emergency,* he has been an opposition leader since 1977, resigning as president of the *Janata Party* in 1988. By most accounts, probably retains ambitions to national if not prime ministerial office.

Chief Minister. The equivalent of the prime minister in the government of Indian states.

Communist Party of India (CPI). The Communist Party in India, characterized by a pro–Soviet stance, has been at times willing to cooperate with the Congress (I). Its electoral strength has been in decline for many years.

Communist Party of India (Marxist) (CPI(M)). The stronger segment of the Communist Party of India after the split of 1964. The CPI(M) has run the government of the state of West Bengal since 1977, and competes with the Congress (I) for power in Kerala.

Congress (I) Party. Party of Prime Minister Rajiv Gandhi and the dominant Indian national party since Independence. Congress is the principal inheritor of the mantle of the independence movement. The "I" stands for Indira Gandhi, who led this faction after a Congress Party split in 1977.

Dalit. Literally meaning "ruined, trampled," this term has come to refer to "untouchables," or members of *scheduled castes.*

Devi Lal. Chief minister of Haryana and a leader of the *Lok Dal (B).*

Directive Principles of State Policy. A section of the Constitution, seen as equivalent to the stipulation of Fundamental Rights, that set out the obligations of the Indian state to its citizens, which are to be legislated by parliament: for example, a right to education.

Doordarshan. India's state television network. No privately-owned television stations are allowed in India, but Doordarshan has begun contracting with private companies for programming.

Dravida Munnetra Kazhagam (DMK). Tamil nationalist party, led by M. Karunanidhi.

Emergency. Declared by Mrs. Gandhi's government in June 1975, it lasted 21 months; opposition leaders were jailed, press censorship imposed, and the constitution amended to restrict the judiciary.

Fairfax. A Washington area investigative agency employed by the Finance Ministry under *V.P. Singh* to pursue inquiries about the alleged foreign exchange and customs violations of Reliance Industries, a textile firm.

Five–Year Plans. Formulated by the Planning Commission and approved by Parliament, these analyze the economic situation of the country and set out both broad goals and specific guidelines for investment and other economic policy, for both public and private sector. The First Plan covered the 1951–56 period. The current Plan is the seventh, covering 1985–1990.

Foreign Exchange Regulation Act (FERA). Law regulating foreign investment in India. Foreign ownership is normally limited to 40 percent except in certain high technology industries.

Gandhi, Rajiv. Born in 1944, he is the elder son of Indira and Feroze Gandhi. A commercial airline pilot, Rajiv entered politics after the death of his brother Sanjay in 1980, and was selected as prime minister after the assassination of his mother on October 31, 1984. He led the *Congress (I)* party to a landslide victory in the December 1984 general elections.

Golden Temple. Holy seat of Sikh religion, located in Amritsar, Punjab. The Golden Temple has been a center of Sikh militant activity.

Gurdwara. Sikh temple.

Gurkhaland. The new state which the *Gurkha National Liberation Front* demands be created from part of the present Indian state of West Bengal. In July 1988, an agreement which will provide for some autonomy of a new "Gurkha Hill Council" within West Bengal has been reached by the Gurkhaland leader, Subhas Ghising, the Chief Minister of West Bengal, and the Government of India.

Gurkha National Liberation Front (GNLF). Militant organization based in the Darjeeling area of the state of West Bengal that demands the creation of a separate state for Nepalis in India, known as *Gurkhaland,* as well as the adoption of Nepali as an official language.

Hegde, Ramakrishna. *Chief minister* of Karnataka and leader of the ruling *Janata Party;* one of the major opposition leaders, considered to be a potential prime minister.

Indian Institutes of Technology. Located in Kanpur, Kharagpur (West Bengal), Madras, Delhi, and Bombay, with students selected through a highly competitive national examination, these were set up with international collaboration and retain world-class standards.

Indian Peace Keeping Force (IPKF). Units mainly of the Indian Army sent into the northern and eastern provinces of Sri Lanka under the Sri Lanka–India accord of July 1987, initially to disarm the LTTE and the other guerrilla groups. When that provision of the accord broke down, the IPKF fought the LTTE in pitched battles in Jaffna, and since has attempted to maintain law and order. The IPKF remains in Sri Lanka at the pleasure of the Sri Lanka government.

Indo–Sri Lanka Accord. See Sri Lanka Accord.

Indo–Soviet Treaty of Peace and Friendship. A 20–year treaty signed in 1971 which commits India and the Soviet Union to consult in the event of threats to each other's security.

Jaffna. City and district in the north of Sri Lanka in which the Tamils are the overwhelming majority.

Janata Party. One of the principal opposition parties, and ruling party in Karnataka. Janata headed a national government coalition in 1977–79, the only non–Congress party to do so since Independence.

Jan Morcha. "People's movement" founded in October 1987 by V.P. Singh and others expelled from the *Congress (I)* in April 1987, as a non–party opposition group.

Jan Sangh. Hindu-chauvinist party formed in 1951 with strength mainly in North India. Much of its political cadre is drawn from the *Rashtriya Swayamsevak Sangh.*

Jati. Caste or sub-caste unit that defines acceptable interactions in marriage, dining, and other caste–related practices.

Jayewardene, J.R. President of Sri Lanka and leader of the United National Party; in power since 1977.

Kharif. The autumn crop; larger than the *rabi* crop, it is heavily dependent on monsoon rains.

Liberation Tigers of Tamil Eelam (LTTE). Leading Sri Lankan Tamil militant group which seeks a separate state for Sri Lankan Tamils on the island of Sri Lanka. After the breakdown of the *Sri Lanka Accord,* continued to fight the *Indian Peace Keeping Force* and conduct terrorist operations against Sinhalese in the Eastern Province of Sri Lanka.

Lok Dal. Break-away faction of the *Janata Party* formed in 1979 due to opposition to *Rashtriya Swayamsevak Sangh* involvement in the Janata Party. Has now split into the Lok Dal (A), led by Ajit Singh, the son of the late Charan Singh, a former prime minister, and the Lok Dal (B), led by H.N. Bahuguna.

Lok Sabha. Lower house of India's bicameral parliament.

McMahon Line. Northeastern border of India with China charted by British cartographers but undemarcated. It is recognized by India as the legitimate border with China. China disputes this border and overran it in the 1962 Sino–Indian war.

Meerut. City and district 50 miles north of Delhi, in the state of Uttar Pradesh. Site of frequent Hindu–Muslim clashes.

Mizoram. A former union territory, granted statehood after the 25 June 1986 signing of the Mizoram Accord between Prime Minister Gandhi and Mizo National Front (MNF) leader Laldenga. The MNF had been leading a guerrilla movement for Mizo autonomy, and took power in the new state in the February 1987 election.

Monopolies and Restrictive Trade Practices Act (MRTP). Law regulating firms that command a major share of the market in their product. Reducing this act's application has been a major element in Rajiv Gandhi's program of economic liberalization.

National Conference (F). Dominant party of Jammu and Kashmir, led by *Farooq Abdullah*.

Navodaya Vidyalayas (NV). Literally, model or "new rise" schools to be established in every rural district under Rajiv Gandhi's new educational plan. These government–funded boarding schools will begin at grade six and provide free tuition and living expenses for students who gain admission.

Nehru, Arun. Former minister of state for internal security and cousin of Rajiv Gandhi. He was removed from office by the prime minister in October 1986 because of his opposition to Gandhi's policies of reconciliation, especially in Punjab and Mizoram. After his expulsion from the Congress(I) in 1987, he became a leader, with *V.P. Singh* and others, of the *Jan Morcha*.

Operation Bluestar. Military assault on the *Golden Temple* in June 1984 to flush out Sikh extremists using the temple as a refuge. Operation Bluestar led to widespread Sikh alienation and protest.

Operation Brasstacks. Indian military maneuvers of record magnitude along the Pakistan border from November 1986 to January 1987. The size of the maneuvers and Pakistan's response of deploying its troops near the border created a war scare in both countries.

President. In India, the equivalent of a constitutional monarch, who gives formal assent to bills, but whose powers are severely restricted. Elected by members of Parliament and the state legislatures for a five–year term. The term of Giani Zail Singh ended in July 1987; he was replaced by the Congress(I) candidate, *R. Venkataraman*.

President's Rule. Suspension of a state's assembly and direct rule of the state by the central government through the centrally appointed governor. Although President's Rule is intended to be put into effect when a state of emergency exists, it has sometimes been used by the center to topple opposition–controlled state governments.

Provincial Armed Constabulary (PAC). The state–level armed police force of Uttar Pradesh, implicated in the massacre at *Meerut* in May 1987.

Punjab Accord. July 1985 agreement primarily between the central government and the states of Punjab and Haryana intended to resolve the crisis created by Sikh grievances over treatment of their community and the state of Punjab by the central government. Under the Accord, the sharing of river waters was to be adjudicated between the two states, Sikhs discharged from the army after *Operation Bluestar* were to transfer their joint capital, *Chandigarh,* to Punjab in return for the transfer of some Hindi-speaking areas of Punjab to Haryana. The agreement remains largely unimplemented.

Rabi. The winter-spring crop; now grown to a great extent on irrigated land.

Rajya Sabha. Upper house of India's bicameral parliament.

Ramachandran, M.G. (MGR). Chief minister of Tamil Nadu and leader of *All India Anna Dravida Munnetra Kazhagam* until his death on December 24, 1987.

Rao, N.T. Rama. Chief minister of the state of Andhra Pradesh and leader of its ruling *Telugu Desam* party. His move to assist the backward classes of his state by extending reservations for education and jobs has led to clashes between upper and lower castes.

Rashtriya Swayamsevak Sangh (RSS). Militant Hindu organization associated with the *Jan Sangh* party. The RSS draws its membership mainly from urban and lower middle classes and seeks the consolidation of a Hindu nation.

Sati. The suicide, whether voluntary or achieved through social pressure, of a wife by burning on her husband's funeral pyre. Outlawed since the nineteenth century, it still can occur, and did, spectacularly, in Rajasthan in September 1987. That *sati* provoked large demonstrations for and against the practice, and ultimately the passage of a more stringent law against it.

Scheduled Castes and Scheduled Tribes (SC/ST). List of "untouchable," or "harijan," castes and tribes drawn up under the 1935 Government of India Act and subsequently revised. Legislative seats as well as government posts and places in educational institutions are reserved for members of these castes and tribes.

Sharma, Shankar Dayal. Vice–President of India, succeeding *R. Venkataraman;* elected to a five–year term in August 1987.

Shekhar, Chandra. See Chandrashekhar.

Shiv Sena. Militant nativist communal organization based largely in the towns of northern India. It was founded in Bombay in 1966 to agitate against South Indian immigrants to the state of Maharashtra.

Siachen Glacier. Disputed area in the mountains of Kashmir and the site of many recent minor skirmishes between India and Pakistan.

Sikh, Sikhism. The religion of Sikhism was founded in the sixteenth century by the first Guru, Nanak, drawing on Hindu devotionalism and Islam. Persecuted by the later Mughal emperors, Sikhs developed into a martial community, led by the tenth and last Guru, Gobind Singh; a Sikh kingdom in central Punjab was defeated by the British in the mid–19th century.

Simla Agreement. Peace pact signed in 1972 by India and Pakistan, formally ending the 1971 war between India and Pakistan over Bangladesh and affirming the line of control between India and Pakistan in Kashmir.

Singh, V.P. Former finance and defense minister under Rajiv Gandhi, Singh ran into political difficulties resulting in his April 1987 ouster from government because of his efforts to hunt down tax evaders and eliminate corruption from India's government arms deals. He was the principal architect of India's new liberal economic policy and is considered by some to be a potential prime minister, particularly after his victory in June 1988 in the contest to fill the seat vacated by *Amitabh Bachchan* in Allahabad. The leader of the *Jan Morcha*.

South Asian Association for Regional Cooperation (SAARC). Organization formed in 1985 to enhance regional cooperation in social, economic, and cultural development. The SAARC members are Bangladesh, Bhutan, India, the Maldives, Nepal, Pakistan, and Sri Lanka. The third SAARC Summit was held in Kathmandu, Nepal, in November 1987.

Sri Lanka Accord. Signed by Prime Minister Gandhi and president J.R. Jayewardene on July 28, 1987 in Colombo, the accord provided for the ending of the guerrilla war, insured by Indian armed forces which were to disarm the *Liberation Tigers of Tamil Eelam (LTTE)* and other Tamil extremists; and for the holding of elections to newly–empowered provincial assemblies in which Tamils would gain significant autonomy. The accord continues in effect, though the LTTE have conducted terrorist attacks against civilians and the *Indian Peace Keeping Force,* and Sinhalese opposition groups have conducted terrorist attacks against Sri Lanka government policy supporters.

Telugu Desam. Ruling party in the state of Andhra Pradesh, formed in 1982 and led by *N.T. Rama Rao*. This party survived a 1984 attempt by the center to install a *Congress (I)* chief minister in place of Rama Rao, marking a trend of resiliency of opposition–led state governments.

Tohra, Gurcharan Singh. Leader of the powerful, separatist-oriented Shiromani Gurdwara Prabandhak Committee (Sikh Temple Management Committee), jailed for sedition in December 1986. Tohra had previously supported the *Punjab Accord.*

United Akali Dal (UAD). A segment of the old *Akali Dal,* somewhat less moderate than the Akali Dal (L).

Varna. The four broad hierarchical categories of the Hindu caste system. In descending order of status, the *varna* are Brahmin, Kshatriya, Vaishya, and Shudra. Untouchables fall below these categories.

Venkataraman, R. *President* of India for the 1987–1992 term. A respected Congress(I) politician, who had most recently served in the cabinet as defense minister, he was vice president of India for a brief period before his election as president.

Zia ul–Haq. The late president of Pakistan and Chief of its Army Staff, Zia ruled Pakistan since a coup in 1977 that overthrew the government of Zulfiqar Ali Bhutto. He was killed in an airplane crash on August 17, 1988.

About the Contributors

James Manor is Professorial Fellow and Director of Research at the Institute of Development Studies, University of Sussex, England. He has taught at Yale, Harvard, Leicester, and London Universities and has written numerous studies of the politics of India and Sri Lanka. His most recent book is *The Expedient Utopian: Bandaranaike and Ceylon* (forthcoming).

T.N. Srinivasan is Samuel C. Park, Jr. Professor of Economics at Yale University. He is a consultant at the Development Research Center of the World Bank, and his numerous publications include *Foreign Trade Regimes and Economic Development: India* (with J.N. Bhagwati) and *Rural Poverty in South Asia* (forthcoming).

Thomas Perry Thornton is Adjunct Professor at the Johns Hopkins University School of Advanced International Studies in Washington, D.C. Among his publications are: *The Challenge to U.S. Policy in the Third World: Global Responsibilities and Regional Revolution, Communism and Revolution,* and *The Third World in Soviet Perspective.*

Raju G.C. Thomas is Professor of Political Science at Marquette University and a research fellow at the Defense and Arms Control Studies Program, Massachussetts Institute of Technology. He is author of *The Defense of India: A Budgetary Perspective of Strategy and Politics* and *Indian Security Policy,* and editor of *The Great Power Triangle and Asian Security.*

Krishna Kumar is Professor at the Department of Education at Delhi University. His most recent study, *The Political Role of Education,* was carried out on a Fellowship of the Nehru Memorial Museum and Library, New Delhi. His other books include *Social Character of Learning* and *Raj Samaj Aur Shiksha* (in Hindi).

William A. Blanpied, currently on the staff of the Graduate School of International Relations and Pacific Studies at the University of California, San Diego, is on leave of absence from the U.S. National Science Foundation, where he serves as Senior Policy Analyst for International Programs. His published papers include "India's Scientific Development," and "Pioneer Scientists in Pre–Independence India."

Index